Law for Pharmacy Technicians

Nora Rock

2011
Emond Montgomery Publications
Toronto, Canada

Emond Montgomery Publications Limited
60 Shaftesbury Avenue
Toronto ON M4T 1A3
http://www.emp.ca/college

Printed in Canada.
First printing August 2010.

We acknowledge the financial support of the Government of Canada through the Canada Book Fund for our publishing activities.

Acquisitions and development editor: Bernard Sandler
Marketing manager: Christine Davidson
Director, sales and marketing, higher education: Kevin Smulan
Supervising editor: Jim Lyons
Copy editor: Francine Geraci
Photo researchers: Francine Geraci and Kathleen D. Davis
Proofreader: Diane Gula
Production editor: Tara Wells
Indexer: Paula Pike
Cover image: ugurhan/iStockphoto

Library and Archives Canada Cataloguing in Publication

Rock, Nora, 1968-
    Law for pharmacy technicians / Nora Rock.

Includes index.
ISBN 978-1-55239-366-6

    1. Pharmacy technicians—Legal status, laws, etc.—Canada—
Textbooks.   2. Pharmacy—Law and legislation—Canada—
Textbooks.   3. Drugs—Law and legislation—Canada—Textbooks.   I. Title.

KE2714.P4R63 2010   344.71'0416   C2010-904042-2
KF2915.P4R63 2010

Contents

CHAPTER 4 Overview of the Regulation of Drugs and Other Controlled Substances

CHAPTER 1

Introduction to the Law Governing Pharmacy Technicians

A pharmacy technician who works with a pharmacist in the retail setting has many opportunities to provide a high level of service to the general public.

LEARNING OBJECTIVES

After completing this chapter, you should be able to:

- List some of the qualities and special responsibilities of a professional.

- Make an argument for the status of pharmacy technicians as professionals.

- Describe at least four settings in which pharmacy technicians may practise.

- Discuss some of the practice issues unique to particular settings, such as the online pharmacy and the pharmacy serving a long-term care facility.

- Explain the roles of the pharmacist, the designated pharmacy manager, the pharmacy technician, and other pharmacy personnel.

- Discuss the pharmacy's status as both a business and a professional practice and the challenges of integrating these two roles.

INTRODUCTION

Are Pharmacy Technicians Professionals?

The *Compact Oxford English Dictionary* defines a professional as "a person having impressive competence in a particular activity." Besides impressive competence, there are many other attributes we associate with professionals in our society, including doing an activity for pay, not as a hobby; possessing recognized or standard qualifications; performing work to an expert, rather than a beginner, standard; being worthy of the public trust; being a member of a self-regulated occupation; and adhering to a code of conduct that takes into account not only one's own reputation, but also the reputation of the profession as a whole.

Not all occupations are recognized as professions. Being a pharmacist certainly is. But what about being a pharmacy technician?

Before answering that question, you might ask yourself why the public puts special faith in professionals. Common sense dictates that while a do-it-yourself approach is fine for certain tasks, others—such as pouring a foundation for a house, performing a root canal operation, or mounting a defence in a criminal trial—are best left to a professional. What sets these professional tasks apart is not only the level of difficulty involved, but also the "downside risk" of doing a poor job: a house built on a shaky foundation is liable to fall down; a kitchen-table root canal might cause serious pain or an infection; and representing oneself in a criminal case might lead to prison. The more serious the consequences of our incompetence, the more likely we are to rely on a professional.

What are the consequences of incompetence in a pharmacy technician? The most obvious is **medication error**. There are thousands of drugs available on the market today, with a very wide range of effects on the body, but a narrow range of visual differentiation—many drugs look very much alike. Telling drugs apart from one another, dispensing them appropriately, and considering the implications of ingesting them are not only critically important tasks; they are also difficult. Because pharmacy technicians are involved with many of the steps in these tasks, their work bears many of the hallmarks of professional practice.

The role of pharmacy technicians is still evolving, and is not yet widely understood by the general public. It's understandable, therefore, that not everyone currently views pharmacy technicians as professionals. But there are important indicators within the pharmacy industry that pharmacy technicians are moving toward professional status. For example:

medication error
an error that occurs during the process of prescribing, transcribing, dispensing, administering, or monitoring a drug

- *Regulation/self-regulation:* As of 2010, registered pharmacy technicians are regulated by the Ontario College of Pharmacists (OCP; hereafter called "the College"). The form of regulation provided by the College is known as self-regulation, because pharmacy technicians are elected to the regulatory body and play a role in setting standards that will apply to themselves and their colleagues. Self-regulation is a key indicator of an occupation's professional status.
- *Registration:* Now that registration is available, many Ontario pharmacy technicians are likely to opt for registering with the College—a step that requires them to meet educational and certification standards. Many other

professions—for example, the medical, dentistry, and legal professions—
require registration with a regulating body as a prerequisite for practice.

- *Standardized training and education:* To qualify for registration, new
  Ontario pharmacy technicians must prove that they have successfully
  completed locally accredited education and practical training programs, or
  that their foreign credentials (including credentials from another province)
  are at least equivalent to the Ontario standard. Pharmacy technicians
  already working in Ontario must complete bridging programs to ensure
  that their skills meet the current standards. Many existing professions
  depend on accredited education and training programs to establish the
  competence needed for professional practice.
- *Standardized examinations:* To ensure that all pharmacy technicians have
  minimum qualifications, those who choose to register with the College
  must pass two separate exams—a (national) Pharmacy Examining Board of
  Canada (PEBC) qualifying exam, and a (provincial) Jurisprudence Exam
  that focuses on federal and Ontario pharmacy law.

Now that the regulation, registration, and certification of pharmacy technicians
has been fully implemented in Ontario, it will be difficult for anyone to argue that
pharmacy technicians are not professionals. Consider, for example, Standard One
from the College's "Proposed Standards of Practice for Registered Pharmacy
Technicians":

> The pharmacy technician practises within legal requirements and ethical princi-
> ples, demonstrates professional integrity, and acts to uphold professional stan-
> dards of practice.

What Are the Special Responsibilities of a Professional?

Because members of the public place special faith in professionals and rely on their
competence, professionals have big shoes to fill. Among other things, professionals
are expected to:

- have special or expert knowledge;
- be familiar with new and emerging information and best practices in the
  industry;
- know and comply with all laws and regulations that govern the industry;
- be dedicated to public service (customer service);
- use good judgment;
- act in the best interests of the public;
- act in the best interests of professional colleagues and the profession in
  general;
- have a code of ethics and adhere to it; and
- have personal integrity and be governed by it.

If pharmacy technicians hope to be viewed as professionals, they must live up
to these high expectations. This textbook is intended to help you meet at least some
of those challenges. After completing this course, you will be familiar with the laws
and regulations that govern pharmacy in Ontario at the present time. You will learn

that the law, and work practices designed to maintain compliance with it, changes often, and that pharmacy technicians are responsible for maintaining the currency of their knowledge.

You will also learn about the policy aspects of laws, and about how the government strives to protect the public interest. The role of the College as a protector of the public will be introduced, as will the topics of ethical decision making and the conduct expected of a pharmacy professional.

First, however, the pharmacy itself will be introduced, with an overview of the many different settings in which pharmacy technicians practise.

THE PHARMACY

Introduction

While the essential work of pharmacy professionals is fairly consistent, pharmacists and pharmacy technicians practise in a wide range of settings. Those most familiar to the public are chain drugstores with pharmacy departments, and independent pharmacies unaffiliated with medical practices or other businesses. However, many pharmacy technicians work in other settings: in hospital or medical clinic pharmacies, in travel clinics, in nursing homes or long-term care facilities, or in pharmacy departments in large department stores like Walmart or Zellers. While the setting in which a pharmacy technician works makes no difference in terms of the need for training, competent practice, and the role of laws and regulations, it can have other effects on the job. For example, the clientele served by a pharmacy in a walk-in clinic will likely be quite different from that served by a pharmacy in a nursing home. The variety of pharmacy types are described below.

Independent, Freestanding Community Pharmacies

The independent community pharmacy is the most traditional form of pharmacy practice. Independent pharmacy practices (and their predecessors, which include the practices of compounders, midwives, alchemists, shamans, and other practitioners who worked with healing plants) date back to the distant past, and have existed in cultures around the world. There have always been individuals with an interest in the properties of drugs who have developed expertise in that field; and there have always been consumers eager for access to those drugs.

The independent pharmacy—which is often owned by a pharmacist—still exists. Independent pharmacies often develop a loyal customer following but, particularly in larger communities, they face significant competitive challenges. Chain drugstores and department store-based pharmacies attract customers by offering a recognizable brand and one-stop shopping. To compete, many independent pharmacies strive to provide a higher level of service, tailored carefully to their customers' needs. It can be rewarding to work as a pharmacy technician in these settings.

Chain Drugstore Pharmacies

Pharmacies in chain drugstores are quickly becoming the dominant form of community pharmacy practice. Easy access to prescription medication and **over-the-counter (OTC) drugs**, cosmetics, and sundries in a single location appeals to customers, as does dealing with a trusted retail brand: customers know what to expect when they shop. Economies of scale allow chain retailers to offer attractive pricing, both on the cost of OTC drugs and cosmetics, as well as on dispensing—another factor that attracts customers.

Because busy chain drugstores enjoy brisk business, there is often a need in these settings for pharmacy technicians. There may also be opportunities, as the profession evolves, for expanded responsibilities—for example, patient counselling—for pharmacy technicians working in chain drugstore pharmacies.

Pharmacies in Department Stores

A natural extension of the chain drugstore phenomenon is the inclusion of pharmacies in department stores. Department stores like Zellers and Walmart strive to offer customers access, in a single store, to a very wide range of goods—clothing, housewares, hardware, and even food. Cosmetic and personal health products have always been an important part of department store offerings, and including a pharmacy in the personal care department has been, for many department stores, a logical development.

If a pharmacy is part of a larger store, the law requires a barrier that prevents public access to the area where drugs are stored. This area must be designed so that it can be locked any time the pharmacist is out.

Hospital Pharmacies

Hospital pharmacies, as the name suggests, are generally located within hospitals. They provide drugs and services to hospital inpatients (for example, patients recovering from surgery, or those admitted to the mental health ward) and also to outpatients who visit the hospital for treatment (for example, for chemotherapy to treat cancer).

There are important differences between community pharmacy practice and hospital pharmacy practice. A hospital pharmacist is generally considered a member of a patient's interdisciplinary health-care team—along with physicians, nurses, physiotherapists, anesthesiologists, and others. The hospital pharmacist is considered the pharmaceutical expert on that team, and may be given considerable authority with regard to determining a patient's drug needs. She will often have access to patient information that a community pharmacist would never see—for example, medical records, diagnosis, and treatment notes. Hospital pharmacists may make their own notations in patients' charts and participate in conferences about patient care.

A pharmacy technician who works in support of a hospital pharmacist may, in turn, have enhanced access to patient information and enhanced responsibilities with respect to work tasks. For example, pharmacy technicians in many hospital pharmacies have primary responsibility for drug dispensing and distribution.

over-the-counter (OTC) drugs
medicines that are sold directly to consumers without a prescription from a health-care professional

In its brochure about hospital pharmacy practice, the Canadian Society of Hospital Pharmacists (n.d.) cites the following advantages, for pharmacists, to practising pharmacy in a hospital:

- greater opportunities for direct patient care;
- playing a role in maintaining care continuity during patient transfers from hospital to home or other care settings;
- enhanced access to continuing education opportunities;
- opportunities to participate in research;
- opportunities to serve on patient care committees;
- opportunities to teach pharmacy students and pharmacy technicians and to educate other hospital professionals about their area of expertise; and
- better opportunities to network and share expertise with pharmacists in other settings and jurisdictions. (Canadian Society of Hospital Pharmacists, n.d.)

Working in support of a hospital pharmacist can mean that some of these benefits will trickle down to pharmacy technicians, who will gain an enhanced understanding of the role of pharmacy in a patient's broader medical care, and who will be exposed to a wider range of health-care professionals than would be the case in a community pharmacy setting. Pharmacy technicians may also be exposed to practice areas—such as pharmaceutical research—that are not part of the community pharmacy experience.

Pharmacies in Clinics

For the convenience of patients, many medical clinics incorporate a pharmacy into their services. These clinic-based pharmacies offer a number of advantages:

- Patients can fill prescriptions without having to travel to a pharmacy elsewhere.
- Where the clinic offers specialized services—for example, specialized diabetes care or travel medicine—having a pharmacist with expertise in these areas, and who stocks drugs typically prescribed to these patients, can mean a higher level of pharmacy service.
- Pharmacist familiarity with the preferences, handwriting, etc., of a smaller pool of prescribing physicians can help limit medication errors.
- Pharmacist familiarity with a small complement of physicians can help support communication about patient needs, drug reactions, and so on, providing more of a true team-based approach to patient care.

A pharmacy located in a clinic requires sufficient dedicated space to satisfy all legal regulations and College policies. For example, the College has a policy requiring that all pharmacies maintain a "professional products area" where OTC drugs are displayed for sale. This area must be within 10 metres of the dispensary (so that the pharmacist can be near enough to offer advice). The College's Professional Products Area guideline (OCP, 1994) further states that a pharmacy layout must offer an area in which a pharmacy can provide patient counselling with "reasonable acoustical privacy"—in other words, where the conversation is not likely to be overheard. Meeting these two requirements can be a challenge in clinics with little available space.

Clinics in Pharmacies

While it is common in Canada to find pharmacies in medical clinics, the reverse arrangement—where a medical clinic is situated in, and operates as part of, a retail pharmacy—is not yet a feature of our pharmacy landscape. This arrangement, however, is gaining popularity in the United States, where companies like MinuteClinic and Take Care Health Systems operate.

Pharmacy-based medical clinics offer on-the-spot diagnosis of certain common medical conditions, like ear infections, bronchitis, and skin conditions. Specified fees (for example, $62 for a swimmer's ear diagnosis) apply, and diagnoses are often made by nurse practitioners, who are qualified to write prescriptions that can be filled immediately by the pharmacist.

Pharmacy-based clinics have implications, positive and negative, for pharmacists. Some critics feel that the space requirements of these clinics can put pressure on pharmacies. On the positive side, these clinics may provide opportunities for pharmacists to offer more consultative services to customers (essentially, the pharmacist becomes a member of the diagnostic and treatment team). This may help promote the public's respect for the value of pharmacy services, and also a deeper understanding of the pharmacist's role.

One of the features that make pharmacy-based clinics attractive to US consumers is low cost. Because Canadian public health-care programs—such as the Ontario Health Insurance Plan (OHIP)—cover the full cost of all of the diagnoses offered by MinuteClinic and its competitors, there is little incentive to launch pharmacy-based clinics in Canada at the moment. ◇

Pharmacies Serving Nursing or Long-Term Care Homes

Pharmacists who provide services to residents of long-term care facilities have distinct responsibilities as members of the interdisciplinary team responsible for resident care. The College has developed a standard (OCP, 2007) that outlines those responsibilities.

Pharmacies that serve long-term care facilities often incorporate innovative services designed to meet the special needs of the elderly or of patients who must take multiple medications on a continuing basis. For example, some of these pharmacies use special packaging to group medications together by dosing time, a practice that easily allows patients or caregivers to determine which medications must be taken at a particular time, and to identify forgotten doses. Pharmacy technicians may need to assist with preparing medication for this special packaging—a task that requires a thorough understanding of the patient's needs and careful attention to detail. In some cases, drugs are packaged by computerized machinery with which the pharmacy technician must be familiar.

Internet Pharmacies

As anyone who receives Viagra spam in their email can attest, the sale of drugs online began as soon as the general public gained access to the Internet in the early 1990s. Internet-based pharmacies have since flourished, and Canada has been near the leading edge of this trend. At its most recent peak, between 2000 and 2006, some researchers estimated that US purchases from Canadian online pharmacies were worth more than $1 billion per year.

While changes to the US Medicare plan and a rising Canadian dollar, among other factors, have led to a decrease in those sales in recent years, there are still hundreds of online pharmacies claiming to be based in Canada.

Not all online pharmacy business is scrupulous. There has been criticism, inside and outside the pharmacy industry, of the practices of some of these pharmacies. The most important criticisms levelled at online pharmacies focus on the absence, in some cases, of a true physician–patient relationship between the physician who writes prescriptions for drugs bought online, and the patient-consumer.

Sometimes, a person who seeks to buy drugs from an online source never meets the prescribing physician in person. Instead, the consumer may be asked to fill out a very basic health questionnaire. There is no opportunity for a true consultation with a physician, and there is nothing to stop consumers from lying about their health status.

Of course, a patient who visits a doctor in person may also lie. However, there are better opportunities, in a traditional prescribing relationship, for the physician to assess not only the patient's health, but also his or her credibility. Also, where the patient visits a "live" pharmacist, yet another chance arises for an assessment.

Other criticisms of some online pharmacies have included:

- the fact that some of the pharmacists running these pharmacies are not properly licensed to prescribe drugs;
- the fact that it's difficult for patients to be certain that they are receiving legitimate, untampered-with medication in an appropriate dosage, and not contaminated or past its sell-by date;
- the lack of opportunity for appropriate counselling of the patient at the time of dispensing; and
- the lack of opportunity for followup to determine whether the patient is tolerating the medication well.

Despite these concerns, there are some online pharmacies that offer convenience, high standards of practice, and scrupulous service. The challenge, for the general public, is identifying these "safe" pharmacies.

Health Canada has published a guide, "Buying Drugs over the Internet" (Health Canada 2009), that provides tips for patients who wish to minimize the risks associated with the purchase of drugs online. These tips include buying from an online pharmacy that has a "bricks and mortar" physical pharmacy associated with it and provides contact/address information for that pharmacy; buying only drugs that have a **Drug Identification Number (DIN)** issued by Health Canada; and buying only from Canadian pharmacies.

Drug Identification Number (DIN)
a number assigned by Health Canada to every product defined as a drug under Canada's *Food and Drugs Act*

In addition to these strategies, consumers may look for further indicators. To assist the public in safely buying drugs online, the US National Association of Boards of Pharmacy (NABP) has created a program for certifying "Verified Internet Pharmacy Practice Sites" (VIPPS). The VIPPS seal is available to online pharmacies that meet a long list of criteria designed to protect patients' health. In 2003, the NABP entered into an agreement with Canada's National Association of Pharmacy Regulatory Authorities (NAPRA) that permits NAPRA to administer the VIPPS certification program in Canada. For a summary of the VIPPS criteria, see Appendix B at the end of this textbook.

Other Settings

Finally, a few pharmacists work in settings not described above. Some, for example, work for the Canadian Forces. The Canadian Forces do not, at the current time, employ pharmacy technicians.

Other pharmacists work in veterinary pharmacies. In the field of animal health, the line between veterinary medicine and pharmacy is somewhat blurred, with both veterinarians and pharmacists engaged in drug compounding. Guidelines on this subject have been published by the College of Veterinarians of Ontario (2007).

PHARMACY STAFF AND THEIR ROLES

Introduction

The efficient running of a pharmacy depends on the coordinated work of a number of different specialists: pharmacists (including a pharmacist who acts as a designated manager), pharmacy technicians, pharmacy aides, clerks, and customer service personnel. These workers may also interact during the workday with other employees who work in the same setting—for example, doctors and nurses in a medical clinic, or retail staff and managers in a chain drugstore or department store. Understanding your own role and the roles of people with whom you work helps promote good relations and raise the profile of pharmacy services.

The Pharmacist

According to the Ontario *Pharmacy Act*, **pharmacy** is "the custody, compounding and dispensing of drugs, the provision of non-prescription drugs, health care aids and devices and the provision of information related to drug use" (s. 3).

The pharmacist is the person with primary responsibility for the delivery of professional pharmacy services. He or she (and in large pharmacies, there may be more than one pharmacist) may not physically complete every pharmacy task; for example, the pharmacist may **delegate** the task of checking a drug delivery to ensure the order is complete. Most pharmacists play a hands-on role with respect to some duties and delegate others. Nevertheless, the pharmacist remains personally responsible for the work of the pharmacy and the well-being of its customers.

Under Ontario law, pharmacists are permitted to engage in "authorized acts." The *Pharmacy Act* specifies that a pharmacist who is a registered member of the Ontario College of Pharmacists can "dispense, sell or compound a drug or supervise the part of a pharmacy where drugs are kept" (s. 4). At the present time, pharmacists cannot fully delegate those acts to a pharmacy technician or other staff member who is not a pharmacist; however, legislative and regulatory preparations are being made to allow "remote dispensing"—a topic that will be discussed in Chapter 2 (Box 2.3).

In the meantime, a pharmacy technician can assist with these tasks; however, the technician cannot do so without a pharmacist's supervision, because the government and the College view these tasks as requiring a pharmacist's professional judgment. In order to meet the requirements of the law, pharmacists currently must personally:

pharmacy
the custody, compounding, and dispensing of drugs; the provision of non-prescription drugs, health-care aids, and devices; and the provision of information related to drug use

delegate
legally assign to a subordinate health professional (in Ontario, under the *Registered Health Professions Act*)

- counsel clients about both prescription and OTC drugs;
- investigate any perceived problem with the safety or therapeutic appropriateness of a prescription;
- make decisions related to dosage substitution (for example, deciding to dispense pills in a smaller dosage unit because the patient cannot swallow the larger size—such as instructing the patient to take two 250-milligram tablets instead of one 500-milligram tablet at dosing times);
- make decisions about special preparations and compounding (for example, preparing a liquid form of a drug that was prescribed in tablet form, or combining two ingredients in a skin cream); and
- undertake any other task that requires the use of professional judgment.

In its protocol on delegating the tasks of dispensing and compounding (OCP, 1995), the College states that only a pharmacist can autonomously compound, dispense, or sell controlled substances. While aspects of these tasks can be delegated to pharmacy technicians or aides, the College takes the position that only the technical aspects of compounding and dispensing can be handled by technicians. Included in "technical aspects" would be counting out pills or physically preparing admixtures. Cognitive—non-technical—aspects of dispensing and compounding are those aspects of the job that require the exercise of professional judgment—for example, in the words of the protocol mentioned above, "assessing the therapeutic appropriateness of a prescription."

In order to qualify to practise pharmacy, a candidate must complete an Ontario Bachelor of Science in Pharmacy university degree or foreign equivalent (including degrees from other provinces). This educational requirement takes between four

---

FACTS AND TRENDS   BOX 1.2

Prescribing Pharmacists?

The scope of pharmacy technician practice is not the only hot topic in pharmacy these days. In Canada, pharmacists are not permitted, strictly speaking, to prescribe medications—only to dispense them. However, the line between prescribing and dispensing is not absolutely clear.

Consider, for example, a situation in which a pharmacist fills a prescription for Tylenol 3 for an elderly patient. Pharmacists know well that the codeine in Tylenol 3 can cause troublesome constipation, especially in the elderly. In an effort to prevent this side effect, the pharmacist might, when presenting the drug to the patient, point out (even hold out by hand) an OTC constipation remedy and recommend that the patient take this product along with the prescription. This activity, while not technically pharmacist prescribing, is very similar in nature—the only distinction is that the pharmacist-recommended product is an OTC drug.

Pharmacists also come close to prescribing when they make autonomous decisions to adjust a prescription dose, dosage schedule, or delivery format; or when they allow a patient to purchase a supply of emergency medication.

The Canadian Pharmacists Association (CPhA) supports an expanded role for pharmacist prescribing. For more information, see the association's "Position Statement on Pharmacist Prescribing" (CPhA, 2007). ◈

and five years. After graduation, candidates must pass provincial and national examinations, apply for registration with the College, and maintain and upgrade their pharmacy knowledge through continuing education and lifelong learning.

Pharmacists registered with the College are the only individuals authorized, in Ontario, to use certain alternative job titles, including "apothecary," "druggist," "pharmacist," or "pharmaceutical chemist" (*Pharmacy Act*, s. 10). There are amendments to the legislation that are awaiting proclamation (waiting to be declared in force by Parliament) that will also make it illegal, once pharmacy technicians are registered with the College, for non-members to call themselves "pharmacy technicians."

The Designated Manager (DM) or Owner-Manager

Section 146(1.1) of the *Drug and Pharmacies Regulation Act* (DPRA) states:

> 146 (1.1) Every owner of a pharmacy shall designate a designated manager for the pharmacy, and file notice of the designation with the College in accordance with the regulations.

The **designated manager** is the manager who is legally responsible for the pharmacy's compliance with all applicable laws and standards. It is illegal to operate a pharmacy that does not have a designated manager in place.

Designated managers must:

- register as such with the College (any change of designated manager must be communicated to the College);
- post their name and certificate of registration in a prominent location in the pharmacy;
- come before the discipline committee, if they are asked to do so, to respond to a complaint that the pharmacy has failed to comply with the law; and
- keep a record of every purchase and sale of a drug referred to in the *Schedules to the Controlled Drugs and Substances Act* (Canada) or the *Schedule to the Narcotic Control Regulations* (Canada).

As the person responsible for a pharmacy's legal compliance, the designated manager is legally responsible "for every offence against this Act committed by any person in the employ of or under the supervision of the owner or designated manager with the owner's or designated manager's permission, consent or approval, express or implied" (DPRA, s. 166).

designated manager
a pharmacist who has been appointed by the pharmacy owner or operator as having the ultimate legal responsibility for the pharmacy's compliance with laws, standards, and guidelines

Relief Pharmacists

Relief pharmacists are not employed full-time by a particular pharmacy, but choose instead to make themselves available for temporary work assignments at pharmacies that are short-staffed—for example, because the regular pharmacist is away sick or is on vacation.

Relief pharmacists must be registered with the College and must meet all the same educational and qualifying requirements of regularly employed pharmacists. Subject to any restrictions on their licences, relief pharmacists are authorized to do any act permitted by law for a pharmacist, including dispensing, compounding, and supervising other staff, including pharmacy technicians.

For a pharmacy technician, working with a relief pharmacist can pose certain challenges. Individuals vary in their work habits, expectations, and the way in which they delegate and supervise work. To work successfully with a relief pharmacist, a pharmacy technician must be prepared to be flexible, to listen carefully to instructions, and to be willing to collaborate in new ways. If the relief pharmacist is replacing the only pharmacist in a particular pharmacy, the pharmacy technician will be an important resource: because she is familiar with the organization of the dispensary and the procedures and systems in place, she will likely be needed to answer questions, explain procedures, and advise the relief pharmacist of the pharmacy's priorities for the day. She may also serve as the liaison between the relief pharmacist and other employees (including pharmacy aides), suppliers, and even prescribing physicians.

The Pharmacy Technician

As of 2010, registration of pharmacy technicians is likely to bring some changes to the profession. Now that pharmacy technicians are self-regulated, members of the profession will likely be called upon to develop or update certification conditions, educational requirements, professional standards, best practices, codes of conduct, and guidelines for discipline. This textbook outlines the current scope of practice and legal status of pharmacy technicians, and also provides some insight into potential changes to the profession.

Currently, pharmacy technicians may, under direct supervision, assist a pharmacist with the following dispensing tasks:

- receiving a written prescription or request for prescription refill from the patient or representative, and ensuring completeness of the information on the prescription;
- establishing and maintaining patient profiles in the database;
- selecting the appropriate prescription container, preparing prescription labels, and applying labels and auxiliary labels (for example, a label directing the patient to avoid dairy products while taking the medication) to the container;
- counting, pouring, weighing, measuring, reconstituting, and mixing medications;
- preparing specialty products;
- pricing prescriptions;
- maintaining packaging and dispensing equipment; and
- in institutional settings, replenishing medications for nursing units, night cupboards, emergency boxes, and cardiac arrest kits.

In health-care pharmacy settings, a pharmacy technician's role can be somewhat different, with a greater level of autonomy with respect to some dispensing tasks. For more information, you may want to review the College's "Protocol for Delegating Dispensing and Compounding in Health Care Facilities" (OCP, 1995).

Pharmacy technicians often carry out non-dispensing tasks of a more clerical nature. These tasks may include:

- preparing receipts, invoices, and other forms and communications;
- filing;
- preparing and reconciling third-party billings;
- answering the telephone;
- preparing and maintaining records;
- managing inventory and ordering drugs (including checking orders); and
- restocking drugs and other supplies.

Table 1.1 compares and contrasts the respective scopes of practice of pharmacists and pharmacy technicians.

Table 1.1   Scopes of Practice: Pharmacists and Pharmacy Technicians

Pharmacists	Pharmacy Technicians
<ul><li>have responsibility for patient care through direct assessment and intervention</li><li>are health professionals who practise within a knowledge-based environment in which they use high-level critical thinking, specialized knowledge of drug therapy, and professional judgment appropriate to the pharmacist role to offer and optimize patient care</li><li>are accountable for direct patient care knowledge</li><li>practise in accordance with professional registration and licensure and professional standards within their jurisdiction</li><li>possess both broad-based and pharmacy-specific knowledge</li><li>mentor pharmacists, pharmacy students or interns, pharmacy technicians, and others</li><li>take responsibility for their continuing professional development and commit to lifelong learning</li></ul>	<ul><li>have responsibility for patient care and to the circle of care through collaborative relationships with pharmacists</li><li>are health professionals who use their knowledge, skills, abilities, and attitudes to think critically, solve problems, make decisions, and generate professional judgments appropriate to the pharmacy technician role that optimize patient care</li><li>recognize and differentiate practice situations within the collaborative relationship in which they make decisions and take action independently, those that require pharmacist intervention, and those that are team-based in nature</li><li>are accountable for respecting and supporting the role, rights, and responsibilities of patients, pharmacy technicians, the pharmacy team, health-care providers, and others</li><li>practise in accordance with provincial/territorial professional requirements, standards, bylaws, and policies</li><li>possess pharmacy-specific knowledge, skill, abilities, and attitudes related to technical and distributive aspects</li><li>act as mentors to pharmacy technicians, pharmacy technician students, and others</li><li>collaborate with and are an integral part of the health-care team</li><li>take responsibility for their continuing professional development and commit to lifelong learning.</li></ul>

Source: NAPRA, 2007, p. 7.

Dispensary Assistants and Other Pharmacy Workers

Besides pharmacists and pharmacy technicians, some pharmacies employ other personnel. These individuals may have a wide range of titles, but they fall into two general categories: employees who work with the public, and employees who help maintain the dispensary.

Both categories of "other pharmacy workers" differ from registered pharmacy technicians in important respects. These workers, while very much needed in busy pharmacies, will have a narrow scope of practice in that they are not permitted to complete "authorized acts" independently.

Unregulated pharmacy workers require supervision at all times. When they work in the dispensary—for example, taking inventory, placing and checking orders, stocking supplies, keeping records—they must defer to a pharmacist on any matter involving professional judgment. Pharmacists are responsible for the quality of their work and so are likely to check it carefully.

When unregulated pharmacy employees work with the public, their work does not extend to patient counselling because that task requires professional judgment. They may, however, be able to provide other kinds of customer service—for example, entering demographic data into the computer, answering phones, working the cash register, and booking client appointments for medication reviews. Where unregulated workers work closely with the public, a pharmacist should always be close by in case a customer asks a question that requires the pharmacist's expertise.

Non-Pharmacy Workers

In some settings, pharmacy technicians may have contact with non-pharmacy workers. For example, in a big chain drugstore, retail sales staff may need to consult with pharmacy staff about such matters as the organization of displays, the use of floor space and waiting areas, and the stocking of store shelves. While retail staff typically make most of the decisions about store organization, pharmacy staff may need to advise the retail staff about legal requirements and regulatory guidelines—for example, the College requirement to display OTC drugs no farther than 10 metres from the dispensary.

Retail staff may also, on occasion, direct or refer customers to the pharmacy, or to displays of OTC drugs. Maintaining a good working relationship with retail staff will ensure that those staff understand to whom these referrals should be made. New retail staff may not realize, for example, that pharmacists are available to give advice not only about prescription drugs, but also about OTC medicines.

THE PHARMACY AS HYBRID: A BUSINESS AND A PROFESSIONAL PRACTICE

This textbook emphasizes professionalism in pharmacy technician practice. However, some people believe that professional services and business objectives are not entirely compatible.

Service professionals pride themselves on taking the welfare and interests of their clients to heart by "putting the client first." Businesspeople, rightly or wrongly, are sometimes accused of putting profit first—often by focusing on economic self-interest.

The business of selling medication is a very lucrative one. For ill people, medication is a necessity, not a discretionary expense, and most people value their health very highly. While criticism sometimes appears in the media related to the profits made by big drug companies, it's important to remember that if drugs were not profitable, researchers would have little incentive to continue looking for cures for the diseases that ail humanity.

A pharmacy is a retail business that cannot survive without making a profit. That is a fundamental truth. In order to retain the public's trust, pharmacists and pharmacy technicians must embrace business values, but they must do so within the bounds of professionalism. This textbook will help you, as a pharmacy technician, develop a richer understanding of what it means, in practice, to do just that.

KEY TERMS

delegate
designated manager
Drug Identification Number (DIN)
medication error
over-the-counter (OTC) drugs
pharmacy

REFERENCES

Canadian Pharmacists Association (CPhA). (2007, August). CPhA position statement on pharmacist prescribing. Retrieved May 11, 2010 from http://www.pharmacists.ca/content/about_cpha/who_we_are/policy_position/pdf/CPhA%20position%20statement%20Pharmacist%20Prescribing%20Final2%20August%2007.pdf.

Canadian Society of Hospital Pharmacists. (n.d.). Hospital pharmacy: Imagine the possibilities. Retrieved May 11, 2010 from http://www.cshp.ca/productsServices/otherPublications/pharmbrochure_e.asp.

College of Veterinarians of Ontario. (2007, September). Guidelines for the compounding of veterinary drugs. Retrieved May 13, 2010 from http://www.cvo.org/uploadattachments/Drugcompounding.pdf.

Drug and Pharmacies Regulation Act. 1990. RSO 1990, c. H.4.

Health Canada. (2009, November). Buying drugs over the Internet. Retrieved May 11, 2010 from http://www.hc-sc.gc.ca/hl-vs/iyh-vsv/med/internet-eng.php.

National Association of Pharmacy Regulatory Authorities (NAPRA). (2007, September). Professional competencies for Canadian pharmacy technicians at entry to practice. Retrieved May 11, 2010 from http://www.ocpinfo.com/ Client/ocp/OCPHome.nsf/object/Pharmacy+Technician+Competencies +Profile/$file/PT_Competencies.pdf.

Ontario College of Pharmacists (OCP). (n.d.). Proposed standards of practice for registered pharmacy technicians: Summary. Standard one. Retrieved May 11, 2010 from http://www.ocpinfo.com/client/ocp/OCPHome.nsf/object/ Proposed_For_Techs/$file/Proposed_For_Techs.pdf.

Ontario College of Pharmacists (OCP). (1994, February). Standards, policies and guidelines: Professional practice area. Retrieved May 11, 2010 from http://www.ocpinfo.com/client/ocp/OCPHome.nsf/web/ Professional+Products+Area.

Ontario College of Pharmacists (OCP). (1995, June). Protocol for delegating dispensing and compounding in health care facilities. Retrieved May 11, 2010 from http://www.ocpinfo.com/client/ocp/OCPHome.nsf/web/Protocol +for+Delegating+Dispensing+&+Compounding+in+Health+Care+ Facilities.

Ontario College of Pharmacists (OCP). (2007, January). Standards, policies and guidelines: Standards for pharmacists providing pharmacy services to licensed long-term care facilities. Retrieved May 11, 2010 from http://www.ocpinfo.com/client/ocp/OCPHome.nsf/web/ Standards+for+Long-Term+Care+Facilities.

Pharmacy Act. 1991. SO 1991, c. 36.

Registered Health Professions Act. 1991. SO 1991, c. 18.

REVIEW EXERCISES

Discussion Questions

1. Why might you, as a pharmacy technician, wish to be viewed as a professional? What are the advantages of professional status? Are there any disadvantages?

2. There has been a strong trend, in the pharmacy business, toward locating pharmacies within larger retail businesses. Do you believe that this trend is beneficial or not beneficial to the industry as a whole? Explain.

Review Questions

1. List five attributes associated with professionals in our society.

2. List at least five responsibilities of a professional.

3. List at least five different settings in which a pharmacy technician may practice.

4. Which modern practice setting is most similar to the settings in which the ancestors of pharmacists—alchemists and healers, for example—used to practise?

5. What challenges do independent community pharmacies face, and how can they meet those challenges?

6. Which features of chain drugstore pharmacies make them especially attractive to consumers?

7. What regulations exist to safeguard the drugs stored in pharmacies that are located in department stores?

8. What aspects of practice make hospital-based work attractive to many pharmacy technicians?

9. List at least four ways in which medical clinic-based pharmacies may differ from typical community pharmacies.

10. Where might you find more information about the College's guidelines for the delivery of pharmacy services to the residents of long-term care facilities and nursing homes?

11. How can members of the public assure themselves that an online pharmacy meets the standards approved by the pharmacy industry?

12. Is a pharmacy legally responsible for the quality of dispensing work done by pharmacy technicians?

13. What is a designated manager?

14. Can dispensary assistants or other pharmacy aides do the same work as pharmacy technicians?

15. Why should pharmacy technicians make an effort to familiarize themselves with non-pharmacy workers in retail settings?

CHAPTER 2

The Regulation of Pharmacy Professionals

According to Ontario law, pharmacy technicians must work under the direct supervision of a licensed pharmacist.

LEARNING OBJECTIVES

After completing this chapter, you should be able to:

- Name three statutes that regulate the practice of pharmacy in Ontario.

- Explain the purpose of the *Regulated Health Professions Act*.

- Explain where to find the *Health Professions Procedural Code* and summarize its purpose.

- Understand the objectives and application of the *Pharmacy Act* and the *Drug and Pharmacies Regulation Act*.

- Describe the role of the Ontario College of Pharmacists.

- Summarize the current regulatory status of Ontario pharmacy technicians and discuss the journey toward self-regulation for that profession.

INTRODUCTION

Health is precious. Without it, people may lose enjoyment in work, social activities, and recreation, and therefore experience reduced quality of life. In recognition of the importance of health, all Canadian provincial and territorial governments impose some regulation and control over the provision of health-care services. While some health-care services are fairly new to regulation, pharmacy has long been regulated in Ontario and around the world.

Before 1991, health-care services were regulated, in Ontario, through a patchwork of laws (laws are also commonly known as "statutes" or "legislation"; all three terms will be used in this textbook). Pharmacy, for example, was regulated under the *Health Disciplines Act*, which has since been repealed ("taken off the books"; made inapplicable), and the *Drug and Pharmacies Regulation Act*, which remains in force.

In an effort to harmonize and simplify the regulation of health-care services, the Ontario government, in 1991, passed (brought into force) the *Regulated Health Professions Act* (RHPA). The RHPA is intended to assist the Minister of Health and Long-Term Care ("the Minister") in discharging his or her duty to:

> ensure that the health professions are regulated and co-ordinated in the public interest, that appropriate standards of practice are developed and maintained and that individuals have access to services provided by the health professions of their choice and that they are treated with sensitivity and respect in their dealings with health professionals, the Colleges and the Board. (RHPA, s. 3)

The RHPA is a "generalist statute"; that is, it provides a structure for the regulation of many different health professions, including medicine, dentistry, pharmacy, and midwifery, among others. You will learn more about the objectives and application of the RHPA later in this chapter.

Because the RHPA provides only general regulation, many health professions are also subject to a profession-specific statute. In the case of pharmacy, this is the *Pharmacy Act*. Now that pharmacy technicians are a self-regulated profession, this statute may be amended to govern their specific role in the pharmacy field; alternatively, a new statute that governs pharmacy technicians specifically may eventually be passed. The *Pharmacy Act* is discussed later in this chapter.

The RHPA provides that each regulated health profession in Ontario will be governed by a College (although a College can govern more than one profession). In the case of pharmacists, pharmacy students and interns, and pharmacy technicians, the governing College is the Ontario College of Pharmacists (www.ocpinfo.com). To permit true self-regulation of the pharmacy technician profession, pharmacy technicians will have a role in developing membership criteria and standards, guidelines, procedures, rules, and a disciplinary system for pharmacy technicians within the College generally. For example, amendments to the *Pharmacy Act*, 1991 proclaimed December 15, 2009 (s. 7(1)(a)) provide that between two and four members of the 17-member Council of the College will, from now on, be pharmacy technicians. The role of the College is discussed later in this chapter.

The *Drug and Pharmacies Regulation Act* (DPRA) was once a long and detailed statute with six parts and over 150 provisions. When the RHPA was passed in 1991, most of the DPRA was repealed because the subject matter covered by those provisions was incorporated into the RHPA. In its current form, the DPRA has, as its primary objective, the accreditation and regulation of pharmacies (and only indirectly, pharmacists and pharmacy technicians). Section 139 of the DPRA states that "no person shall establish or operate a pharmacy unless a certificate of accreditation has been issued in respect thereof." The DPRA is discussed later in this chapter.

Finally, the profession of pharmacy is affected by other statutes—for example, at the federal level, the *Controlled Drugs and Substances Act* and the *Food and Drugs Act*, and at the provincial level, the *Personal Health Information Protection Act*. These statutes and others will be discussed in later chapters of this textbook.

FACTS AND TRENDS

BOX 2.1

Legal Citations

You will notice that some of the statute names mentioned in this textbook and listed in the References at the end of each chapter are followed by numbers and letters; for example, the *Pharmacy Act* is followed by "SO 1991, c. 36." This "code" is called a *citation*. It provides information about the law and where to find it in a book or online. Here's how to make sense of the abbreviations.

1. The letters at the beginning of the citation identify the **jurisdiction** of the statute—the parliamentary body that created the law, and the political unit to which it applies.

   - "SO" stands for Statutes of Ontario.
   - "RSO" stands for Revised Statutes of Ontario.

   Similar abbreviations indicate the provincial statutes of other provinces—for example, "SM" refers to the statutes of Manitoba.

   - "SC" stands for Statutes of Canada.
   - "RSC" stands for Revised Statutes of Canada.

2. The year that follows the jurisdiction abbreviation indicates the year in which the law was proclaimed.

3. The "c." stands for "chapter" and reflects the way in which laws are numbered by the parliament that proclaimed them.

   - Statutes are numbered starting from "1" each year, as they are passed; the first law passed in 1991 would be numbered "c. 1," while the 36th statute passed by the Ontario government in 1991 would be numbered "c. 36."
   - Some chapter numbering includes an alphabetic letter reference. The letter matches the first (or most important) word in the statute (not counting "the"). The number indicates the order in which the statute was passed. For example, the *Fisheries Act* is cited "RSC 1985, c. F-14."

Understanding legal citations can help you locate statutes in books; however, you won't be completely lost without citations. Current statutes can now easily be located online, using keyword searches. There are a variety of sources, but the most up-to-date websites are those of the pertinent governments.

For Ontario statutes, see www.e-laws.gov.on.ca; for federal statutes, see http://laws.justice.gc.ca. ◈

jurisdiction
the parliamentary body that created a law, and the political unit to which it applies

THE REGULATED HEALTH PROFESSIONS ACT

Introduction

The primary function of the RHPA is to create a mechanism for the supervision, by the Minister, of the regulated health professions. The list of health professions regulated under the RHPA is set out in Schedule 1 to the statute. Pharmacy is on the list; the work of pharmacy technicians is not, at least not as a profession separate from pharmacy. However, the RHPA's application to pharmacists has relevance to pharmacy technicians because they do work delegated to them by pharmacists.

The RHPA gave the Minister the power to create the Health Professions Regulatory Advisory Council (HPRAC). The Advisory Council is made up of between five and seven members appointed by the Lieutenant Governor-in-Council (with the Minister's recommendations). It has the following mandate:

- to advise the Minister whether unregulated professions should be regulated, and whether currently regulated professions should no longer be regulated;
- to suggest amendments to the RHPA, a health profession Act or a regulation under any of those Acts; and to suggest new regulations;
- to investigate and oversee the quality assurance programs implemented by Colleges;
- to investigate and advise the Minister of its conclusions about any matter the Minister refers to it; and
- to monitor each College's patient relations program and to advise the Minister about its effectiveness. (HPRAC, 2007)

The Advisory Council acts as a liaison between the Minister and the individual councils of the Colleges affected by the RHPA, assisting the Minister in carrying out his or her powers with respect to those Colleges. The Minister's powers include the ability to:

(a) inquire into or require a Council to inquire into the state of practice of a health profession in a locality or institution;

(b) review a Council's activities and require the Council to provide reports and information;

(c) require a Council to make, amend or revoke a regulation under a health profession Act or the *Drug and Pharmacies Regulation Act*;

(d) require a Council to do anything that, in the opinion of the Minister, is necessary or advisable to carry out the intent of this Act, the health profession Acts or the *Drug and Pharmacies Regulation Act* … . (RHPA, s. 5.1)

Controlled Acts

controlled act
in Ontario, under the *Regulated Health Professions Act*, a specific act or procedure that may be performed only by a specific health professional

Section 27(2) of the RHPA contains a list of **controlled acts** that can be done only by:

1. a person who, as a member of a regulated profession, is authorized to do the act; or

2. a person to whom the act has been delegated by a member of a regulated profession who is authorized to do it.

Acts related to pharmacy that are included in the list are:

8. Prescribing, dispensing, selling or compounding a drug as defined in the Drug and Pharmacies Regulation Act, or supervising the part of a pharmacy where such drugs are kept.

Section 28 of the RHPA, which deals with the delegation of controlled acts, is of special interest to pharmacy technicians. This section provides that any delegation of a controlled act by or to a member of a regulated profession must take place

---

FACTS AND TRENDS   BOX 2.2

Legislation, Regulations, and Policies

This textbook discusses a wide range of documents that have implications for pharmacy technicians. What are the differences among them?

Legislation (also called statutes or laws) is introduced into a parliament—either the federal House of Commons, or the parliament of a provincial or territorial government—and is passed by a formal vote. Changes to legislation must also be formally introduced in this way. Legislation is typically administered (applied and enforced) by the government ministry most closely associated with the subject matter of the legislation—for example, the *Regulated Health Professions Act* is administered by the Ontario Minister of Health and Long-Term Care, while the *Controlled Drugs and Substances Act* is administered by the federal Ministry of the Attorney General.

Legislation can contain schedules (often, lists or tables), codes (bodies of rules), and other appendixes. If they are part of the statute, these appendixes have the force of law.

Many statutes contain **offences** that can be charged when a person covered by the legislation does something contrary to it, or fails to do something required by it. People found guilty of an offence may be subject to a fine or even imprisonment.

Regulations are another form of government-created law. They are made "under" statutes—that is, under the authority of a statute to support its administration. Regulations provide technical details or instructions that elaborate on a statute's more general provisions. For example, a statute may state that a person cannot engage in an activity (such as driving a car on a highway) unless that person obtains a licence. In contrast, the details about what the licence should say, and how it may be obtained, would be contained in regulations made under the statute.

Unlike statutes, regulations need not be voted into force by a parliament; the government simply publishes and adopts them. They do, however, have the force of law and must be followed. Anyone violating a regulation may be charged with an offence under the regulation's parent statute.

Policies—which can include guidelines, codes, rules, statements of expectations, and other documents—may be created by governments or non-governmental bodies, such as corporations, associations, and colleges. Policies are designed to make members, customers, or the general public aware of an organization's rules and processes.

Anyone violating a policy may lose a privilege (for example, the right to obtain a licence or register for a program) or be subject to a penalty—for example, a fine or the loss of membership in the policy-making organization. ◈

legislation
laws introduced into a parliament and passed by a formal vote

offences
acts or omissions committed that run contrary to a statute

regulations
laws created under a statute to support its administration

policies
guidelines, codes, rules, and statements of expectations created by governments or non-governmental bodies

in accordance with the regulations that govern delegation within that profession. In the case of pharmacy, delegation of work to pharmacy technicians is covered by section 149(1)(d) of the *Drug and Pharmacies Regulation Act*, which is discussed later in this chapter.

A notable exception to the prohibition against controlled acts by non-members is an emergency that requires first aid. In fact, in some facilities such as hospitals and long-term care homes, pharmacists prepare caches (emergency drug boxes) of certain drugs commonly required in emergencies (for example, cardiac arrest), even when such drugs have not previously been prescribed for the patient.

Engaging in a controlled act without authority—without being a member of a regulated profession authorized to do the act, or a person to whom the act was properly delegated—is an offence. Anyone who commits this offence can be charged under section 40(1) of the RHPA, and upon conviction may be fined up to $25,000, imprisoned for up to one year, or both. A conviction for a second such offence can lead to a fine of up to $50,000, imprisonment for one year, or both.

If a person violates section 27 (controlled acts) with the blessing and knowledge of his or her employer, the employer can also be charged. For example, a corporate director of a company that employs a person who violates section 27 can also be charged, provided that the director "approved of, permitted, or acquiesced in" the violation.

Finally, it is an offence for a person to "procure employment" for another who will be performing controlled acts without authority, when the procurer knows this is likely to happen. For example, it would be an offence for an employment agency to knowingly arrange employment as a pharmacist for a person who is not registered as such.

Confidentiality and Privacy

Section 36 of the RHPA states that regulated health professionals must keep confidential all information that they collect in the course of their work, except under certain prescribed circumstances. For example, they can divulge the information to their own lawyer if they are subject to prosecution, or if they are specifically required to do so under a statute.

Confidentiality goes both ways: the RHPA also imposes limits on the purposes for which the Minister can request information about regulated health professionals, and on the ways the Minister can use this information.

The RHPA is not the only statute that imposes confidentiality requirements. Other privacy legislation—for example, the *Personal Health Information Protection Act*—also applies. Privacy and confidentiality are further discussed in Chapter 3.

The Health Professions Procedural Code

The *Health Professions Procedural Code* ("the Code"), which appears as Schedule 2 to the RHPA, is a document longer than the RHPA itself. Section 4 of the RHPA states that the Code is considered a part of each health profession statute (including the *Pharmacy Act*).

The Code includes a list of objectives for each regulatory College. The objectives imposed on the Colleges by the Code are as follows:

1. To regulate the practice of the profession and to govern the members in accordance with the health profession Act, this Code and the *Regulated Health Professions Act, 1991* and the regulations and by-laws.

2. To develop, establish and maintain standards of qualification for persons to be issued certificates of registration.

3. To develop, establish and maintain programs and standards of practice to assure the quality of the practice of the profession.

4. To develop, establish and maintain standards of knowledge and skill and programs to promote continuing evaluation, competence and improvement among the members.

4.1 To develop, in collaboration and consultation with other Colleges, standards of knowledge, skill and judgment relating to the performance of controlled acts common among health professions to enhance interprofessional collaboration, while respecting the unique character of individual health professions and their members.

5. To develop, establish and maintain standards of professional ethics for the members.

6. To develop, establish and maintain programs to assist individuals to exercise their rights under this Code and the *Regulated Health Professions Act, 1991*.

7. To administer the health profession Act, this Code and the *Regulated Health Professions Act, 1991* as it relates to the profession and to perform the other duties and exercise the other powers that are imposed or conferred on the College.

8. To promote and enhance relations between the College and its members, other health profession colleges, key stakeholders, and the public.

9. To promote interprofessional collaboration with other health profession colleges.

10. To develop, establish, and maintain standards and programs to promote the ability of members to respond to changes in practice environments, advances in technology and other emerging issues.

11. Any other objects relating to human health care that the Council considers desirable. (*Health Professions Procedural Code*, s. 3)

Another important objective, which is reinforced by section 1.1 of the Code, is "to encourage the reporting of [sexual] abuse, to provide funding for therapy and counselling for patients who have been sexually abused by members and, ultimately, to eradicate the sexual abuse of patients by members."

One of the most important provisions of the Code is section 3(2), which states that the College has a duty, in carrying out the objectives listed above, to protect the public interest. This provision makes it clear that where the interests of College members and the interests of the public conflict, the College must take the side of the public. Because the College provides a great deal of support and information for members of the pharmacy and pharmacy technician communities, it is easy to assume that the College is an advocate for the profession, and exists to protect its members. This is a false, and potentially dangerous, assumption. The College's role as a protector of the public interest is discussed more fully later in this chapter.

The Code provides that, in order to support the achievement of its objectives (listed above), each College must establish seven different committees, namely:

- Executive Committee;
- Registration Committee;
- Inquiries, Complaints, and Reports Committee;
- Discipline Committee;
- Fitness to Practise Committee;
- Quality Assurance Committee; and
- Patient Relations Committee.

The Code contains detailed procedural provisions that are designed to guide the way in which a College carries out its objectives. For example, sections 13 through 24 of the Code, which take up several pages of text, provide guidelines on how to manage registrations, including the following situations:

- what happens when a College has concerns about a person's eligibility for registration;
- the basis upon which conditions can be imposed on a registration;
- what members can do if they feel that they have been unjustly denied registration;
- the role of the Fairness Commissioner, a person who is appointed under the *Fair Access to Regulated Professions Act*, and who intervenes in situations in which someone claims he or she is being unfairly prevented from registering as a member of a regulated profession;
- what happens when someone is discovered to have registered, or has attempted to register, fraudulently (this is an offence);
- what information the College is required to keep in the register; and
- the rules for public access to that information, and for the protection of the privacy of members.

Other topics covered in detail by the Code include:

- complaints and reports (made by the public about members, and how these complaints and reports are handled);
- discipline of members by the College;
- procedures for handling situations in which a member is suspected to be incapable of carrying out his or her professional duties;
- appeals from College decisions to courts of law (appeals outside the professional regulation system into the court system);
- procedures for reinstating suspended members;
- procedures for investigations;
- guidelines for the work of the Quality Assurance Committee of a College;
- guidelines for the establishment and management of a Patient Relations Program;
- procedures for making reports (complaints) about health professionals and guidelines for handling these reports;
- rules for funding counselling and other member-support programs; and
- rules for the management of health profession corporations.

Covering all the procedures related to these topics is beyond the scope of this textbook. Pharmacy technicians need not be familiar with such details unless they face them in practice. However, pharmacy technicians must have a general understanding of the kinds of topics covered in the Code so that they know where to retrieve this information if they need it. Some of the above-listed topics—for example, complaints and discipline—are discussed later in this textbook, and specific provisions of the Code will be mentioned then. For now, readers should simply review the list above—and perhaps also the Table of Contents of the Code (see RHPA, 1991 in the References at the end of this chapter)—to develop an understanding of the Code's scope.

THE PHARMACY ACT

The Act

The *Pharmacy Act*, 1991 ("the PA") is the specific "health profession Act" (as described in the RHPA) that applies to pharmacists. In some respects, it also regulates the work of pharmacy technicians. The PA defines the practice of pharmacy as:

> the custody, compounding and dispensing of drugs, the provision of non-prescription drugs, health care aids and devices and the provision of information related to drug use. (PA, s. 3)

The PA provides that the Ontario College of Pharmacists regulates all pharmacists in practice in Ontario, and that no person who is not a registered member of the College can practise pharmacy, present him- or herself as a pharmacist, or use certain titles, including "apothecary," "druggist," or "pharmaceutical chemist." The title "pharmacy technician" will soon be added to the list of restricted titles now that pharmacy technicians are registered.

Using one of these titles without being a member of the College, or representing oneself as qualified to practise pharmacy in Ontario without being a member, is an offence. The penalty is similar to that imposed under the RHPA for performing a controlled act without authorization: up to $25,000 for a first offence and $50,000 for a second.

In addition to the list of objectives included in the PA by the *Health Professions Procedural Code* (see above), the PA lists two other objectives:

1. To regulate drugs and pharmacies under the *Drug and Pharmacies Regulation Act*.

2. To develop, establish and maintain standards of qualification for persons to be issued certificates of accreditation.

As is required by the RHPA, the PA establishes a Council for the College of Pharmacists. As of December 2009 there is a requirement that between two and four members of the nine- to 17-member Council "hold a certificate of registration as a pharmacy technician." This requirement provides true self-regulation for pharmacy technicians.

The PA also establishes the College's Accreditation Committee.

Two regulations have been made under the PA: a "general" regulation (O. Reg. 202/94) and a "professional misconduct" regulation (O. Reg. 681/93).

The General Regulation

The general regulation prescribes classes of registration for members of the College. Prior to 2010, the available classes were "Pharmacist," "Registered Pharmacy Student," and "Intern." After 2010, when the College registers the first members of the new class "Pharmacy Technician," either the general regulation will be amended, or a separate regulation will be introduced providing for the registration of pharmacy technicians.

The general regulation sets out the conditions of registration for the existing classes, and describes what happens when an individual fails to live up to those conditions (in brief, that person is required to surrender his or her certificate of registration, but remains subject to discipline for any actions that occurred before the certificate was surrendered).

It is likely that the general conditions for registration—the ones that apply to all three classes that existed prior to 2010—will apply to pharmacy technicians as well. Those general conditions are as follows:

1. The applicant must be able to speak and write in English or French with reasonable fluency.

2. The applicant must not have been found guilty of an offence under any Act regulating the practice of pharmacists or relating to the sale of drugs, or of any criminal offence.

3. The applicant must not be the subject of a current proceeding relating to an offence under any Act regulating the practice of pharmacists or relating to the sale of drugs, or relating to any criminal offence.

4. The applicant must not have been the subject of a finding of professional misconduct, incompetence, or incapacity in Ontario or any other jurisdiction in relation to pharmacy or any other health profession and must not be the subject of any current professional misconduct, incompetence, or incapacity proceeding in Ontario or any other jurisdiction in relation to pharmacy or any other health profession.

5. The applicant must be a Canadian citizen or must hold the appropriate authorization under the *Immigration and Refugee Protection Act* (Canada) to permit the applicant to engage in the practice of pharmacy in Canada as a pharmacist, registered pharmacy student or intern.

6. The applicant's past and present conduct affords reasonable grounds for the belief that the applicant will practise with decency, honesty and integrity and in accordance with the law … ." (O. Reg 202/94, s. 28(1))

Any time applicants whose registration has not been completed—or members of the College who have successfully registered—do anything to place themselves in violation of any of these conditions, they are obliged to give notice to the College.

For example, if a person moves to Ontario from Alberta and applies to register as a pharmacist in Ontario, then subsequently learns that disciplinary proceedings have been commenced against him by the College of Pharmacists of Alberta, he must advise the Ontario College of the proceedings, which may affect his Ontario registration.

Besides meeting the six general conditions listed above, applicants who want to register with the College as pharmacists (that is, not as students, interns, or pharmacy technicians) must meet additional criteria. A person who wishes to register as a pharmacy technician in Ontario must be a new graduate of a Pharmacy Technician Education Program accredited by the Canadian Council of Accreditation for Pharmacy Programs (CCAPP), or, if she or he is already in practice, must have completed an equivalent degree and a "bridging" (refresher) program. Any domestic or foreign degree that is acceptable, for exam eligibility purposes, to the Pharmacy Examination Board of Canada (PEBC) will generally be accepted by the College. The applicant must pass the PEBC qualifying exam before applying to the College for membership.

Besides having a recognized degree and passing the PEBC exam, all applicants must pass the College's Jurisprudence Exam (which tests familiarity with Ontario law). Applicants must also show proof that they have completed 48 weeks of inservice training approved by the Council while registered as a registered pharmacy student or intern, or an equivalent period of training (for example, in another province or country).

The College requires applicants' practical experience to be recent. If the practicum was completed more than three years after the applicant's graduation, took more than three years to complete, or if the applicant is applying more than three years after completing that requirement, he or she may need to complete an additional "refresher" practicum to be eligible for registration.

Pharmacists can register in two different streams:

- Part A registrants are those who engage in direct patient care.
- Part B registrants engage in non-direct patient care.

Since becoming self-regulated, pharmacy technicians must now meet a set of registration requirements of their own. These are discussed in greater detail at the end of this chapter.

Other topics covered by the general regulation include the procedures for Council meetings and disciplinary hearings, and advertising rules (restrictions on how pharmacies and pharmacists can advertise drugs, and drug and dispensing prices).

Finally, the general regulation establishes the College's Quality Assurance Program. This program, which is administered by the College's Quality Assurance Committee, oversees the profession's continuing education program.

The College expects both pharmacists and pharmacy technicians to keep their knowledge current and their skills fresh by participating in continuing education. For example, it requires all pharmacists to use its "Learning Portfolio and Professional Profile" (OCP, n.d. (a)), and may ask them to produce their portfolios for review on request by the Quality Assurance Committee.

Besides promoting continuing education, the Quality Assurance Committee monitors the competence of pharmacists and provides **remediation** to those who fall short of the profession's competence standards. This remediation is different from discipline. It is not punitive in nature or intent, but is designed to provide guidance to those members of the College who may be struggling with the demands of the profession.

Pharmacists in need of remedial help are identified through practice reviews. Pharmacists registered under Part B are subject to practice reviews only if they are referred to the Quality Assurance Committee by the Inquiries, Complaints, and

remediation
practice assistance, study, and skill development imposed by the Ontario College of Pharmacists Quality Assurance Program on professionals who do not meet standards of competence

Reports Committee or the Executive Committee (usually after a complaint). Pharmacists registered under Part A can be subject to practice review upon referral by the Complaints or Executive committees, or the College may select them at random.

If a practice review reveals problems with a pharmacist's judgment, knowledge, or skill, the pharmacist must undergo remediation to address the deficiencies. If a follow-up assessment shows appropriate improvements, the pharmacist will be allowed to return to practice. If the pharmacist fails to undergo remediation or does not improve, the College can place conditions, restrictions, or limitations on his or her certificate of registration. If the pharmacist has not successfully received remediation by expiry of the term of conditions (up to six months), the restrictions can be extended for one further term. After expiry of the second term, the pharmacist is referred to the Executive Committee. The Executive Committee conducts its own review, and the pharmacist's certificate of registration may be revoked.

There is a separate, dedicated remediation process for pharmacists who have been the subject of complaints about behaviour or remarks of a sexual nature.

Now that pharmacy technicians are eligible for registration, a system of practice reviews and remediation will likely be established for them.

The Professional Misconduct Regulation

The professional misconduct regulation (O. Reg. 681/93) established under the PA sets out a list of 32 different acts, each of which constitutes professional misconduct under clause 51(1)(c) of the *Health Professions Procedural Code*. That clause provides that a Discipline Committee panel can find a member guilty if the member does anything defined in the regulations as an act of professional misconduct. The acts that qualify as professional misconduct fall into five categories. Some of these acts are unlikely to be committed by pharmacy technicians because they relate to tasks done only by pharmacists.

Although professional misconduct by a pharmacy technician had not been defined at the time this textbook was written, the definition will likely overlap with the list of acts that constitute misconduct by a pharmacist. For this reason, the list appears here in its entirety. A careful review of it will prepare the pharmacy technician for practice problems before they occur. The best protection against an accusation of professional misconduct is to avoid practice pitfalls in the first place.

The first category of professional misconduct includes acts that relate to "the practice of the profession and the care of, and relationship with, patients":

1. Contravening a term, condition or limitation imposed on the member's certificate of registration.

2. Failing to maintain a standard of practice of the profession.

3. Abusing a patient, verbally or physically.

4. Practising the profession while the member's ability to do so is impaired by any substance.

5. Dispensing or selling drugs for an improper purpose.

6. Discontinuing professional services that are needed, without reasonable cause, unless,

    i.   the patient requests the discontinuation,

    ii.   alternative services are arranged, or

    iii. the patient is given a reasonable opportunity to arrange alternative services.

7. Practising the profession while the member is in a conflict of interest.

8. Breaching an agreement with a patient relating to professional services for the patient or fees for such services.

9. Failing to reveal the exact nature of a remedy or treatment used by the member following request to do so by a patient or his or her agent. (O. Reg. 681/93, s. 1)

The second category relates to "representations about members":

10. Inappropriately using a term, title or designation in respect of the member's practice.

11. Inappropriately using a term, title or designation indicating a specialization in the profession.

12. Using a name other than the member's name, as set out in the register, in the course of providing or offering to provide services within the scope of practice of the profession … . (O. Reg. 681/93, s. 1)

The third category relates to record-keeping and reports:

13. Failing to keep records as required respecting the member's patients.

14. Falsifying a record relating to the member's practice.

15. Signing or issuing, in the member's professional capacity, a document that the member knows contains a false or misleading statement … . (O. Reg. 681/93, s. 1)

The fourth category of professional misconduct focuses on inappropriate business practices:

16. Submitting an account or charge for services that the member knows is false or misleading.

17. Charging a fee that is excessive in relation to the service provided.

18. Providing a prescriber with prescription blanks, a professional diary, an appointment book or other gift, whether or not imprinted with the name of a member or the name of a pharmacy.

19. Sharing fees with any person who has referred a person to a member or to a pharmacy, or receiving fees from any person to whom a member has referred a person.

20. Participating in a lease of premises for a pharmacy that permits any person other than a member or the owner of the pharmacy to participate in the revenue of the pharmacy except by way of a rent normal for the area in which the premises are located … . (O. Reg. 681/93, s. 1)

The fifth and final category gathers together a group of miscellaneous acts of professional misconduct:

21. Contravening the Act, the *Drug and Pharmacies Regulation Act*, the *Regulated Health Professions Act*, 1991 or the regulations under those Acts.

21.1 Permitting, consenting to or approving, either expressly or by implication, any act that contravenes Ontario Regulation 121/97 in respect of prescription services at a pharmacy operated by a corporation of which the member is a director.

21.2 Contacting or communicating with, or causing or permitting any person to contact or communicate with potential patients, in person, by telephone or by facsimile machine, in an attempt to solicit business.

22. Contravening, while engaged in the practice of pharmacy, any federal or provincial law or municipal by-law with respect to the distribution, sale or dispensing of any drug or mixture of drugs.

23. Influencing a patient to change his or her will or other testamentary instrument.

24. Entering into any agreement that restricts a person's choice of a pharmacist without the consent of the person.

25. Returning to stock or again selling or dispensing a drug previously sold or dispensed and delivered.

26. Knowingly permitting the premises in which a pharmacy is located to be used for unlawful purposes.

27. Permitting, consenting to or approving, either expressly or by implication, the commission of an offence against any Act relating to the practice of pharmacy or to the sale of drugs by a corporation of which the member is a director.

28. Refusing to allow a duly appointed inspector to enter, at a reasonable time, the pharmacy in which the member is engaged in the practice of pharmacy for the purpose of an inspection.

29. Offering or distributing, directly or indirectly, a gift, rebate, bonus or other inducement with respect to a prescription or prescription services.

30. Engaging in conduct or performing an act relevant to the practice of pharmacy that, having regard to all the circumstances, would reasonably be regarded by members as disgraceful, dishonourable or unprofessional … . (O. Reg. 681/93, s. 1)

If a member is found guilty of one of these acts, the possible consequences are described in section 51(2) of the *Health Professions Procedural Code*. The panel may make an order:

1. Directing the Registrar to revoke the member's certificate of registration.

2. Directing the Registrar to suspend the member's certificate of registration for a specified period of time.

3. Directing the Registrar to impose specified terms, conditions and limitations on the member's certificate of registration for a specified or indefinite period of time.

4. Requiring the member to appear before the panel to be reprimanded.

5. Requiring the member to pay a fine of not more than $35,000 to the Minister of Finance.

5.1 If the act of professional misconduct was the sexual abuse of a patient, requiring the member to reimburse the College for funding provided for that patient under the program required under section 85.7.

5.2 If the panel makes an order under paragraph 5.1, requiring the member to post security acceptable to the College to guarantee the payment of any amounts the member may be required to reimburse under the order under paragraph 5.1 … .

THE DRUG AND PHARMACIES REGULATION ACT

The primary purpose of the *Drug and Pharmacies Regulation Act* (DPRA) is the regulation of retail pharmacies. The DPRA requires a pharmacy to have a certificate of accreditation in order to operate (s. 139). Hospital pharmacies, and certain other kinds of operations that dispense drugs (for example, veterinary offices) are exempt from the accreditation requirement.

Certificates of accreditation for Ontario pharmacies are issued by the Registrar of the College of Pharmacists, after the Accreditation Committee has received, reviewed, and approved an application from the representatives of a proposed pharmacy. No retail business that lacks a certificate of accreditation can describe itself (for example, via signage) as a pharmacy, drug store, drug department, drug sundries store or department, drug mart, or purveyor of medicines (or the French equivalent of these terms) (DPRA, s. 147).

As noted in Chapter 1, the DPRA requires that pharmacies designate a manager who will have primary responsibility for complying with the DPRA. That manager's name (along with the certificate of accreditation) must be posted prominently in the pharmacy in a place where the public can see it.

The DPRA is the statute that provides the legal authority for pharmacy technician engagement in acts that constitute "controlled acts" under the RHPA. Section 149 of the DPRA provides the authority for pharmacist delegation of dispensing tasks, under supervision, to pharmacy technicians and others:

149 (1) Subject to subsection (2), no person shall compound, dispense or sell any drug in a pharmacy other than,

(a) a pharmacist;

(b) an intern acting under the supervision of a pharmacist who is physically present;

(c) a registered pharmacy student acting under the supervision of a pharmacist who is physically present; or

(d) *a pharmacy technician acting under the supervision of a pharmacist who is physically present*. [emphasis added]

(2) Where a pharmacist or an intern is present in the pharmacy and available to the purchaser for consultation, subsection (1) does not apply to the sale in a pharmacy of a drug listed in Schedule III.

The DPRA provides important rules regarding the technical aspects of drug prescribing. For example:

- Nobody can dispense one drug while claiming it is another drug (s. 150).

FACTS AND TRENDS　　　　　　　　　　　　　　　　　　　BOX 2.3

Amendments Pave the Way for Remote Dispensing

In 2009, the Ontario government passed amendments to the DPRA that, when proclaimed, will provide standards for remote dispensing. Remote dispensing is the dispensing of drugs—for example, by a pharmacy technician—from a location supervised by a pharmacist who is not physically present at the time of dispensing.

The new provision, not yet in force, is DPRA s. 149(3):

Remote dispensing locations

149 (3) The requirement in clause (1)(d) that a pharmacist be physically present to supervise does not apply with respect to a remote dispensing loca-tion, as long as a pharmacist is actively supervising the pharmacy technician mentioned in that clause and,

　　(a) a certificate of accreditation has been issued permitting the operation of the remote dispensing location; and

　　(b) the remote dispensing location is operated in accordance with the regulations.

A new regulation providing for the accreditation and operation of remote dis-pensing locations was ratified by the Council of the College of Pharmacists on March 8, 2010. This proposed regulation—which was not yet in force at the time this textbook was written—would replace, and in some cases amend, existing regulations 551/90, 545/90, and 297/96 made under the DPRA. ◇

- Drugs listed in Schedule I of the *Controlled Drugs and Substances Act* (CDSA)—that is, opiates—must not be mailed unless by registered mail, or by some other traceable and auditable manner that requires the signature of the patient or his or her agent (s. 152).
- Records must be kept, as prescribed by regulations, of the sale or dispensing of all drugs listed in the schedules to the CDSA or the schedule to the *Narcotic Control Regulations* (Canada) (s. 153).
- Prescriptions cannot be filled unless they are recorded in a prescribed format, and the records must include certain information (for example, the drug's name, manufacturer, directions for use, name and address of the prescriber, etc.) (s. 156).
- Prescription containers must include prescribed markings (s. 156).
- Ontario pharmacists can fill prescriptions from other Canadian jurisdictions if they believe that the patient who presents the prescription requires the drug (s. 158).
- Drugs cannot be sold wholesale to anyone who is not allowed to sell them by retail (s. 160).

Like many statutes, the DPRA contains offence provisions. Section 165 states that any person who contravenes "any provision of this Act or the regulations for which no penalty is otherwise provided is guilty of an offence and on conviction is liable" to pay a fine of up to $25,000 for a first offence and up to $50,000 for a sub-sequent offence (for a corporation, $50,000 for a first offence and up to $200,000 for

FACTS AND TRENDS

BOX 2.4

New Amendments Expand Scope of Practice for Pharmacists

On May 11, 2009 Premier Dalton McGuinty and (then) Ontario Minister of Health and Long-Term Care David Caplan introduced the *Regulated Health Professions Statute Law Amendment Act, 2009* (Bill 179).

When passed into law, the amendments contained in this Act will expand the scope of practice of several health professions, including physiotherapy, midwifery, nurse practitioners, and pharmacy. Many of the provisions relating to pharmacy came into effect on December 15, 2009.

The objective of the amendments is to improve Ontarians' access to health-care services by reducing wait times and eliminating unnecessary consultations. For example, one of the proposed changes would permit pharmacists, under certain circumstances, to prescribe drugs to patients. ◇

a subsequent offence). Section 166 states that every pharmacy owner or designated manager ("or either of them") is personally liable for an offence committed by anyone in the pharmacy. This provision underscores the importance of supervision of dispensing activities, and the responsibility associated with being a designated manager.

THE COLLEGE

The College as Champion of the Public Interest

As you have read, the Ontario College of Pharmacists is the self-regulatory body that governs the practice of pharmacy. It has existed since 1871. As of 2010, the College also governs the work of those pharmacy technicians who choose to register as such.

Both the RHPA (s. 3) and the *Health Professions Procedural Code* (s. 3(2)) require the College to regulate the practice of pharmacy in the public interest. This means that if the interests of the public are at risk, the College must act to protect them—even if a member must be disciplined.

Acting in the best interests of the public also benefits the profession. By ensuring fair access to high-quality pharmacy services, and handling complaints and concerns promptly and satisfactorily, the College preserves the overall reputation of the profession of pharmacy. Maintaining the public's trust in and respect for pharmacists and pharmacy technicians helps ensure the public's continued use of pharmacy services, justifies reasonable compensation for services provided, and supports the expansion of pharmacists' scope of practice.

The College expresses its mission as follows:

The mission of the Ontario College of Pharmacists is to regulate the practice of pharmacy, through the participation of the public and the profession, in accordance with standards of practice which ensure that our members provide the public with quality pharmaceutical service and care. (OCP, n.d. (c))

The College and the Law

The objectives, mandate, and procedures of the College are governed by the RHPA and the *Pharmacy Act*. The College is required to support the profession's compliance with the law by providing mechanisms to address problems with competence, professionalism, and ethics. Because pharmacists and registered pharmacy technicians are self-regulated professions, the College assumes responsibility for enforcing the laws that apply to them.

The Council

The College's activities are overseen by a Council. In 2010, the College had 17 community or hospital pharmacy representatives, one for each of 17 electoral districts in Ontario. It also had 10 public (non-pharmacist) members, plus two academics—the Dean of Pharmacy of the University of Toronto and the Hallman Director (Director of Health Sciences and Pharmacy) of the University of Waterloo.

The Council meets four times a year, acting much like a board of directors for the College. It appoints the members of the seven committees prescribed by the *Health Professions Procedural Code*: Executive, Complaints, Discipline, Fitness to Practise, Patient Relations, Quality Assurance, and Registration. The College has five other committees as well: Accreditation, Professional Practice, Finance, Compensation, and Communications. These committees carry out different aspects of the Council's mandate.

Resources for Members

Besides conducting practice reviews and offering remediation to struggling members, the College publishes a newsletter to communicate pharmacy news, the results of disciplinary hearings, and guidance on practice and ethical issues. District meetings and a breakfast meeting series help bring members up to date on developments in the pharmacy professions.

Through its website, the College provides links to the laws, policies, bylaws, and guidelines that apply to the profession of pharmacy and the work of pharmacy technicians. It archives reports and statistics relevant to pharmacy work and also maintains a directory of continuing education programs of interest to members, as well as self-assessment tools.

Resources for the Public

As protector of the public interest, the College accepts complaints from the public. A section of its website is designed to assist members of the public in reporting problems with pharmacists. It explains the complaint process, the disciplinary system, and what the public can expect. Members of the College, too, may lodge complaints about other members, if necessary, although approaching a colleague directly about a concern is usually an appropriate first step.

Complaints and Discipline

When the College receives a complaint about a pharmacist, as a first step, a representative of the Complaints Committee may call the pharmacist to attempt an informal resolution of the problem. If this approach fails to satisfy the complainant, a formal complaint may be lodged. The complainant must put the complaint in writing and mail, fax, or deliver it to the College. A form for filing complaints is available on the College's website.

Each complaint is assigned to either a Complaints Officer or an Investigator. After collecting supporting material from the complainant, the Complaints Officer or Investigator will send a Notice of Complaint to the pharmacist. The Notice of Complaint includes the patient's original letter or form. After receiving the notice, the pharmacist has 30 days in which to file a response. Some parts of the response may be compulsory—for example, the pharmacist may be required to send in copies of certain documentation. A statement of the pharmacist's side of the story is not compulsory but can help resolve the complaint.

Upon receiving the pharmacist's response, the College conducts its investigation, which can include reviewing documents, interviewing the complainant and the pharmacist, and (with the patient's written permission) speaking with other health-care providers involved in the case.

The results of the investigation are forwarded to the Complaints Committee which, after reviewing the results, can do any of the following:

- Take no further action if the pharmacist's conduct and actions meet reasonable and acceptable standards of practice, or if there is insufficient information for the Complaints Committee to take action.
- Caution the pharmacist about his or her practice or conduct, either in writing or in person before the Complaints Committee. The Complaints Committee discusses its concerns with the pharmacist and makes suggestions that it believes the pharmacist should take to avoid future difficulties.
- Provide guidance to the pharmacist on how to improve his or her practice. Sometimes, if the investigation has revealed a practice deficiency on the part of the pharmacist, the pharmacist will enter into an agreement with the College to undertake relevant and useful remedial educational programs or upgrading. The pharmacist's compliance with this agreement will be monitored by the College.
- Refer the pharmacist to the College's Executive Committee for incapacity proceedings (that is, concerns about the pharmacist's health).
- Refer specified allegations of professional misconduct or incompetence (related to the complaint) to the Discipline Committee. (OCP, n.d. (a))

If the complaint is not referred to the Discipline Committee (the majority of complaints are not), all information about the complaint is kept confidential. Should a member wish to appeal a decision of the Complaints Committee, she or he may begin an appeal to the Health Professions Appeal and Review Board.

If a pharmacist is referred to the Discipline Committee, a hearing and formal decision follows. In serious cases, disciplinary proceedings can lead to temporary suspension, or even a permanent ban from pharmacy practice. Discipline and appeals from complaints and disciplinary decisions are discussed in greater detail in Chapter 6.

Now that pharmacy technicians are eligible for registration with the College, the complaints and disciplinary process—with any necessary modifications—will apply to them as well.

TOWARD SELF-REGULATION AND PROFESSIONAL STATUS FOR PHARMACY TECHNICIANS

In Ontario

Registration with the College became available to eligible pharmacy technicians beginning in 2010. As pharmacists expand their own roles, they require more sophisticated technical support. Elevating pharmacy technician practice to a regulated profession is a means of ensuring high and consistent standards of competence for pharmacy technicians, allowing pharmacists to have confidence in new hires.

Registration also paves the way for self-regulation. Like pharmacists, pharmacy technicians will play an important role in defining their profession, developing educational standards, registration criteria, practice guidelines, and a code of ethics. Self-regulation is a key marker of professional status, and will likely raise the profile of pharmacy technicians in the eyes of the public. Now that registration is offered, the *Pharmacy Act* will be amended to make it illegal for people who are not registered as pharmacy technicians to represent themselves as such.

The movement to seek self-regulation has grown over many years. The first formal step was a 2002 request by the College that the Ontario Ministry of Health and Long-Term Care consider supporting self-regulation for pharmacy technicians. That request triggered an invitation from the Ministry for a proposal describing such a plan. The proposal was then submitted for evaluation by the Health Professions Regulatory Advisory Committee (HPRAC).

In 2006, HPRAC recommended that pharmacy technicians be registered as a separate class of professionals with the College of Pharmacists as a move toward self-regulation. To permit this to happen, supporting legislation was needed. That legislation came in the form of amendments to existing statutes: the *Regulated Health Professions Act*, the *Pharmacy Act*, and the *Drug and Pharmacies Regulation Act*. The amendments (along with other amendments affecting other professions) were introduced in Bill 171, the *Health Systems Improvement Act*. That bill received royal assent (came into force) on June 4, 2007 (although some provisions come into force at a later date, after the necessary regulations have been made).

With the necessary legislation in place, the College still had a great deal of preparatory work to do. While government approval was still pending (awaited), the College created a Pharmacy Technician Working Group to begin discussing such key issues as the following:

- a Pharmacy Technician Profile (what a pharmacy technician should be expected to know and do);
- educational requirements for pharmacy technicians;
- criteria for extending accreditation (the College's recognition or endorsement) to pharmacy technician education programs;
- "bridging programs" for pharmacy technicians already in practice, to permit them to bring their knowledge up to date in preparation for registration;
- development of a Jurisprudence Exam to test candidates' understanding of the (mostly provincial) laws that apply to the work of a pharmacy technician;

- standards of practice for pharmacy technicians; and
- a code of ethics for pharmacy technicians (currently, the College's *Code of Ethics* is shared by pharmacists and pharmacy technicians; see Appendix E at the end of this textbook).

Table 2.1 lists the registration requirements for pharmacy technician graduates and practitioners.

The College accepted the first Ontario pharmacy technician registrations in early 2010.

Table 2.1   Requirements for Registration: Pharmacy Technicians

Graduates (2008 or later) of a CCAPP Accredited Pharmacy Technician Education Program	Pharmacy Technicians Already in Practice
Structured Practical Training Program	OCP Certification Program (discontinued in 2008) *or* the PEBC Evaluating Exam
PEBC Qualifying Exam (both components)	Bridging Education Program
OCP Jurisprudence Exam	PEBC Qualifying Exam (both components)
	OCP Jurisprudence Exam

National Initiatives

Ontario is not the only province in which pharmacy technicians are seeking self-regulation. Alberta permitted the first such registrations in 2008. Other provinces are at varying stages in the journey toward self-regulation.

If pharmacy technicians become registered and self-regulated, most stakeholders believe that the standards for that status should be as consistent as possible across the country. A number of initiatives have emerged in support of this goal. For example, the Canadian Pharmacists' Association, with funding from the federal Foreign Credential Recognition Program, hosted a "National Dialogue on Pharmacy Technicians" in January 2008.

The Canadian Council for Accreditation of Pharmacy Programs (CCAPP), an organization once devoted to the accreditation of programs for pharmacists, has now turned its attention to pharmacy technicians and developed criteria for the accreditation of pharmacy technician education programs. The CCAPP has published a list of 31 programs, 19 of which are in Ontario, that have been awarded either "Provisional Status" or "Qualifying Status" (for programs still under development, but which promise to meet the accreditation criteria) (CCAPP, 2010).

Another important national initiative has been the development by the Pharmacy Examining Board of Canada (PEBC) of a national entry-to-practice examination for pharmacy technicians. The PEBC has been administering practice entry exams for pharmacists for more than 40 years. It has now turned its attention to pharmacy technicians, and the first pilot Qualifying Exam was administered to a test group of pharmacy technicians in August 2009.

After an evaluation of the pilot, the PEBC instituted a two-tiered examination process. Pharmacy technicians who have graduated from an accredited education program will be allowed direct access to the Qualifying Exam; those who are already in practice, or who did not complete their education through an accredited program, will be required to pass an Evaluating Exam (the sitting fee, $350) before they are permitted to sit the Qualifying Exam. (There is an additional requirement that those candidates have completed 2,000 hours of practice within the 36 months preceding the exam.)

The PEBC exam has two components:

- a written, multiple-choice component (sitting fee, $375); and
- an Objective Structured Performance Exam (sitting fee, $900).

The Objective Structured Performance Exam (OSPE) is designed to measure proficiency with applied tasks, for example, interaction with patients and the checking of prescriptions. It will be administered with the help of assistants assuming the roles of patients, pharmacists, and others.

Successful completion of the exam requires that the candidate pass both components.

KEY TERMS

controlled act
jurisdiction
legislation
offences
policies
regulations
remediation

REFERENCES

Canadian Council for Accreditation of Pharmacy Programs (CCAPP). (2010, February). Pharmacy technician programs—List of accredited programs. Retrieved May 12, 2010 from http://www.ccapp-accredit.ca/news/.

Controlled Drugs and Substances Act. 1996. SC 1996, c. 19.

Drug and Pharmacies Regulation Act. 1990. RSO 1990, c. H.4.

Fair Access to Regulated Professions Act. 2006. SO 2006, c. 31.

Food and Drugs Act. 1985. RSC 1985, c. F-27.

Health Professions Regulatory Advisory Council (HPRAC). 2007. *Welcome to the HPRAC website*. Retrieved May 12, 2010 from http://www.hprac.org/en/.

Health Systems Improvement Act. 2007. SO 2007, c. 10.

Ontario College of Pharmacists (OCP). (n.d. (a)). The complaints process unveiled. Retrieved May 12, 2010 from http://www.ocpinfo.com/client/ocp/ OCPHome.nsf/d12550e436a1716585256ac90065aa1c/6e54166adc27efdf852 5716f004c05a6?OpenDocument.

Ontario College of Pharmacists (OCP). (n.d. (b)). The learning portfolio and professional profile. Retrieved May 12, 2010 from http://www.ocpinfo.com/ client/ocp/OCPHome.nsf/d12550e436a1716585256ac90065aa1c/f7da1b2ce df4094e85256c32006f08e9?OpenDocument.

Ontario College of Pharmacists (OCP). (n.d. (c)). Mission statement. Retrieved May 12, 2010 from http://www.ocpinfo.com/client/ocp/OCPHome.nsf/web/ About+OCP.

Personal Health Information Protection Act. 2004. SO 2004, c. 3.

Pharmacy Act. 1991. SO 1991, c. 36.

Regulated Health Professions Act. 1991. SO 1991, c. 18.

Regulated Health Professions Act. 1991. Table of contents. Retrieved May 12, 2010 from http://www.e-laws.gov.on.ca/html/statutes/english/elaws_ statutes_91r18_e.htm#BK0.

Regulated Health Professions Statute Law Amendment Act, 2009 (Bill 179) 2009. SO 2009, c. 26 (royal assent December 15, 2009).

REVIEW EXERCISES

Discussion Questions

1. What are the benefits of self-regulation for professionals? Why is it better for health professions to take charge of the regulation of their own members, instead of leaving that task up to the government?

2. Ontario's conditions for registration as a pharmacist (which will likely serve as the model for registering as a pharmacy technician) currently allow the College to deny applicants who have been subject to practice restrictions and suspensions in other jurisdictions. Is this condition fair?

3. Registration as a member of the Ontario College of Pharmacists is challenging and expensive: pharmacy technicians must attend accredited schools (or prove that their training is equivalent), meet strict conditions, and pass costly examinations. Once they become members of the College, they are subject to a public complaints process, and if they break the rules, to discipline. Is registration worth it? Why or why not?

Review Questions

1. List three laws that regulate the work of pharmacists and pharmacy technicians.

2. What was the purpose of the *Regulated Health Professions Act* when it was introduced in 1991?

3. After reviewing the statement of purpose of the RHPA on page 22, list four objectives for the government's oversight of regulated health professions.

4. Which government-appointed body acts as a liaison between regulated health profession colleges and the Minister of Health and Long-Term Care? List two aspects of that body's mandate.

5. Which controlled acts does the RHPA reserve only to pharmacists or their authorized delegates (people to whom pharmacists can assign supervised work)?

6. What are the consequences of performing a controlled act without authority?

7. Where can you find the *Health Professions Procedural Code*? Which statute should it be read with, and why?

8. How does the *Health Professions Procedural Code* inform the *Pharmacy Act* (that is, what does it add)?

9. How will the Council of the College of Pharmacists of Ontario change to permit the self-regulation of pharmacy technicians?

10. Where can you find the general conditions for registration as a member of the Ontario College of Pharmacists? Do these apply to pharmacy technicians?

11. What is "remediation," and why (and how) does it apply to pharmacists?

12. Where can a pharmacist find the list of actions and omissions that constitute professional misconduct?

13. What are the possible consequences for a pharmacist who is found guilty of professional misconduct?

14. Which kinds of pharmacy operations are governed by the *Drug and Pharmacies Regulation Act* (DPRA)?

15. In order to dispense and sell drugs legally to the public, what must a retail pharmacy obtain from the College?

16. What person, within the retail pharmacy, is primarily responsible for compliance with the DPRA?

17. List at least three matters governed by the DPRA and the regulations made under it.

18. The College of Pharmacists is required to protect the interests of the public. How can this benefit the profession?

19. What are some of the resources that the College makes available to its members?

20. Are pharmacy technicians who are already in practice automatically registered with the College?

CHAPTER 3

Professional Pharmacy Services

Pharmacy technicians prepare prescriptions for patients at the Sunnybrook Hospital pharmacy in Toronto.

LEARNING OBJECTIVES

After reading this chapter, you should be able to:

- Explain what is meant by "scope of practice" and why it is important to practise within it.

- Describe the legislation, regulations, and guidelines that help define a pharmacy technician's scope of practice.

- Understand which controlled acts (and sub-tasks) that pharmacy technicians, under the supervision of a pharmacist, may perform.

- Describe the privacy legislation that governs pharmacy technician practice.

- Understand the importance of good customer service and how it can contribute to business success, patient safety, and reduction of complaints against pharmacy staff.

- Explain some of the common differences between retail pharmacy technician work and the work of pharmacy technicians in hospital pharmacies.

INTRODUCTION

As you have learned, the potential impact of pharmacological care on human health and well-being has led Canada's provincial and federal governments to develop a detailed scheme of regulation for the pharmacy industry.

Although the following chapter touches on many aspects of pharmacy work, this textbook is not designed to teach you how to accomplish those technical and customer service tasks. Rather, its purpose is to describe how legal requirements inform, shape, and constrain the way in which pharmacy technicians and pharmacists do their day-to-day work.

scope of practice
the decisions, actions, and procedures that are permitted for a licensed professional

This chapter addresses the important issue of **scope of practice**. Working within the approved scope of practice for one's profession is one of the simplest and most effective ways to stay on the right side of the law. A pharmacy technician's scope of practice can differ depending upon the setting in which she or he works—hospital-based pharmacy technicians have a scope of practice substantially different from that of pharmacy technicians in retail settings. For that reason, these two settings are discussed separately in this chapter.

Besides scope of practice, you will learn about other important issues here: reporting and record-keeping requirements, confidential information management, customer service, working with technologies, and working with other health-care professionals, such as physicians.

PROFESSIONAL SERVICES IN THE RETAIL PHARMACY

Scope of Practice in Retail Pharmacies

When this textbook was being written, the scope of practice for both pharmacists and pharmacy technicians was somewhat of a "moving target." New legislation had just been introduced that would pave the way for remote dispensing (see Chapter 2, Box 2.3). Remote dispensing will, if it becomes a reality, require new skills and procedures for pharmacists and will have an impact on the work of pharmacy technicians, because the pharmacist will delegate the actual physical task to a pharmacy technician. Thus, the pharmacy technician will be the only registered health professional who deals with the patient "in person."

The proposed introduction of remote dispensing is a good example of how a change in the scope of practice of one profession—pharmacy—affects the scope of practice of another: the work of pharmacy technicians. This current phase of rapid evolution in the delivery of pharmacy services makes it more important than ever that pharmacy technicians clearly understand the range and the limits of their work.

How Practice Standards and Competencies Help Establish Scope of Practice

As you read in Chapter 2, Ontario pharmacy technicians get the authority to dispense and sell drugs (under a pharmacist's supervision) from section 149(1)(d) of the *Drug and Pharmacies Regulation Act* (DPRA). This statute, however, provides few specific details about the day-to-day activities and responsibilities of pharmacy technicians. Filling in those details falls, appropriately, to the Ontario College of Pharmacists ("the College"; OCP) (and in other provinces, to other provincial Colleges).

In preparation for the registration of pharmacy technicians as a class of self-regulated professionals, the College's Pharmacy Technician Working Group developed a statement of proposed standards of practice (OCP, n.d.). This document sets out six practice standards and provides examples—in the form of case studies—of how these standards might be met in a retail pharmacy setting. These standards are "proposed" because they were developed before pharmacy technicians were eligible for registration. While the College's original plan was to update and then formalize these standards, the College has since expressed an intention to adopt, in place of its own draft standards, a document currently titled "Professional Competencies for Canadian Pharmacy Technicians at Entry to Practice" prepared by the National Association of Pharmacy Regulatory Agencies (NAPRA), once that agency, in turn, has released the revised version of that document.

In the meantime, the College's standards — which are similar to the NAPRA competencies in many respects — remain a useful guideline for pharmacy technicians, especially when considered in conjunction with the NAPRA competencies in their current form. The current "Proposed Standards of Practice for Registered Pharmacy Technicians" appears as Appendix D in the back of this textbook.

The National Association of Pharmacy Regulatory Authorities (NAPRA) includes members from regulatory colleges across the country. As noted above, NAPRA has developed a list of nine "professional competencies" for pharmacy technicians (NAPRA, 2007). These "competencies" reflect NAPRA's expectations about what newly graduated (and in some provinces, registered) pharmacy technicians will be trained and prepared to do in their work.

The College's proposed standards and the NAPRA Competencies, considered together, form a good overview of the general scope of pharmacy technician work in Canada as it exists on the eve of the first pharmacy technician registrations.

The College's six proposed standards are as follows:

Standard One
The pharmacy technician practises within legal requirements and ethical principles, demonstrates professional integrity, and acts to uphold professional standards of practice.

Standard Two
The pharmacy technician, as a member of the pharmacy team and in compliance with relevant legislation and established policies and procedures, uses knowledge and skills to receive, renew, and transfer/copy prescriptions and to document.

Standard Three
The pharmacy technician, as a member of the pharmacy team, uses knowledge, skills, and established policies and procedures to enter demographic and prescription data into the patient profile or health record.

Standard Four
The pharmacy technician, in collaboration with the pharmacist, designated manager, or hospital pharmacy manager, prepares pharmaceutical products for release and documents.

Standard Five

The pharmacy technician, in collaboration with the pharmacist, designated manager, or hospital pharmacy manager, performs distributive and quality assurance functions to ensure safety, accuracy, and quality of supplied products.

Standard Six

The pharmacy technician, as a member of the pharmacy team, uses knowledge and skills and follows established policies and procedures to communicate with patients or their agents, pharmacists, and other healthcare providers. (OCP, n.d.)

In the proposed standards document, the College provides "operational components" that explain each of the six standards by relating them to a pharmacy technician's day-to-day work. For example, Standard One states that a pharmacy technician must practise "within legal requirements." The operational component associated with this standard (1.1) provides an expanded description of exactly how the pharmacy technician must comply:

The pharmacy technician complies with federal and provincial regulatory bylaws, standards of practice, policies and guidelines, practice expectations, and where provided, workplace policies and procedures ... . (OCP, n.d.)

Operational Component 1.1 goes on to explain that a pharmacy technician must keep current about changes to legislation, and must recognize "the right, role, and responsibility of regulatory bodies to establish and monitor professional standards, ethical guidelines, and practice expectations."

The standards and their associated operational components will be touched on throughout this book where they are relevant to specific issues.

Some of the operational components deal specifically with the scope of pharmacy technicians' authority and their role. Operational Component 1.3 provides that:

1.3.2 The pharmacy technician recognizes and practises within the limits of his or her professional role and personal knowledge and expertise ... .

1.3.3 The pharmacy technician accepts responsibility for his or her decisions and actions ... [and]

1.3.5 The pharmacy technician collaborates with the pharmacist in enabling the patient to achieve his or her health care goals and to support optimal patient care.

Other standards and operational components describe, in detail, key work tasks that can be delegated to a pharmacy technician. These work tasks will be discussed below.

The nine NAPRA entry-to-practice competencies are as follows:

1. Legal, Ethical, and Professional Responsibilities

    Pharmacy technicians meet legal, ethical, and professional responsibilities in the performance of their practice. ...

2. Professional Collaboration and Team Work

    Pharmacy technicians work in collaborative relationships within health care teams to optimize patient safety and improve health outcomes. ...

3. Drug Distribution: Prescription and Patient Information

   Pharmacy technicians promote safe and effective drug distribution by receiving, gathering, entering, and storing prescription and patient information so that this information can be accessed and retrieved readily. …

4. Drug Distribution: Product Preparation

   Pharmacy technicians promote safe and effective drug distribution by preparing products in a manner that ensures patient safety through the accuracy and quality of the product. …

5. Drug Distribution: Product Release

   Pharmacy technicians promote safe and effective drug distribution by releasing and distributing products in a manner that ensures patient safety. …

6. Drug Distribution: System and Inventory Controls

   Pharmacy technicians collaborate in the management of systems for drug distribution and inventory control to ensure patient safety and the safety, accuracy, quality, integrity, and timeliness of the products. …

7. Communication and Education

   Pharmacy technicians communicate effectively with patients, pharmacists, and other health care team members, and educate, where appropriate, in order to promote and support optimal patient care and well-being. …

8. Management Knowledge and Skills

   Pharmacy technicians apply management knowledge, principles, and skills. …

9. Quality Assurance

   Pharmacy technicians collaborate in developing, implementing, and evaluating quality assurance and risk management policies, procedures, and activities. … (NAPRA, 2007)

As you can see, the NAPRA competencies are organized somewhat differently from the College's standards. On closer examination—and especially after reading the "competency units" (subheadings associated with each competency) and the associated explanatory material, it becomes clear that the content of the OCP standards and the NAPRA competencies overlap substantially, and are generally consistent.

There are, however, some important exceptions. For example, the explanatory material associated with NAPRA Competency 7 (Communication and Education) provides that pharmacy technicians can "[a]ssist patients to select and use drug administration devices, diagnostic and monitoring devices, home health aids, and other non-drug measures" (7.2.4), while the operational component (6.1.2) associated with the College's communication standard (Standard Six) specifies that a pharmacy technician "refers all therapeutic issues, questions, and queries to the pharmacist." It would seem that assisting a patient to "select" a device—for example, a blood sugar monitor—is a task permitted by NAPRA, but one that falls outside an Ontario pharmacy technician's permitted scope of practice, because the College's standards would likely characterize the selection of these devices as a therapeutic "issue," "question," or "query."

FACTS AND TRENDS

BOX 3.1

Distinguishing Pharmacist and Pharmacy Technician Roles

Because pharmacists and pharmacy technicians work in close cooperation but are subject to different legal scopes of practice, it is important to understand the key distinctions between the roles of these two professionals. In the introduction to its entry-to-practice competencies, NAPRA provides a useful comparison of the pharmacist's and pharmacy technician's roles (Table 3.1).

Table 3.1 Summary of NAPRA Competencies at Entry to Practice

Pharmacists	Pharmacy Technicians
1. Have responsibility for patient care through direct assessment and intervention	**1.** Have responsibility for patient care and to the circle of care through collaborative relationships with pharmacists
2. Are health professionals who practise within a knowledge-based environment in which they use high-level critical thinking, specialized knowledge of drug therapy, and professional judgment appropriate to the pharmacist role to offer and optimize patient care	**2.** Are health professionals who use their knowledge, skills, abilities, and attitudes to think critically, solve problems, make decisions, and generate professional judgments appropriate to the pharmacy technician role that optimize patient care
3. Are accountable for direct patient care knowledge	**3.** Recognize and differentiate among practice situations within the collaborative relationship in which they make decisions and take action independently, those that require pharmacist intervention, and those that are team-based in nature
4. Practise in accordance with professional registration and licensure, and professional standards within their jurisdiction	**4.** Are accountable for respecting and supporting the role, rights, and responsibilities of patients, pharmacy technicians, the pharmacy team, health-care providers, and others
5. Possess both broad-based and pharmacy-specific knowledge.	**5.** Practise in accordance with provincial/territorial professional requirements, standards, bylaws, and policies

Source: NAPRA, 2007. ◈

The fact that the NAPRA and College guidelines diverge on this device-selection issue should signal that this is an area of controversy within the pharmacy technician's scope of practice. In proposing to adopt the NAPRA competencies in place of its own draft standards, the College may be moving toward an expanded scope of duty for pharmacy technicians; however, it is important to keep in mind that the College has expressed an intention to adopt not the current version of the NAPRA competencies, but a future revised version. For this reason, it is essential that, on becoming registered as a pharmacy technician, you determine which set of guidelines is endorsed by the College at the relevant time, and that you review those standards or competencies carefully so that you have a clear understanding of the rules in your province.

It is clear that, when the members of NAPRA and the College created these codes of practice, they were mindful that work in a pharmacy is multifaceted, and that it incorporates not only technical tasks but also business practices. This holistic view of pharmacy work has been embraced by judges. For example, in *Rissi v. Ontario College of Pharmacists*, the court found that a pharmacist's obligation to meet standards of ethics and professionalism extended not only to the technical tasks of dispensing drugs, but also to business decisions (the case involved a professional misconduct ruling based on business tax evasion). The judge in *Rissi* made it clear that "practicing pharmacy involves more than merely dispensing pharmaceutical products" (para. 17). As you will learn below, customer service is also an aspect of the professional practice of pharmacists and pharmacy technicians, and high standards of professionalism and ethics apply to customer service work just as they do to technical dispensing tasks.

Finally, regardless of legislation or guidelines, professionals are *not* within their scope of practice when they do something that requires them to act beyond the limits of their training, experience, knowledge, or skills. NAPRA Competency 1.2.3(iv) emphasizes that at all times, a pharmacy technician must "practise within personal limits of knowledge, skills, and abilities." In practical terms, the meaning of this standard is simple: if you have been asked to do something you don't understand, or don't feel comfortable doing, ask questions and ask for help. Admitting your inexperience with a new task makes you more, not less, competent and professional in your work.

Authorized Acts

INTRODUCTION

The activities described in the following sections are the "authorized acts" that can be delegated (under supervision) by pharmacists to pharmacy technicians. Each activity is discussed in the College's proposed standards, the NAPRA competencies, or both.

RECEIVING AND DOCUMENTING A PRESCRIPTION FROM A PATIENT

The operational components that support the College's Standard Two state that when receiving a prescription from a patient, a pharmacy technician must:

- check the prescription for authenticity;
- confirm that the prescription complies with all legal requirements;
- use health-care lists to determine the privileges of the prescribing physician;
- verify the accuracy and completeness of the demographic and prescription data;
- verify the clarity of the strength, dosage, and scheduling information;
- advise the physician of any potential therapeutic problems, allergy potential, or changes in dosage, strength, or patient medical condition; and
- complete appropriate documentation related to receiving and recording the prescription.

While it is impossible to know for certain that a prescription is authentic, a pharmacy technician is expected to use professional judgment to review the prescription for potential "red flags" (drug misspellings, prescriptions not written on personalized or properly filled-out prescription pads, unusual dosages or therapy durations, prescriptions that appear tampered with, etc.) and to report these to the pharmacist. Pharmacy technicians are also expected to investigate the prescribing privileges of all prescribing physicians. Many pharmacies have access to a list of local physicians and other prescribers, with information about each one's prescribing privileges.

Sometimes the person presenting the prescription will be a repeat customer and familiar to the pharmacy technician. In other cases, the person will be a newcomer. If the pharmacy technician does not recognize the customer, two important first questions should be: "Is this prescription for you?" (helps prevent breaches of confidentiality if someone other than the patient presents the prescription); and "Have you had a prescription filled at this pharmacy before?" (alerts the pharmacist about the need to create a new patient file).

Upon receipt of a prescription, pharmacy staff may need to make a decision about whether dispensing an interchangeable product (a generic drug) may be appropriate in the circumstances. Providing generic products often saves the patient money, and may be mandated (required or preferred) under the terms of the patient's drug coverage. The legal aspects of dispensing interchangeable products are governed by the *Drug Interchangeability and Dispensing Fee Act* (DIDFA) and the regulations made under it. The DIDFA explains that a drug product can be treated as interchangeable as long as:

- it is designated as interchangeable by "the executive Officer [of Ontario's public drug benefit programs] in the Formulary [a formulary that the executive officer is required to manage]"; and
- the dispensing of an interchangeable drug is not contrary to the physician's prescription instructions (for example, in cases where the physician has prescribed a named drug with the notation "no substitutions" or "no sub").

A pharmacy that offers interchangeable products must post a special notice explaining that these products might be substituted for a named drug, and that the patient has the right to request a generic where one is available. The precise form of this notice is described in Regulation 936 ("Notice to Patients") made under the DIDFA.

RECEIVING AND DOCUMENTING A PRESCRIPTION FROM A PHYSICIAN

It is important to know that pharmacy technicians are not currently authorized to receive *verbal* prescriptions for drugs listed under Schedule 1 of the *Drug and Pharmacies Regulation Act*. According to Regulation 551 made under the DPRA:

56. (1) A verbal prescription for a drug referred to in Schedule I established by Ontario Regulation 297/96 (General) made under the [DPRA] shall only be accepted by,

      (a) a pharmacist;

      (b) an intern; or

      (c) a registered pharmacy student under the direct supervision of a pharmacist ... .

Schedule I of the DPRA contains a very wide range of drugs. Many retail pharmacies, out of caution, have a policy that prohibits pharmacy technicians from receiving any verbal prescriptions from physicians (despite the fact that the College's Operational Component 2.2.2 discusses the receipt of orally transmitted prescriptions by pharmacy technicians).

Regardless of who presents the prescription—the patient, the patient's agent, or a prescribing physician—the pharmacy technician is required to give the prescription to a pharmacist for review (and confirm that this review has actually taken place) before he or she can begin preparing the product. Having a system in place whereby the pharmacist checks a box on a checklist, or places the prescription in a "checked" box or location, is a useful way to confirm that the prescription has been reviewed and deemed ready to fill.

Even after the pharmacist has checked a prescription, errors are possible. The pharmacist cannot always detect every single problem (medication conflict, forged prescription, double doctoring, etc.) with a prescription. Oversights happen. Having a pharmacy technician in the pharmacy provides an important opportunity to reduce oversight errors, and so pharmacy technicians must always use their own independent judgment when filling a prescription, even after the prescription has been reviewed by the pharmacist. Whenever a pharmacy technician has a legitimate concern about a prescription, it is *always* appropriate to bring that concern to the attention of the pharmacist, rather than simply deferring to the fact that the pharmacist has checked the prescription.

MANAGING THE PATIENT'S RECORD

Both the College's proposed standards and the NAPRA competencies recognize a role for pharmacy technicians in the management of a patient's record. After receiving a prescription from a patient, pharmacy technicians are expected to review the existing data in the patient's (usually computerized) record, and to add details of the new prescription.

Before collecting and recording any patient demographic information (for example, the patient's age), the pharmacy technician must explain the purpose for collecting the information and obtain the patient's consent to collect it. Patient confidentiality is discussed below.

FACTS AND TRENDS

BOX 3.2

The Electronic Health Record (EHR)

In February 2009, federal Minister of Health Leona Aglukkaq confirmed the government's ongoing support for the expansion of the electronic health record (EHR) health information management system.

The EHR system allows for the creation, for Canadian patients, of a single electronically stored health record that compiles a wide range of health information, including health history, diagnoses, health testing history, and prescriptions. The system, developed by the non-profit corporation Canada Health Infoway, is designed to allow patients to grant access to their records, on consent, to health-care providers—including pharmacists.

The government hopes that the system will improve access to health care by reducing duplication, allowing better transmission of important health information (for example, drug allergies and sensitivities), and tracking tests, inoculations, and vaccinations. Similar systems are in place in at least eight other countries.

Currently, only a minority of Canadians have EHRs. In late 2009, Ontario's portion of the EHR initiative was plagued by a scandal related to government spending on the program. If government support for this project continues, working with EHRs may become a day-to-day reality for pharmacy technicians. If EHRs are implemented in your area, you will need to learn how to obtain patient consent to access the system, and how to use the information it contains. ◈

The information appropriate to a patient record is described in the DPRA. Operational Component 2.1.1 further explains that a pharmacy technician can collect information related to:

> known patient risk factors for adverse drug reactions, drug allergies, or sensitivities, known contraindications to prescription drugs, non-prescription drugs, natural health products and complementary and alternative medicines, and other medications or treatments the patient is currently taking that may contribute to their condition or interact with suggested therapy.

Once collected, prescription and demographic information must be entered into the patient's record accurately, and in a format that will be understood by all users. Depending on the policies of the particular pharmacy, this may include using appropriate abbreviations for drugs, dosages, and other details. Pharmacy technicians are expected to be familiar with these abbreviations or, when they encounter an unfamiliar one, to ask for advice. Many drugs are similarly named, and minor differences in abbreviations can represent major deviations. For these reasons, the competent and accurate entry of prescription and demographic information is not merely a clerical concern but a matter of patient safety.

PREPARING THE PRESCRIPTION FOR RELEASE TO THE PATIENT

The College's proposed Standard Four provides that "[t]he pharmacy technician, in collaboration with the pharmacist, designated manager, or hospital pharmacy manager, prepares pharmaceutical products for release and documents."

Preparing products for release involves a number of tasks. The first tasks usually include the technical aspects of compounding, reconstituting, measuring, and counting drugs. While carrying out these tasks, it is not enough for the pharmacy technician simply to follow instructions. She must also exercise professional judgment. For example, NAPRA Competency 4.1.1(vi) provides that the pharmacy technician must "ensure the integrity, stability, and where applicable, sterility of products, for example, by checking expiry dates, colour, odour, etc."

In addition to the technical aspects of dispensing, there are other practical tasks: the pharmacy technician must select packaging (which can include child-proof packaging or special packaging for those who have limited dexterity, or divided-dose packaging that promotes compliance), prepare labels, choose and affix auxiliary warning or instructional stickers, print handouts (if the use of these is a policy of the pharmacy), and choose administration devices.

How these tasks are managed depends a great deal on several factors:

- pharmacy technologies—for example, in many pharmacies, some aspects of dispensing, such as pill-counting, are automated;
- pharmacy policies—for example, some pharmacies provide detailed product handouts for patients; and
- demographics—for example, pharmacies that cater to seniors may stock packaging that addresses special needs (easy-to-open packaging, large-print labels).

There is one aspect of dispensing, however, that is—or should be—common to all pharmacies: a formal quality-control procedure for checking prepared products before distribution to patients. Both the College's proposed standards and NAPRA's competencies emphasize that under no circumstances should a prepared product be permitted to go out to the patient without being carefully checked (and compared against the original prescription) by the pharmacist or a pharmacy student or intern. Now that Ontario pharmacy technicians are eligible for registration, a second registered pharmacy technician may be permitted to perform this review (see the College's proposed Operational Component 4.3; OCP, n.d.).

In some cases, additional checks will be appropriate earlier in the process. For example, if preparing the prescription requires calculations, proposed Operational Component 4.2.2 states that the pharmacy technician should ask a pharmacist or another pharmacy technician to check the preparing technician's calculations before proceeding with the preparation.

Whenever a check is performed—whether of a finished product or at an earlier stage—the fact that the review took place, and the name of the person who checked the product, should be documented.

From a legal perspective, a pharmacy technician must be careful, while carrying out product preparation activities, to comply with all applicable legislation and regulations. The *Drug Interchangeability and Dispensing Fee Act* (DIDFA) applies to some aspects of dispensing, particularly with respect to the selection of interchangeable drugs. Pharmacy technicians have a legal responsibility to maintain accurate knowledge of drug interchangeability, or to consult with a pharmacist should there be any uncertainty about a proposed substitution.

RELEASING THE PRESCRIPTION TO THE PATIENT

Before a pharmacy technician releases any product to a patient, he or she must ensure that the prepared product has been independently double-checked by another pharmacy staff person.

The pharmacy technician must also check to ensure that all the required information appears on the product packaging. This information should include:

- the pharmacy's prescription identification number;
- the name of the prescriber;
- the name of the patient;
- the name and manufacturer of the drug;
- the dosage strength and number of units or quantity of liquid/cream/lotion;
- the date the drug was dispensed;
- clear instructions for use; and
- the number of refills remaining, if any.

The packaging should also bear supplemental instructional or warning stickers, where appropriate.

The patient must be issued a receipt or invoice that bears the same information as the packaging, as well as information about drug and dispensing costs. The DIDFA states:

> 10. Every person who dispenses a drug pursuant to a prescription shall provide with the drug, in the manner prescribed by the regulations, particulars of the amount charged.

The "Notice to Patients" regulation made under the DIDFA further elaborates on this requirement:

> 4. (1) A person who dispenses a drug pursuant to a prescription shall provide a receipt to the person to whom the drug is supplied at the same time that the drug is supplied that sets out the amount being charged in respect of,
>> (a) a dispensing fee;
>> (b) the cost of the drug; and
>> (c) the total price of the prescription.

Even if all these requirements are met, situations may arise in which it is not appropriate for a pharmacy technician to complete the release of a drug independently. All therapeutic inquiries from patients must be handled by a pharmacist, not a pharmacy technician. Whenever a pharmacy technician anticipates that a patient may need clarification about instructions or questions about treatment, a pharmacist must be consulted. To avoid confusion, and to promote good communication with patients, many pharmacies have a policy that the pharmacist should handle most, if not all, releases of product to patients.

Sales and Billing

Sometimes pharmacy technicians perform the billing and sales aspects of dispensing, under the supervision of the pharmacist.

Particularly when the patient requires no counselling about the prescription (for example, in the case of a routine refill), the pharmacy technician may be the sole direct contact with the patient in the course of the dispensing transaction. When presenting the bill and receiving payment, the pharmacy technician is authorized to answer questions about such issues as:

- dispensing fees;
- prescription cost;
- differences in cost as between generic and brand-name drugs;
- the extent of the patient's insurance coverage, coverage limits, and coverage details; and
- acceptable methods of payment.

The pharmacy technician must be prepared to address all such inquiries.

Insurance coverage for drugs and pharmacy products are discussed in Chapter 5.

With respect to dispensing fees, these are set by the pharmacy. The DIDFA provides that after determining its "usual and customary dispensing fee," a pharmacy must file this fee with the Registrar of the College of Pharmacists. Once the filing is received, the maximum fee is in force, and the pharmacy must make a new filing any time it chooses to raise the fee.

Dispensing fees vary from pharmacy to pharmacy. Often, larger chain pharmacies and pharmacies located in department stores offer lower dispensing fees than do independent pharmacies. Volume of business makes this possible. However, a high volume of business at chain or department store pharmacies often means that the pharmacists who work there have less time available for patient counselling, for reviewing the patient record, and for other services. Because the dispensing fee reflects such professional services, the higher fee charged by independent pharmacies is often justified. Pharmacy technicians should be prepared to describe the kinds of services that are recovered through dispensing fees and to justify the fee charged by their own pharmacy.

Once a pharmacy has established a dispensing fee, it must post a notice disclosing this fee where the public can read it (usually near the cash register). The notice should read as follows:

> *Our usual and customary fee for professional services when dispensing a drug product is _____.*

Under normal circumstances, the pharmacy may not charge a fee higher than the posted fee, though it can charge a lower one if appropriate. However, Regulation 935 made under the *Pharmacy Act* provides that:

> [a] person may charge more than the person's usual and customary dispensing fee for a product that is supplied pursuant to a prescription if the person explains why a fee in excess of the usual and customary fee is being charged prior to the dispensing of the prescription and the charging of the additional fee is not an act of professional misconduct under section 1 of Ontario Regulation 681/93 made under the *Pharmacy Act*, 1991. (s. 5)

In general, a pharmacist will be permitted to charge a fee higher than the posted fee only when the services rendered exceed the normal range. For example, if the patient requests, and the pharmacist creates, a special compound or preparation (a dye-free version of a reconstituted drug that is normally coloured, for example), and preparation of the drug requires extra effort or time, a higher dispensing fee may be warranted; but the pharmacist (or pharmacy technician who receives the instructions) should explain the increased fee *before* preparing the drug.

It is illegal to use inappropriate profit-generating tactics, such as charging a higher dispensing fee when dispensing a less-expensive generic drug to "even out" the cost, or dispensing the prescription in batches less than the total prescription amount in order to charge multiple dispensing fees. (In some cases, however, where insurance coverage dictates the dispensing of smaller batches, or where a pharmacist's professional judgment dictates that a smaller batch should be dispensed, dispensing less than the full prescription at once can be justified.)

The drug cost, the dispensing fee, and any other charges (for example, taxes and shipping costs) must be set out separately on the customer's bill.

Non-compliance with dispensing fee and cost disclosure rules is an offence that, if proven, can result in a fine of up to $25,000 for an individual or $100,000 for a corporation.

Customer Service

Both the College's proposed standards and the NAPRA competencies make it clear that the pharmacy technician profession includes not only technical functions, but also customer service.

In the early 1990s, the Court of Appeal of British Columbia issued a judgment in the case of *Li v. College of Pharmacists of British Columbia*, which seemed to suggest that providing rude and unhelpful customer service did *not* constitute professional misconduct on the part of a pharmacist. The pharmacist in that case was disciplined by his College for treating four different pharmacy clients (some of whom had questions about non-prescription products, including camera film) with extreme rudeness and disrespect, in one case demanding that a customer leave the pharmacy.

The court, however, overturned the College's disciplinary order, quoting the lower court judge's finding:

> I cannot conceive that the intention of the Legislature was to empower the College to pass judgment on the personal idiosyncrasies of its members, offensive as these may be to some members of the public. Short temper, intemperate language, and rude behaviour must surely be regulated by business considerations, not by the College.

In the years that followed, the *Li* decision was approved by some courts and rejected by others. In the 2006 decision in *Tardif c. Nammour*, a Quebec court called a pharmacist's actions, in ordering a patient out of his pharmacy and threatening to remove her, "reprehensible," and awarded the patient damages (compensation) of $500.

A close reading of the College's proposed standards and the NAPRA competencies for pharmacy technicians makes it evident that regulators consider discourteous and insensitive treatment of patients to be unprofessional and grounds for discipline. Operational Component 1.2.1, which expands on the College's Standard One, prescribes a customer service approach that respects patient diversity, preserves patient dignity, and guarantees "quality care":

1.2.1 The pharmacy technician acts in the best interest of the patient and the public by:

- Reflecting on personal values and attitudes and examining their influence on interactions with the patient, the patient's agent, members of the pharmacy team, and other healthcare providers
- Respecting diversity
- Protecting patient rights to quality care, dignity, privacy, and confidentiality.

Operational Component 6.2 also prescribes a flexible, culturally sensitive approach to patients:

The pharmacy technician communicates using effective and appropriate communication skills while respecting the patient's personal, cultural, and educational differences. When interacting with the patient/patient's agent the pharmacy technician demonstrates flexibility in recognizing the unique qualities of each patient/patient's agent to find workable communication solutions.

In addition, NAPRA Competency 1.1.1 reminds pharmacy technicians that patients have a right to be heard, and to participate in decisions related to their own health:

1.1.1 Be accountable to patients.

    i. advocate on behalf of patients.
    ii. involve patients in decision making.
    iii. respect patients' rights to make their own choices.
    iv. consider patient-specific circumstances.

Good, attentive customer service is not merely a matter of manners. Maintaining good relationships with patients can improve safety by making it more likely that the patient will ask questions, report side effects, or disclose potential problems with compliance. For example, a patient who is comfortable speaking with the pharmacy technician may reveal that he has trouble swallowing large pills. This disclosure may prompt the pharmacy technician to speak with the pharmacist about dispensing smaller-dose pills, with amended dosing instructions.

Paying close attention to patients may also allow pharmacy staff to identify potential risks to health. For example, a patient who repeatedly asks for refills prior to the appropriate interval may have a substance abuse problem, or may be sharing his prescription with others. Or an adult may be inappropriately dosing a child with antihistamines (for example, Gravol or Benadryl) to make the child sleep. Pharmacy staff who suspect child abuse have a non-delegable statutory duty to report these suspicions to police, as provided by section 72 of the *Child and Family Services Act*.

Finally, good patient care means taking the time to reflect on individual patient circumstances and needs, instead of simply treating patients like customer files. One example of customer-focused decision making would be asking an elderly patient, who appears to have arthritis in her hands, whether she would prefer easy-to-open packaging.

Good customer service can also help pharmacy personnel. If pharmacy personnel are courteous and helpful, patients will be less likely to challenge dispensing fees. Or, in the event of a medication error, patients who have had good care from their pharmacy personnel may be less likely to escalate an error into a formal complaint against the pharmacy team.

Privacy and the Management of Confidential Information

INTRODUCTION

An important issue related to customer service is the protection of patient privacy and the appropriate management of confidential information. Pharmacy technicians are privy to highly sensitive and confidential patient health information, and are required, both ethically and by law, to effectively protect that information. Operational Component 6.1.6, which relates to the College's Standard Six, requires that "[t]he pharmacy technician maintains confidentiality of patient information"; NAPRA Competency 1.1.2 states that a pharmacy technician must "[p]rotect patient confidentiality according to applicable federal and provincial/territorial privacy legislation."

In Canada, privacy legislation exists at both the federal and provincial levels:

- At the federal level, confidential information is governed by the *Privacy Act* and the *Personal Information Protection and Electronic Documents Act*.
- At the provincial level, confidential information is governed by the *Freedom of Information and Protection of Privacy Act*, the *Municipal Freedom of Information and Protection of Privacy Act*, and the *Personal Health Information Protection Act*.

For pharmacy technicians—who are typically not legal experts—the prospect of reading, understanding, and complying with five different privacy statutes may seem daunting. However, the following four points will help clarify the issue:

1. Much of the content of these statutes relates to situations and activities (for example, standards for information storage) for which pharmacy technicians will not generally be responsible.
2. The statutes overlap substantially in terms of information they cover.
3. Focusing on compliance with the very strict *Personal Health Information Protection Act* (PHIPA) will automatically lead pharmacy workers to comply with the other legislation.
4. Most retail pharmacies have—or should have—detailed policies for the protection of patient privacy, and these will have been developed according to the requirements of the legislation.

Table 3.2 summarizes the customer and patient service aspects of Canada's confidential information protection scheme.

Table 3.2 Information Protection: Customer and Patient Service

1.	Know or determine what information you legitimately need to collect in order to serve and protect your patient.
2.	Ensure that your patient understands the purpose(s) for which you are collecting the information.
3.	Obtain your patient's consent to collect information.
4.	Collect and record only the information you need and no more.
5.	Protect the confidential information you have collected (for example, with technologies that protect computer data, and by keeping written materials out of sight of others).
6.	Use confidential information only for the purposes you have disclosed to the patient, and for no other purposes.
7.	Before sharing a patient's confidential information with any other party (for example, a family member of the patient—including the patient's spouse—or a new physician), obtain the patient's specific *written* consent to do exactly what you want to do (in other words, the consent must describe the information you want to disclose and the person to whom you want to disclose it).
8.	Destroy confidential information completely when it is no longer needed.
9.	If you break any of the above rules (for example, you accidentally disclose information), report the incident to a supervisor and to the patient.

The following sections provide a brief overview of the relevant legislation, and a discussion of its implications for pharmacy staff.

THE PRIVACY ACT

The federal *Privacy Act* governs the handling of confidential information by federal government departments and agencies. It applies to over 150 agencies, including the following health-related entities:

- the Department of Health;
- the Assisted Human Reproduction Agency of Canada;
- the Canadian Institutes of Health Research;
- the Federal Public Service Health Care Plan Administration Authority;
- the Patented Medicine Prices Review Board; and
- the Public Health Agency of Canada.

Pharmacy technicians who work at or with these agencies, or who work in pharmacies that provide services to them, may need to be familiar with the *Privacy Act* and follow policies and procedures that support compliance with it.

THE PERSONAL INFORMATION PROTECTION AND ELECTRONIC DOCUMENTS ACT

The *Personal Information Protection and Electronic Documents Act* (PIPEDA) applies to a wide range of transactions and records involving confidential information. However, because its application and objectives are substantially similar to those of the Ontario *Personal Health Information Protection Act* (PHIPA), the PHIPA applies instead to transactions and records in the health sector (which includes pharmacy).

THE FREEDOM OF INFORMATION AND PROTECTION OF PRIVACY ACT AND THE MUNICIPAL FREEDOM OF INFORMATION AND PROTECTION OF PRIVACY ACT

The *Freedom of Information and Protection of Privacy Act* (FIPP Act), a provincial statute, provides rules for the government's handling of people's personal information. The legislation and the regulations made under it regulate the collection, use, disclosure, storage, and disposal of personal information. The Act also gives the public, under many circumstances, the right to access the information held about them by government institutions, and to request corrections to that information.

The FIPP Act is managed by the Information and Privacy Commissioner of Ontario. The Commissioner is appointed by the legislature, but is independent of the ruling government. The Commissioner investigates complaints about the mishandling of individuals' personal information by public sector information gatherers and manages requests for access to information.

When individuals request access to their information, they must first directly approach the agency holding the information. Only when that agency refuses the request, or fails to provide access, should an individual seek recourse from the Information and Privacy Commissioner.

Complaints about mishandling of personal information by private sector information gatherers fall under the (federal) PIPEDA, discussed above, and under the provincial PHIPA, discussed below.

Besides creating a mechanism for allowing individuals access to their own information, the FIPP Act also allows individuals to request access to general government information—that is, information that does not pertain to the individual or other third parties but rather to the government and its dealings.

There are limitations to what the government must disclose. The government may not disclose information that would infringe on the privacy interests of a third party (another individual, for example). It is also not allowed to disclose cabinet records.

An example of the relevance of the FIPP Act to a pharmacy technician might be a case in which a pharmacy patient who receives government-sponsored drug coverage (under the *Ontario Drug Benefit Act*, which is discussed in Chapter 5) is denied coverage for a claim or for a particular drug. The patient might want to apply under the FIPP Act for information about the government's decision and may need the pharmacy technician's help (for example, spelling a drug name or providing an information handout about the drug).

The *Municipal Freedom of Information and Protection of Privacy Act* is substantially similar to the FIPP Act, except that it provides access to personal information held by municipal agencies.

THE PERSONAL HEALTH INFORMATION PROTECTION ACT

The *Personal Health Information Protection Act* (PHIPA) establishes rules for the collection, use, and disclosure of personal health information. Like the *Privacy Act* and the FIPP Act, it also establishes individuals' right to access personal health records held by others and, if appropriate, to correct or amend those records.

The PHIPA regulates "custodians" of personal health information. Custodians include a wide range of organizations, including the "officers in charge" of medical practices, hospitals, pharmacies, ambulance services, boards of health, and more.

Personal health information is broadly defined in the PHIPA. Besides factual details of a person's physical health, it includes also:

- the person's OHIP number;
- details of the person's eligibility for and receipt of health-care services, public health insurance, and drug benefits; and
- the identity of the person's substitute decision maker (for example, one who has power of attorney for personal care over the patient), if any.

Part IV of the PHIPA provides that a "custodian"—which can include a pharmacy or a pharmacy staff person—cannot collect, use, or disclose personal health information about an individual unless the collection, use, or disclosure is necessary and permitted by the legislation, and unless the individual consents.

From a practical perspective, consent to collection, use, and disclosure of personal health information by a pharmacy is usually managed verbally. In some cases, however—for example, if a pharmacy requests access to an electronic health record—consent may be obtained more formally, perhaps by providing the patient with a waiver form that explains the issue of consent. In such a case, the patient's signature on the form constitutes consent provided that it is reasonable to believe that the patient understood the content and legal effect of the waiver.

The PHIPA requires collectors and custodians of personal health information to protect that information. This requirement relates both to paper and to electronic records. The details of how information is to be protected (for example, from theft, destruction, tampering hackers, etc.) may eventually be covered in a regulation made under the PHIPA; at the moment, there are no specific guidelines for guaranteeing protection. If information is lost, illegally accessed, illegally disclosed, or tampered with, the person whose information it is must be notified promptly.

There are good reasons why pharmacy patients might guard the confidentiality of their personal health records, and in particular, those records relating to drug therapy. Some patients are concerned that if employers or potential employers became aware that an employee suffers from a chronic illness (for example, heart disease or diabetes), they might think twice about employing that person because of the risk that he or she might become sick. A person suffering from a communicable disease (for example, HIV/AIDS) might be discriminated against if that status were revealed; and a person being treated for a psychiatric ailment (for example, depression or schizophrenia) might be concerned about stigmatization. Finally, teenage patients who have been prescribed contraceptives might worry about negative reactions from parents. Accidental disclosure of personal health information can have serious consequences for some people; thus, a pharmacy's responsibility as a custodian of personal health information must not be taken lightly.

Each custodian of personal health information is required to appoint a contact person. The contact person handles requests for disclosure of information and inquiries about information management, and receives complaints under the PHIPA. Custodians must prepare and distribute to the interested public a written policy with respect to the handling of personal health information. From a practical perspective, pharmacists or pharmacy technicians may use the distribution of this policy as an opportunity to discuss and obtain the patient's consent to disclosure of personal health information.

Part III of the PHIPA defines consent, and provides that individuals (or their substitute decision maker) have the right to consent, to withhold consent, to give conditional or limited consent, and to **revoke** consent to the disclosure and use of personal health information.

revoke
cancel officially

Part V governs requests for access to information, and entitles individuals to access to their own personal health information records except under certain special circumstances. A person who finds an error in a record of personal health information can request that the custodian correct the error. The custodian must respond, advising whether or not the correction will be made. If the individual objects to a correction not being made, he or she can make a complaint to the Commissioner.

Part VI describes the process by which complaints are brought to the attention of the Commissioner; how the Commissioner reviews (or elects not to review) complaints, including by using powers of inspection; and the orders that the Commissioner can make to resolve a complaint. The complaints process (if the Commissioner decides to proceed with a review) allows both the individual and the custodian to make representations (speak up about their side of the story). A lawyer or a non-lawyer representative can make these representations on behalf of the individual, if he so wishes.

In appropriate cases, the Commissioner can find a custodian or another person guilty of an offence in relation to private records. In general, an offence can be charged only if the custodian "willfully" (intentionally) violated the provisions of the PHIPA. Individuals found guilty of a PHIPA offence can be fined up to $50,000, and corporations found guilty can be fined up to $250,000.

In cases where the Commissioner finds that improper disclosure has caused an invasion of privacy or mental anguish, and all appeals of the order have been completed, the individual can seek compensation through the Ontario Superior Court of Justice.

In 2005, the Commissioner heard a case involving complaints (*Commissioner Initiated Complaints Against Internet Pharmacies*), by a number of US customers, against a Canadian Internet pharmacy. The complaints alleged that the customers had been receiving email solicitations from other Internet pharmacies, and that their content suggested that these other pharmacies had "inside knowledge" about the medications the complainants had ordered in the past.

The Commissioner launched an investigation into the revelation, by the Internet pharmacy, that two of its employees had, in the year prior to the complaints, collaborated to steal the company's client list and sell it to a third party (another Internet pharmacy, which in turn resold the list to two other Internet pharmacies— without disclosing to them that the list was stolen).

Because the theft took place before the PHIPA came into force, the Commissioner did not have jurisdiction to make findings against the original Internet pharmacy (which, in the meantime, had taken steps to improve its information security). The Commissioner did, however, find that the two companies to which the customer list had been resold had used the personal health information of the customers without their consent. This case represents just one of the possible scenarios through which a pharmacy might fall afoul of the PHIPA.

BOX 3.3

CASE

Consent and Disclosure

Pharmacy's Privacy Policy and Practices Considered Exemplary

In an example of how you can never make everyone happy, a pharmacy that enhanced its consent and disclosure policies after the PHIPA was brought into force became the subject of complaints from patients to the office of the Commissioner. Complainants alleged that the consent the pharmacy was seeking was too broad, or that they did not want to be required to read the pharmacy's detailed privacy policy or sign its complicated waiver.

In response to the complaints, the pharmacy took several steps, summarized as follows by the Commissioner:

1. It revised and simplified the language of the consent form.

2. It offered pharmacy patients who were uncomfortable with reading the brochure the option of having a pharmacy employee explain the privacy practices. To this end, the company developed a comprehensive training program for its staff, including a standard script that the employee can read to the pharmacy patient. The script explains the purposes for the collection, use and disclosure of information, and in very straightforward language, outlines with whom the pharmacy shares information, how information is stored, and how the customer can obtain additional information.

3. It offered pharmacy patients the option of providing verbal consent. In such circumstances, the pharmacy employee reads a standard script, asks if the pharmacy has the patient's consent for its practices, and records the person's consent on file.

In addition to this flexible approach, the pharmacy drafted its privacy policy using "straightforward language" and made copies available in all its locations. It also adopted special practices, including providing patient counselling only in private or semi-private areas, and training staff to communicate with patients using an appropriate tone and volume of voice.

The Commissioner, after reviewing the pharmacy's personal information protection program, found that the patients' complaints were without merit and were based on lack of familiarity with the new legislation. The Commissioner praised the pharmacy's program as "exemplary" and a "model for best practice." ◙

Pharmacy technicians employed by retail pharmacies will usually be guided by the store's own detailed policy on the handling of personal health information. Careful adherence to this policy is essential, but it is not a substitute for good judgment. Existing policies can often be improved, and any pharmacy technician who detects a security risk not covered by the policy should speak up.

Documenting, Record-Keeping, and Reporting

There are four important reasons for careful record-keeping in pharmacies:

1. to have accurate records of the medications legitimately dispensed to patients for referral in case of adverse drug events or reactions;

2. to minimize the potential for, and maximize the chances of early detection of, illegal diversion or removal of drugs;

3. to assist in the defence of pharmacy staff who may face charges of incompetence, negligence, or other forms of professional misconduct; and

4. to support the efficient management of drug and supplies inventory.

Pharmacy technicians may, in the settings in which they work, have two general categories of reporting obligations. They may have to keep records and complete reports for the pharmacy's purposes (the four listed above); and they may have to keep records and make reports prescribed by the regulatory agencies in support of the government's scheme of management of controlled drugs and substances.

The reporting obligations that arise when dispensing controlled drugs and substances are discussed in Chapter 4.

With respect to internal reporting obligations, both the College's proposed standards and the NAPRA competencies describe pharmacy technicians' record-keeping duties. Steps in the dispensing process include documenting:

- receipt of a prescription;
- the pharmacist's check of the incoming prescription, and approval to fill it;
- the dispenser's review of a patient's file (for example, for drug sensitivities, interactions, or duplication) before dispensing;
- the review, by an independent checker, of any changes made to the patient's health record;
- independent double-check of any calculations required for dispensing;
- independent double-check of the prepared prescription prior to release to the patient;
- release of the prescription to the patient;
- any feedback from the patient about the prescription (for example, reporting of side effects); and
- any dispensing errors should these be discovered.

See, for reference, the College's Operational Components 2.1.5, 2.2.10, 2.3.3, 4.2.2, 4.2.3, 4.3.5, 4.3.6, 5.3.3, and 6.1.7 (OCP, n.d.).

Another form of documentation essential to pharmacy safety is the reporting to a superior of any suspicions, on the pharmacy technician's part, that drugs have been removed or released illegally (whether by staff, or through fraud or deception on the part of patients), or that any other unethical, illegal, or unsafe activities have occurred. NAPRA Competency 1.2.2 states that a pharmacy technician has a responsibility to:

Question, report, and assist in the resolution of potential and actual unsafe, illegal, unethical, or unprofessional actions or situations.

    i.   identify, report, and correct errors, omissions, and unsafe practices or situations.

    ii.   identify and report conduct that is illegal, unethical, or unprofessional to the appropriate authorities.

    iii.   document the incident and actions taken.

Particularly where suspicions relate to co-workers (or even the pharmacy technician's own superiors), this kind of reporting requires courage and integrity.

In general, when reporting a concern about a staff member's management of pharmacy products, it is a good idea to speak directly with the person first. This step allows the person to clarify his or her actions, which may reveal that the pharmacy technician's concerns were unfounded. If the concerns are founded, confronting the employee may be sufficient to bring an end to the behaviour.

If speaking with the co-worker does not resolve the problem, the pharmacy technician is justified in approaching a superior or making a complaint to the College. It is generally preferable to give one's name when making a complaint, but if a pharmacy technician fears for his or her safety, reputation, or job, it is possible to make an anonymous complaint.

If the drugs concerned are controlled drugs, the pharmacy technician should act quickly to confirm or allay suspicions. An incident of mismanagement or diversion of controlled drugs can result in serious consequences for the pharmacy as a whole, and can affect the reputations and careers of innocent parties who work there.

Inventory Management

Effective management of pharmacy inventory promotes early detection of discrepancies and ensures that when patients need a product, it is available for dispensing. Pharmacy technicians often play an important role in inventory management. They may be involved with:

- inventory review and reconciliation of inventory with dispensing records;
- quality control, including ensuring that expired, defective, or recalled products are removed from inventory;
- deciding which drugs will be stocked by the pharmacy;
- placing drug orders; and
- checking incoming orders for completeness, correctness, and quality.

NAPRA Competency 6.2 provides the following outline of pharmacy technicians' specific responsibilities with respect to inventory management:

  6.2   Manage inventory.

     6.2.1 Employ inventory management systems and strategies that incorporate best practice approaches for ensuring patient safety.

     6.2.2 Determine and maintain inventory requirements sufficient for patient safety and efficient operations.

        i.   set order limits and calculate replenishment orders.

    ii. prepare and place orders for stock and supplies from licensed and legitimate pharmaceutical suppliers/sources and in compliance with relevant legislation.

    iii. acquire, receive, verify, and store stock and supplies purchased and investigate and resolve discrepancies.

    iv. ensure that receipt and storage of all medications complies with legislative requirements and policies and procedures.

    v. identify, report, and remove defective, unsafe, and recalled products.

    vi. dispose of, destroy, or return expired, unusable products, and complete recalls of products according to legislation and policies and procedures.

6.2.3 Audit inventory and report any discrepancies.

    i. reconcile inventory for narcotic, controlled, targeted-controlled substances, and any other products as selected.

    ii. identify, investigate, and report any discrepancies to a pharmacist or appropriate authority.

6.2.4 Maintain an inventory information system so that the information can be retrieved easily.

6.2.5 Complete all documentation pertaining to inventory management including narcotics, controlled, targeted-controlled, investigational, special access, and hazardous drugs.

Should you, as a pharmacy technician, be unfamiliar with any of these tasks or with your pharmacy's procedures for completing them, you should ask for help (or even formal training). A consistent approach to inventory management—one in which all pharmacy staff members complete tasks in the same way—is essential for good and consistent inventory control.

Pharmacy Best Practices

best practice
methods and processes that have been proven to produce optimal results

A **best practice** is a way of doing things that research and experience have shown is most likely to achieve a particular goal. In pharmacy, there are a wide range of possible goals that pharmacists, pharmacy technicians, and others work toward every day. Some examples of pharmacy goals include:

- ensuring patient safety;
- minimizing or eliminating medication errors;
- promoting patient compliance with drug therapy;
- minimizing side effects;
- providing excellent customer service;
- managing inventory effectively;
- earning a profit;
- protecting patient privacy;
- serving the community through health education; and
- creating a positive working environment for pharmacy staff.

Good pharmacy technicians strive every day to improve the service that they offer to their patients. One way to achieve success in this endeavour is to seek out, implement, and develop industry best practices.

The privacy protection program profiled in Box 3.3 is one example of a best practice (or more accurately, a set of best practices). While that particular best practice is quite elaborate, a best practice need not be complicated. Consider, for example, the long-standing practice of placing newly received inventory of a product (product for which the expiry date is farther in the future) behind older product on a retail or stock shelf. This procedure is used by businesses around the world to manage many different kinds of perishable inventory. It's simple, but it's done because it works: it minimizes waste by ensuring that older inventory is sold or dispensed ahead of new. Incorporating as many best practices as possible in the running of a pharmacy ensures that the pharmacy provides the best possible service.

To learn about new best practices as they emerge, pharmacy technicians should regularly read the newsletters or magazines published by the College and by industry associations. They should consider membership in industry associations and attend courses and seminars, where time and funds permit. The College imposes a requirement on all registered pharmacists and pharmacy technicians to pursue continuing education (often called "lifelong learning"). There is a good reason for this requirement: continuing education ensures that pharmacy technicians are exposed to the emerging best practices in their industry.

While the term "best practice" suggests that these practices are patterns of behaviour—and most are—some involve the adoption of new technologies. For example, it is possible to build in to a pharmacy's electronic client database an electronic alert system. These systems are designed to analyze new prescriptions or refills as they are entered into the database, and to compare them both to existing records (for example, records of other prescriptions the patient is taking) or general industry standards (for example, typical doses of various drugs). If the system detects a potential medication error, it generates an alert, and the pharmacy technician (in consultation with the pharmacist) has the opportunity to correct the mistake (for an error in inputting), query the prescriber, or query the patient.

For example, if the patient is already taking one drug, and the new prescription is for a drug that is known to interact with that drug, the pharmacy technician will be alerted. Likewise, if the prescription specifies three times the usual dose of the drug prescribed, an alert will be generated. This system is an example of an automated best practice.

Sometimes, new pharmacy staff—for example, newly registered pharmacy technicians with up-to-date training—bring with them new ideas about how to approach pharmacy work. Rather than resenting these new ideas, a wise pharmacy manager will see the new staff person's fresh perspective as an asset and a potential source of best practices.

Finally, along with best practices, there are also "worst practices" (although this is not a term in regular usage). Some ways of doing things have been proven over time to lower the likelihood of meeting work goals. A simple example of a "worst practice" is understaffing. When a pharmacy has too few staff to keep up with customer demand, the staff become overworked, tired, distracted, and more prone to error. While this is an obvious example of a practice to avoid, there are other, subtler practices and issues that have been associated with problems. Keeping abreast of industry worst practices (for example, by reading the College's discipline cases) is also an important quality-control task for all pharmacy staff.

PROFESSIONAL SERVICES IN HOSPITAL PHARMACIES

Introduction

The College's proposed standards and the NAPRA competencies are intended to apply to all registered pharmacy technicians, regardless of practice setting. However, hospital pharmacies are characterized by different challenges, demands, and work-flow patterns. This section highlights a few of those differences and explains how legal and regulatory requirements apply to hospital-based pharmacy technicians.

Health-Care Workers as Clients

Perhaps the most important difference between hospital and retail practice is that the customer who approaches a hospital-based pharmacy technician for service is typically not a patient, but rather, a health-care worker.

This does not mean that hospital-based pharmacy staff never have contact with patients—they often do (especially pharmacists). In well-run hospitals, pharmacists are viewed as important members of the health-care team, and they often counsel patients directly. Pharmacy technicians typically have less direct contact with patients, but they may encounter them—for example, while delivering medication to a ward.

Having health-care workers as clients has a number of implications. Pharmacy technicians may become familiar with the physicians that they deal with, and may come to anticipate their needs and requests. A good working relationship with pre-scribers can help minimize errors, but it can also lead to increased demands—once a physician has determined that a pharmacy technician is reliable and hard-working, he or she may begin expecting more from the pharmacy technician. On the positive side, the pharmacy technician will enjoy increased autonomy, and may be exposed to learning opportunities (for example, the reasons a physician has chosen one course of treatment over another) that would not be available in a retail setting. On the negative side, the pharmacy technician may be asked to complete tasks that are outside her scope of practice (for example, completing a checklist that is actually the responsibility of the physician to save the physician time). Achieving a good balance between familiarity and formality can be tricky in the hospital environment, and a pharmacy technician must always remain aware of, and work within, the appropriate scope of practice.

An Enhanced Scope of Practice?

One long-established practice in retail pharmacies is that pharmacy technicians can undertake controlled acts (as defined in the *Regulated Health Professions Act* [RHPA]) and the "authorized acts" that support those controlled acts—in other words, compounding, dispensing, and selling drugs—under the direct supervision of a pharmacist who is physically present in the pharmacy.

In hospitals (and a few other institutional settings), however, this rule has not always been followed so strictly. In the past, hospital pharmacies have given an enhanced level of responsibility and autonomy to pharmacy technicians. In some cases, pharmacy technicians have been charged with preparing drugs for distribution to patients under circumstances in which the pharmacist was not physically present in the pharmacy.

This practice is arguably not consistent with the current state of the law. While many of the provisions of the *Drug and Pharmacies Regulation Act* (DPRA) do not apply to institutional pharmacies (hospital pharmacies are exempt from them), the RHPA does apply to pharmacists in hospitals, and now that pharmacy technicians are regulated, it applies to them as well. The RHPA clearly states that only a pharmacist can perform the controlled acts of dispensing, compounding, or selling *unless those acts are properly delegated in accordance with the regulations stipulated by the College.*

What does the College have to say about delegation of controlled acts in institutional pharmacies? Its "Protocol for Delegating Dispensing and Compounding in Health Care Facilities" explains the delegation rule and states:

> The processes of dispensing and compounding drugs consist of technical functions in combination with cognitive functions. *It is the College's position that only the technical aspects of the medication process can be delegated.* For example, tasks not appropriate for delegation would include: assessing the therapeutic appropriateness of a prescription and making a recommendation to a prescriber, developing the compounding formula for an extemporaneously prepared pharmaceutical, etc. (OCP 1995; emphasis in original)

The Protocol goes on to break down the acts of dispensing and compounding into specific tasks, and lists those that it considers to lie within the scope of a hospital pharmacy technician (or pharmacy intern, or other person to whom delegation is acceptable):

1. Delegating "Dispensing a Drug"

    The tasks within "dispensing a drug" which can be delegated are:

    - receiving a written prescription
    - interpreting (i.e., reading) a prescription
    - adjusting an order according to an approved policy (e.g., therapeutic interchange)
    - order entry
    - selecting the drug (i.e., determining product to dispense)
    - reconstituting a product
    - determining expiry date of product
    - repackaging medications (into vial, unit-dose package, syringe, etc.)
    - labeling a product
    - final physical check for accuracy of finished product
    - maintaining (not interpreting) patient profiles
    - maintaining, preparing and operating equipment

2. Delegating "Compounding a Drug"

Drugs which may be "compounded" include non-sterile topical and oral preparations as well as IV admixtures and other sterile preparations. The tasks within "compounding a drug" which can be delegated are:

- selecting ingredients
- performing calculations of quantities
- determining equipment to be used
- physically preparing product according to approved formula and protocol
- carrying out established quality control assessments on product
- final physical check of finished product. (OCP, 1995)

The Protocol also addresses other issues, such as the right of a pharmacist to refuse to delegate an act, and the right of a person to whom the act is delegated to refuse to accept the delegation. The Protocol speaks to the need for facilities to assess the competence of a pharmacy technician before delegation occurs, and to establish a process for monitoring delegation to ensure that it proceeds properly and safely. Finally, the Protocol requires that delegation of controlled acts be documented in writing.

The Protocol is silent on the issue of whether a delegating pharmacist must be physically present in the pharmacy while a pharmacy technician undertakes acceptable compounding and dispensing tasks. In practice, the pharmacist is not always present. Whether or not this situation is acceptable ultimately depends on whether the pharmacist can adequately manage the delegation of controlled acts when he or she is not in the room. The College makes it clear that "[i]n approving the policies and procedures, the pharmacist accepts responsibility for ensuring the procedures are in accordance with standards acceptable to the profession of pharmacy."

As a pharmacy technician, if you find yourself working in a hospital, remember that your own professional responsibilities require you to speak up any time that you feel you are being asked to handle any task that falls outside your training, experience, or technical or ethical comfort level.

Record-Keeping and Reports

Another aspect of practice that may differ in the hospital setting is record-keeping. Hospitals have different record-keeping systems than retail pharmacies, and a greater number of staff may work with records, charts, and checklists that, in a retail pharmacy, would be exclusively reserved for pharmacy staff. A pharmacy technician who moves into hospital practice after retail practice may have to adjust to this change. He may find, however, that the differences in how records are managed in a hospital afford learning opportunities. For example, a pharmacist—perhaps with help from a pharmacy technician—may be entitled, according to the procedures of the hospital, to make independent notes, changes, and amendments to a patient's chart—something that doesn't happen in the retail setting.

An issue that is sometimes controversial in hospital settings is access to drugs. In general, pharmacists prefer to maintain fairly strict control over the flow of drugs; however, practices in some pharmacies allow other staff some limited self-serve access to them. For example, many hospitals maintain a "drug box" or "night cupboard" that is stocked with a small supply of drugs commonly needed in emergencies (such as cardiac care medicines). Non-pharmacy staff have direct access to this cache in emergencies when the pharmacist is not available. Pharmacy technicians and pharmacists should work together to ensure that all staff entitled to access drugs and dispense them to patients maintain appropriate and consistent records.

Health-Care Team Membership

One of the most exciting aspects of practice in an institutional setting is the opportunity for pharmacy technicians to work as members of a patient's health-care team. Pharmacy technicians who work in retail pharmacies see the results of physicians' treatment decisions (in the form of prescriptions), but rarely have an opportunity to gain insights into how physicians arrive at those decisions. Once the prescription is written, the decision about drug therapy has been made, and the pharmacy technician simply plays a role in carrying it out.

In a hospital, however, physicians have direct access to pharmacists—a situation that promotes a flow of professional knowledge in both directions. A pharmacist who has a question about a prescription can ask the physician about it directly (and often informally) as soon as the order is received. This can help reduce errors and improve patient safety.

Professional advice flows in the opposite direction as well. With a pharmacist close at hand, a physician can seek advice about drug therapy choices; the pharmacist, after all, is the expert when it comes to drugs. In a well-run hospital, pharmacy technicians are also seen as experts within their scope of practice. While it's not appropriate for pharmacy technicians to provide an opinion about therapeutic choices, they may be of assistance in solving other problems—for example, by helping a physician choose a drug delivery format (smaller pills, flavoured preparations, preparations free of allergy-causing additives, etc.). Hospital practice has proven that a team-based system of patient care offers important advantages, both for patients and for the members of the health-care team.

KEY TERMS

best practice
revoke
scope of practice

REFERENCES

Child and Family Services Act. 1990. RSO 1990, c. C.11.

Commissioner Initiated Complaints Against Internet Pharmacies. 2005. CanLII 31591 (PCC).

Drug and Pharmacies Regulation Act. 1990. RSO 1990, c. H.4.

Drug Interchangeability and Dispensing Fee Act. 1990. RSO 1990, c. P.23.

Freedom of Information and Protection of Privacy Act. 1990. RSO 1990, c. F.31.

Li v. College of Pharmacists of British Columbia. 1994. CanLII 2943 (BCCA).

Municipal Freedom of Information and Protection of Privacy Act. 1990. RSO 1990, c. M.56.

National Association of Pharmacy Regulatory Authorities (NAPRA). (2007, September). Professional competencies for Canadian pharmacy technicians at entry to practice. Retrieved May 11, 2010 from http://www.ocpinfo.com/ Client/ocp/OCPHome.nsf/object/Pharmacy+Technician+Competencies +Profile/$file/PT_Competencies.pdf.

Ontario College of Pharmacists (OCP). (n.d.). Proposed standards of practice for registered pharmacy technicians: Summary. Retrieved May 11, 2010 from http://www.ocpinfo.com/client/ocp/OCPHome.nsf/object/Proposed_For_ Techs/$file/Proposed_For_Techs.pdf.

Ontario College of Pharmacists (OCP). (1995, June). Protocol for delegating dispensing and compounding in health care facilities. Retrieved May 11, 2010 from http://www.ocpinfo.com/client/ocp/OCPHome.nsf/web/Protocol +for+Delegating+Dispensing+&+Compounding+in+Health+Care+ Facilities.

Ontario Drug Benefit Act. 1990. RSO 1990, c. O.10.

Personal Health Information Protection Act. 2004. SO 2004, c. 3.

Personal Information Protection and Electronic Documents Act. 2000. SC 2000, c. 5.

Pharmacy Act. 1991. SO 1991, c. 36.

Pharmacy's Privacy Policy and Practices Considered Exemplary. 2005 CanLII 27664 (PCC).

Privacy Act. 1985. RSC 1985, c. P-21.

Regulated Health Professions Act. 1991. SO 1991, c. 18.

Rissi v. Ontario College of Pharmacists. 2003. CanLII 19529 (ONSCDC).

Tardif c. Nammour. 2006 CanLII 14618 (QCCQ).

REVIEW EXERCISES

Discussion Questions

1. What is your opinion of the current legally acceptable scope of practice for pharmacy technicians? Do you believe that pharmacy technicians have all the responsibility that they can handle, or do you think that the scope of practice for these professionals should be expanded? Explain.

2. It is fairly common, in a retail pharmacy, to receive a prescription from a person who is not the patient. For example, a child or teen patient's parent may bring in a prescription for the child, or an elderly patient's adult child may bring in a prescription for the patient. How, from the standpoint of confidentiality, should the pharmacy technician handle questions:

   a. about a prescription from a person who arrives alone (for example, without the elderly patient)?

   b. when the patient and agent appear together (and are both within earshot)?

Review Questions

1. What is meant by "scope of practice"?

2. How can a pharmacy technician determine his or her scope of practice?

3. Now that pharmacy technicians are eligible for registration by the Ontario College, if conflicts arise between the College standards and the NAPRA competencies (for example, if the NAPRA competencies permit something that the College standards prohibit), which set of guidelines takes precedence?

4. List at least three things that a pharmacy technician must do after receiving a written prescription from a patient and before dispensing the prescribed drug.

5. Can pharmacy technicians in Ontario accept prescriptions directly from a physician or other prescriber?

6. How might a pharmacy technician use professional judgment when preparing a product for release to a patient? Give at least one example.

7. Which statute provides details of the drug cost and dispensing fee details that must be provided to the patient when a drug is dispensed?

8. Is polite and attentive customer service simply a desirable quality in a pharmacy technician, or is it an aspect of professionalism?

9. List at least two benefits of good customer service.

10. How much and what kinds of personal information is it legal and acceptable to collect from patients?

11. What must a pharmacy technician do before sharing personal health information collected from a patient with any other person?

12. When a pharmacy technician documents dispensing activities, who are the records and reports intended for, and why are they kept?

13. Why is it important to maintain an accurate inventory of products stocked in the pharmacy? Provide at least two reasons.

14. Which aspect of dispensing can pharmacists *not* delegate to pharmacy technicians?

15. How does a hospital-based practice allow a pharmacy technician to be part of the patient's health-care team?

CHAPTER 4

Overview of the Regulation of Drugs and Other Controlled Substances

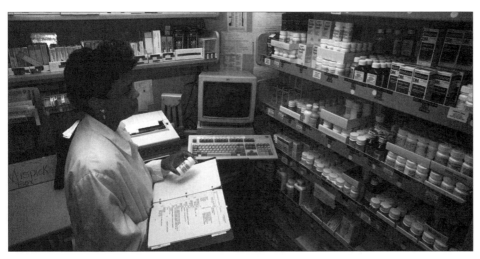

Pharmacy technicians may be expected to check and restock inventory and maintain appropriate records for government-controlled drugs.

LEARNING OBJECTIVES

After completing this chapter, you should be able to:

- List at least six legislative or regulatory sources of guidelines for the management of government-controlled substances.

- Describe the types and categories of drugs that are subject to special government control.

- Understand the special rules that govern the purchase of narcotics by pharmacies.

- Explain the reporting responsibilities borne by pharmacies that deal in narcotics, controlled drugs, and targeted substances.

- Make recommendations about how drugs should be stored by pharmacies.

- Understand the rules for drug refills and prescription transfers for drugs subject to special control.

- Summarize appropriate standards for the return, disposal, or destruction of expired or unneeded drugs.

INTRODUCTION

General

Both the federal and provincial governments play a role in the regulation of drugs and controlled substances designed for human consumption.

The federal government is responsible for establishing criminal laws and for promoting "peace, order, and good government"—a duty that has safety implications. It also regulates many aspects of international trade, imports, and exports, and establishes national health policy.

Provincial governments are responsible for business and commercial transactions (including pharmaceutical sales transactions) within the province; for regulation of professions, such as pharmacists and pharmacy technicians; and for administration of provincial health-care services.

Overlapping spheres of federal and provincial control mean that pharmacy technicians must consult both federal and provincial laws when working with and dispensing substances and products that the two tiers of governments have targeted for regulation.

Three federal statutes create rules for the management of controlled substances:

- the *Controlled Drugs and Substances Act* (CDSA);
- the *Food and Drugs Act* (FDA); and
- the *Excise Act, 2001* (EA) (not to be confused with the *Excise Act*, which regulates substances not generally sold in pharmacies—mainly beer and malt liquor).

At the provincial level, the statutes most relevant to the government regulation of drugs sold in pharmacies are:

- the *Drug and Pharmacies Regulation Act*;
- the *Ontario Drug Benefit Act* (ODBA; discussed in Chapter 5); and
- the *Drug Interchangeability and Dispensing Fee Act* (DIDFA; discussed in Chapter 3).

It is not enough to be aware of just these statutes; important drug rules appear in the regulations made under them. Some key examples:

- the *Natural Health Product Regulations*, the *Food and Drug Regulations*, and the *Medical Devices Regulations* made under the FDA; and
- the *Narcotic Control Regulations*, the *Precursor Control Regulations*, and the *Benzodiazepines and Other Targeted Substances Regulations* made under the CDSA.

schedule
in the context of legislation or regulations, an appendix containing a list, chart, or other collection of data

As if that list were not overwhelming enough, pharmacy staff must also be aware of non-legislative sources of drug policy. In an effort to harmonize the control of drugs in Canada, the National Association of Pharmacy Regulatory Authorities (NAPRA) partnered with the federal Therapeutic Products Directorate (a Health Canada agency) to create a **schedule**—the National Drug Schedule—for the consistent categorization of drugs. This system is discussed below.

Finally, some provincial regulators create policies for the management of drugs, products, and substances. An example of such a policy in effect in Ontario is the College's standard of practice for pharmacies providing access to Methadone Maintenance Treatment (a program of methadone therapy to help patients overcome opiate addiction) (OCP, 2006).

Approach to the Material

The statutes, regulations, and policies referred to above comprise hundreds of pages of detailed, often overlapping, information that, if summarized source by source, would be very difficult for any reader to remember. In addition, many of the details contained in the sources are subject to change. It is common for substances to be added to existing lists, to change categories, or to become **delisted**.

Finally, the way in which legislators organize information is not especially helpful for the pharmacy technician who is trying to perform the day-to-day tasks of maintaining drug inventories and dispensing medicine to patients.

For these reasons, this chapter does not cover the application of these statutes, regulations, and policies individually. Instead, after a very brief introduction to each source of regulation (below), the chapter is organized by reference to the pharmacy tasks that are affected by the legislation, regulations, and policy. These tasks include:

- obtaining permission to sell regulated products;
- ordering products from suppliers and recording receipts into inventory;
- storing products in the pharmacy (whether behind the counter or in patient self-selection areas);
- recording consumer sales;
- transferring prescriptions from pharmacy to pharmacy;
- managing part-fills and refills;
- special transactions (for example, filling prescriptions for a physician's office use, or for a physician's personal use); and
- disposing of pharmaceutical products.

Each discussion of a pharmacy task touches on the rules for handling drugs of various categories.

> **delisting**
> in the context of pharmacy, the process of deregulating a substance by removing it from a list of controlled substances, thereby changing its legal classification

OVERVIEWS OF SOURCES OF DRUG REGULATION

The following sections are very brief introductions to the legislation, regulations, and policies that are described in this chapter.

The Controlled Drugs and Substances Act (CDSA) and Regulations

STATUTE

The CDSA is a federal statute that identifies certain drugs and classes of drugs as subject to government control. The criteria on which drugs are selected relate primarily to human safety; however, certain comparatively safe substances (like cannabis) are subject to stringent control mainly for political and historical reasons.

The CDSA is probably best known by the public as the statute that governs the illegal possession and trafficking of psychoactive drugs. It creates possession, trafficking, import/export, and manufacturing-related offences, and a procedure for prosecuting these.

The legislation also regulates the purchase and sale by pharmacies of substances that have legitimate therapeutic uses, but that if misused can be harmful to human health or, if mismanaged, can contribute to the illegal drug trade.

controlled substance
Any substance, including but not restricted to the category of drugs, that is the subject of government regulation

The CDSA includes a system for the classification of **controlled substances**. Controlled substances are listed in one (or more) of eight schedules of the Act. The rules for the management of these substances are drafted by reference to the schedules—for example, section 5 of the CDSA provides that "[n]o person shall traffic in a substance included in Schedule I, II, III or IV or in any substance represented or held out by that person to be such a substance."

The following is a brief overview of the schedules' content:

Schedule I   Narcotics (opiates, cocaine, phenylpiperidines, amidones, morphine, methamphetamines, and others);

Schedule II   Cannabis and its derivatives;

Schedule III   Amphetamines, psilocybin, lysergic acid, mescaline, methylphenidate, and drugs similar to those;

Schedule IV   Barbiturates, benzodiazepines, anabolic steroids, and drugs similar to those;

Schedule V   Propylhexedrine and its salts;

Schedule VI   Class A and Class B precursors (substances that are commonly used in the manufacture of other controlled substances);

Schedule VII   Cannabis or cannabis resin in an amount of 3 kilograms or greater (for trafficking offences);

Schedule VIII   Cannabis in an amount of 30 grams or less, or cannabis resin in an amount of 1 gram or less (generally, possession that does not establish intent to traffic).

NARCOTIC REGULATIONS

The *Narcotic Control Regulations* made under the CDSA provide that only a "licensed dealer" can "produce, make, assemble, import, export, sell, provide, transport, send or deliver a narcotic" (s. 8(1)). Even for licensed dealers, the import or export of narcotics requires a permit.

Pharmacists and corporations that run pharmacies are eligible to apply for narcotics licenses. The regulations explain the licensing process. Once a license is obtained, the pharmacy must nominate a "qualified person" (and often, also an alternative qualified person) who will take charge of the duties (receiving narcotics into the pharmacy, documenting narcotics transactions, etc.) associated with narcotics management that are imposed by the legislation. Currently, the description of who can be named a qualified person does *not* mention pharmacy technicians, although it does include the phrasing: "a practitioner registered with a licensing body of a province … ." This wording seems to suggest that now that pharmacy technicians are registered, they may be able to act as qualified persons in charge of narcotics. It is more likely, however, that this primary designation will be reserved for pharmacists, with pharmacy technicians occasionally (especially in smaller pharmacies) being named as alternatives.

The "person in charge" rules do not prevent pharmacy technicians from performing certain narcotics control functions (such as recording narcotics transactions on the register); they do, however, prevent anyone who is not properly designated from doing these things without supervision. Where a signature is required (for example, to acknowledge receipt of a shipment of narcotics), the designated person should sign.

Sections 15 through 45 of the *Narcotic Control Regulations* impose procedural and record-keeping requirements on those who purchase, store, compound, and sell products containing narcotics. (Sections 30 through 45 deal specifically with pharmacists.) The details of some of these tasks, if they are relevant to the work of pharmacy technicians, are set out in the pertinent sections of this chapter.

The Food and Drugs Act (FDA)

STATUTE

Also a federal statute, the FDA regulates the export, import, interprovincial trade, manufacture, distribution, advertising, and sale of many categories of products, including:

- food;
- drugs,
- cosmetics;
- natural health products;
- contraceptive devices;
- health-related devices; and
- soaps, toothpastes, and other hygiene products.

Many of the products regulated by the FDA are sold in pharmacies.

One of the key objectives of the FDA is to ensure that products that can affect human health (for example, drugs and some natural health products) are identified as such, and are not confused by the general public with ordinary food or cosmetics. The FDA also makes it illegal to make unsubstantiated claims about the efficacy of products for treatment of certain health conditions, especially serious ones, like cancer. In other words, if legitimate scientific studies on human beings have not established that a product cures, prevents, or reduces symptoms of a disease or condition, the FDA emphasizes that the product's manufacturers, distributors, and retailers cannot advertise it as effective against that disease or condition.

Finally, the FDA regulates the production and distribution of many drugs derived from humans, animals, and microorganisms.

Like the CDSA, the FDA uses schedules to categorize information. Not all of the schedules under the FDA are product lists. There are currently six schedules to the FDA (schedules G and H were repealed in 1996). Of the remaining six, the last two—schedules E and F—are currently empty (blank).

The four remaining schedules can be summarized as follows:

- Schedule A is a list of diseases and health conditions; the FDA's restrictions on unsubstantiated advertising claims relate primarily to these.
- Schedule B is a list of eight "standards" (actually, formularies) approved by the FDA as sources of information for the identification and classification of drugs.
- Schedule C lists radiopharmaceuticals and substances used in the production of radiopharmaceuticals; sale of these is restricted.
- Schedule D lists substances derived from humans, animals, or microorganisms (for example, human blood products, snake venom) that can pose health risks through contamination, spoilage, or other causes. Many of these substances—for example, insulin, glucagon, interferon, and vaccines—are sold in pharmacies.

REGULATIONS

The *Food and Drug Regulations* made under the FDA is an enormous document with detailed rules that pertain to a wide range of goods. Only certain selected provisions apply to drugs and other pharmacy products. For example, section A.01.065(1) sets out rules for the "security packaging" of "drugs for human use," including a wide range of over-the-counter (OTC) products such as medicines and even mouthwash.

The regulations are organized into parts:

- Part A explains how the regulation is administered.
- Part B regulates foods (and to some extent, alcohol).
- Part C regulates non-controlled drugs.
- Part D regulates vitamins.
- Part E regulates certain artificial sweeteners.
- Schedule F lists medicinal ingredients—substances used to create drugs, but that are not regularly prescribed on their own.
- Part G regulates what the FDA considers "controlled drugs"; the list is set out in a schedule and includes some amphetamines, barbiturates, anabolic steroids, and others.
- There are currently no parts H and I (these were repealed).
- Part J regulates a class of controlled drugs described as "Restricted Drugs": these drugs (many of them are amphetamines and other drugs also listed in Schedule III under the CDSA) are identified as at high risk of being abused, necessitating heightened controls.

Many of the parts are subdivided into divisions, with different rules applying to different divisions.

Some of the implications of the *Food and Drug Regulations* are discussed later in this chapter.

The Drug and Pharmacies Regulation Act (DPRA)

The DPRA has already been introduced in chapters 2 and 3 of this textbook. For the purposes of this chapter, the most important aspects of the Act are actually two regulations made under it: RRO 1990 Reg. 551, and O. Reg. 297/96. Both regulations are named—unhelpfully—"general."

The first regulation—Reg. 551—defines "controlled drug" as one that is listed in parts I, II, or III of the schedule of Part G of the *Food and Drug Regulations*. It adopts the definition of "narcotic" from the *Narcotic Control Regulations*, and creates the following new definition for "verbal prescription narcotic":

a substance,

(a) that contains one narcotic drug,

(b) that also contains, in a recognized therapeutic dose, two or more medicinal ingredients that are not narcotic drugs,

(c) that is not intended for parenteral administration, and

(d) that does not contain diacetylmorphine (heroin), hydrocodone, methadone, oxycodone or pentazocine.

As you might guess, the regulation creates rules that make a distinction between these narcotics and other narcotics for the purpose of verbal prescription-taking.

The regulation also creates rules governing prescription refills, transfers of prescriptions to other pharmacies, recording of narcotics transactions, warning labels for certain drugs, and standards for pharmacy facilities (amenities, safety, cleanliness).

FACTS AND TRENDS   **BOX 4.1**

Harmonization on the Horizon for Drug Classification

A new proposed regulation designed to combine, replace, and amend regulations 551/90 and 297/96 was ratified by the Council for the Ontario College of Pharmacists in 2009.

The new regulation, if passed, will harmonize the two previous regulations. It will do this by creating its own version of schedules I, II, III, and U, which are consistent with the organizational scheme of the National Drug Schedule (discussed immediately below), but which are also defined by cross-referencing the *Food and Drug Regulations* and the *Controlled Drugs and Substances Act*. While this change sounds complicated, it actually simplifies the classification of drugs. In effect, the new regulation will allow pharmacists (and pharmacy technicians) to look in a single place—the schedules to this new regulation—to determine how a drug is treated for the purpose of the DPRA.

This harmonization incorporates the definitions and rules about "verbal prescription narcotics" and "controlled substances" that are currently covered in O. Reg. 551 into a more comprehensive and cohesive scheme for drug handling in Ontario.

The new regulation will also make certain other changes: for example, it will update the manner in which pharmacies are accredited to pave the way for remote dispensing. ◈

Some of these rules, to the extent that they apply to the work of pharmacy technicians, will be discussed below.

The second "general" regulation—O. Reg. 297/96—adopts the NAPRA National Drug Schedule for the purpose of the DPRA (more on this immediately below). It regulates certain aspects of the sale of scheduled drugs—for example, section 2.1(1)1 provides that whenever a Schedule I drug is sold, a pharmacist must be present in the pharmacy. The regulation also regulates the advertising of drugs and drug pricing, and includes two schedules of substances (for example, aloe, castor oil, and zinc oxide are on the list) that are deemed not to be drugs for the purpose of the regulations.

The National Drug Schedule (NAPRA Schedule)

Since 1995, the National Association of Pharmacy Regulatory Authorities (NAPRA) has maintained a National Drug Schedule. The schedule (actually, three schedules) was developed to promote the harmonization of drug classification across Canada, to allow for consistent drug prescription and sales rules across the country.

The National Drug Scheduling Advisory Committee (NDSAC), a NAPRA committee, was created to apply the guidelines and factors devised by NAPRA for the classification of drugs. The NDSAC is made up of eight expert members, plus representatives of the Consumers' Association of Canada and Health Canada's Therapeutic Products Directorate. The Committee reviews new drugs (and also existing drugs for which information or patterns of use have changed) and makes decisions about the schedule in which to place them.

The NAPRA National Drug Schedule has been adopted to varying degrees by the different provinces (not at all by Quebec). In Ontario, provincial regulations have been introduced to allow any changes made to a drug's NAPRA classification to become immediately effective in Ontario (see O. Reg. 297/96 under the DPRA, mentioned above). In some other provinces, NAPRA classifications are adopted on a case-by-case basis.

NAPRA's website provides the following overview of the National Drug Schedule scheme:

> The national model consists of three schedules or four categories: Schedule I, Schedule II, Schedule III and Unscheduled, with specific conditions for sale expected for each. NAPRA has developed National Standards of Practice for pharmacists corresponding to the level of professional intervention and advice necessary for the safe and effective use of these drugs by consumers, according to each Schedule.
>
> The model for making drug scheduling recommendations embodies a "cascading principle" in which a drug is first assessed using the factors for Schedule I. Should sufficient factors pertain, the drug remains in that Schedule. If not, the drug is assessed against the Schedule II factors, and if warranted, subsequently against the Schedule III factors. Should the drug not meet the factors for any schedule, it becomes "unscheduled."
>
> "Factors" rather than "criteria" are considered to be more appropriate assessment tools as they are contingent, conditional and dependent. A process using factors allows judgment by reviewers to find the best fit and facilitates a re-evaluation process of scheduled drugs when new knowledge or practice experience emerge.

The factors were initially adapted from established standards for prescription drugs, proposed guidelines for drugs monitored by pharmacists, and the World Health Organization's guidelines for nonprescription drugs, then modified through national consultation.

Unlike the CDSA model, which categorizes drugs more or less by type (derivation and chemical similarity), the National Drug Schedule classifies drugs based on risk to users. The following are some examples of familiar drugs in each National Drug Schedule category:

Schedule I   Amitryptiline, amoxicillin, cannabis, cyclosporine, danazol, diazepam, lovastatin, lithium, methadone, rofecoxib;

Schedule II   Benzocaine for ophthalmic use, codeine in preparations exempted from the CDSA, diphenhydramine, epinephrine emergency injectable (EpiPen, Anapen);

Schedule III   Acetylsalicylic acid 81 milligrams ("baby Aspirin"; now not recommended for children, but typically used for heart disease); benzocaine for teething; cimetidine; clotrimazole for vaginal use; nystatin for topical use;

Unscheduled   Acetylsalicylic acid (ASA) in a standard oral dose; bacitracin for topical use; bile salts; capsaicin; guaifenesin; ibuprofen in a standard oral dose; nicotine patch for smoking cessation.

Different prescription and sale rules apply for each category. Some of these rules are discussed in the relevant sections below.

The Excise Act, 2001 (EA)

The EA regulates certain aspects of the manufacture, purchase, and sale of alcohol products. While provincial legislation regulates most of the details of the retail sale of alcohol to customers, the federal government regulates certain forms of pure alcohol that are poisonous or dangerous when taken internally.

Diluted rubbing alcohol compounds (made from denatured ethyl alcohol) and isopropyl alcohol can be sold in pharmacies. These alcohols, though not safe to drink, are extremely unpalatable and are not commonly abused.

Pure, non-denatured ethyl alcohol is sometimes used by pharmacists for compounding. It can be purchased only from a provincial liquor control board on a pharmacist's written order. Records must be kept of all purchases of straight ethyl alcohol. Records must also be kept of its use in a pharmacy, and there are strict rules for the disposal of ethyl alcohol.

The Natural Health Product Regulations

The *Natural Health Product Regulations* are made under the FDA. They were introduced in 2003 as a vehicle for the federal regulation of products that may be used by consumers to promote human health, but which are not currently regulated (or suitable for regulation) under the CDSA, or that are not designated as products requiring a prescription under the *Food and Drug Regulations* made under the FDA.

The *Natural Health Product Regulations* create two schedules—Schedule 1 and Schedule 2—that list products. The definition of "natural health product" for the purpose of the Act depends on whether the product is listed in Schedule 1 or Schedule 2. The definition (from section 1 of the regulations) follows:

> "natural health product" means a substance set out in Schedule 1 or a combination of substances in which all the medicinal ingredients are substances set out in Schedule 1, a homeopathic medicine or a traditional medicine, that is manufactured, sold or represented for use in
>
> > (a) the diagnosis, treatment, mitigation or prevention of a disease, disorder or abnormal physical state or its symptoms in humans;
> >
> > (b) restoring or correcting organic functions in humans; or
> >
> > (c) modifying organic functions in humans, such as modifying those functions in a manner that maintains or promotes health.
>
> However, a natural health product does not include a substance set out in Schedule 2, any combination of substances that includes a substance set out in Schedule 2 or a homeopathic medicine or a traditional medicine that is or includes a substance set out in Schedule 2.

Whether a substance belongs in Schedule 1 or Schedule 2 (or neither) is determined by the office of the Minister of Health, which issues a product number and a licence that permit distribution of a natural health product. The *Natural Health Product Regulations* explain the process for applying for a product number.

Schedule 1 includes many common vitamins, minerals, probiotics, amino acids, and essential fatty acids. It also includes plants or plant material, algae, bacteria, fungi, and non-human animal material, and extracts or isolates of those materials, provided that the extract or isolate has a primary molecular structure identical to the material from which it was extracted or isolated. Synthetic versions of these substances (except synthetic versions of minerals or probiotics) also make the list.

Schedule 2 creates exceptions to the broad list created by Schedule 1. For example, it excludes anything that would meet the Schedule 1 criteria but that is listed in one of the first five schedules to the CDSA (cannabis is an example). It excludes antibiotics sourced from algae, bacteria, or fungi. It excludes tobacco products, any product that is listed under Schedule C of the FDA (radiopharmaceuticals, etc.), most products listed under Schedule D of the FDA, and any product designed for administration by injection.

Many products regulated under the *Natural Health Products Act* are sold over the counter in pharmacies. The primary responsibility of pharmacy staff with respect to these products is to ensure that any natural health product made available for purchase by the public bears an appropriate product identification number. Pharmacists and other pharmacy staff (including pharmacy technicians) should also endeavour to develop a knowledge of the potential for interaction between natural health products and prescription drugs—for example, many prescription drugs interact with iron or calcium supplements, and a special sticker advising of this interaction is useful for patients who are taking these drugs.

The Precursor Control Regulations

The *Precursor Control Regulations* are made under the CDSA. The regulations divide precursors into two categories, with the following definitions for each):

"Class A precursor" means,

    (a) any substance set out in Part 1 of Schedule VI to the Act; and

    (b) any preparation or mixture referred to in Part 3 of Schedule VI to the Act that contains a substance referred to in paragraph (a).

"Class B precursor" means,

    (a) any substance set out in Part 2 of Schedule VI to the Act; and

    (b) any preparation or mixture referred to in Part 3 of Schedule VI to the Act that contains a substance referred to in paragraph (a). (s. 1)

Schedule VI of the CDSA was introduced earlier in this chapter.

In simple terms, a precursor is a substance, often harmless on its own, but commonly used to create another controlled substance. The potential for use in this manner is the reason for the control of precursors. An example of a precursor is potassium permanganate, an inorganic compound derived from manganese dioxide. The compound is a fairly safe oxidizer that does not create toxic byproducts in the oxidizing process. It has some use as an antiseptic and was historically used to sanitize water.

However, potassium permanganate has a couple of worrisome uses. It can be used to purify cocaine, or to create methcathinone—a substance sold as a street drug sometimes known as qat or "cat." As a result, retailers can sell the compound only under certain conditions—for example, they must not deal exclusively in products used in the creation of chemicals, and are prohibited from selling potassium permanganate in quantities greater than 50 kilograms per transaction. The same rules apply to a number of other substances.

Part 4 of the *Precursor Control Regulations* is addressed specifically to pharmacists. It allows pharmacists to use precursors in compounding. With respect to Class A precursors specifically, pharmacists can sell these—even in excess of the maximum quantities stipulated by the regulations (in some cases, the maximum quantity is zero)—when the precursor is part of a compound or mixture and is sold through retail outlets and under prescription. Pharmacists are required to record the details

---

FACTS AND TRENDS   **BOX 4.2**

Meth Watch Program

The Ontario Pharmacists' Association (OPA) has developed a program called Meth Watch that encourages pharmacy and other retail employees to be aware of transactions that suggest the use of certain substances for the production of crystal methamphetamine ("crystal meth"), a dangerous and addictive street drug.

The most important crystal meth ingredients sold in pharmacies are pseudoephedrine and ephedrine. Law enforcement raids on home crystal meth laboratories have revealed that people engaged in the small-scale production of the drug often use cough and cold products sold in retail outlets in their recipes.

Pharmacies participating in the Meth Watch program post signs alerting the public to their participation, and employees are trained (details of the training program are available at www.methwatch.ca) to recognize "suspicious transactions" and to report these to the police without confronting the consumer. ◈

of Class A precursor prescriptions and sales and to retain copies or records of these prescriptions. The regulation also creates rules relating to refills (none without a prescription) and interpharmacy prescription transfers (these must be documented).

Finally, the regulation requires pharmacists to use reasonable measures to keep Class A precursors secure and to inform the police of any "unusual waste or disappearance" of them.

The Benzodiazepines and Other Targeted Substances Regulations

The *Benzodiazepines and Other Targeted Substances Regulations* is another regulation made under the CDSA. This regulation governs substances that are neither narcotics nor precursors, but that merit special government control.

As is clear from the title, the regulation governs **targeted substances**. These include benzodiazepines and any other substance listed in Schedule 1 to the regulation. Examples of non-benzodiazepines listed in the schedule include fencamfamin, mefenorex, meprobamate, and pipradol.

The regulations create rules for the handling of targeted substances by pharmacists. These rules include guidelines with respect to the reporting, storage, and management of refills and prescription transfers for (and destruction of) targeted substances.

targeted substance
in Canada, benzodiazepines and other drugs included in Schedule 1 of the *Benzodiazepines and Other Targeted Substances Regulations* made under the *Controlled Drugs and Substances Act*

CONTROLLED SUBSTANCES RULES— TASK BY TASK

Introduction

This section explains the various legal requirements imposed by the legislation described above with regard to pharmacy tasks. The phrase "controlled substances" is here used generically to cover not only substances controlled under the CDSA, but also under the FDA, the *Excise Act*, the DPRA, and the regulations discussed above.

Obtaining Permission to Sell Controlled Substances

As you read in Chapter 2, section 139 of the DPRA requires a retail pharmacy to obtain a certificate of accreditation before it begins operation. Accredited pharmacies staffed with properly licensed and registered pharmacists are permitted to sell controlled substances, provided that the pharmacy complies with all applicable regulations. For example, section 72 of O. Reg. 551 made under the DPRA specifies pharmacy amenities and layout—for example, pharmacies must have easy-to-clean storage in certain areas, sufficient floor space, appropriate storage for controlled drugs, and good lighting and ventilation.

In addition, any pharmacy located in a department store that has hours differing from the store's (that is, there are times when the store is open but the pharmacy is not), the pharmacy must have a lockable dispensary.

As explained in Box 4.1, O. Reg. 551 may soon be replaced by a proposed new regulation that covers all these issues with certain amendments—for example, to the accreditation of remote-dispensing pharmacies.

Ordering and Obtaining Products from Suppliers

Pharmacies typically order their products from three kinds of sources: manufacturers, distributors, or—in emergencies—from other pharmacies.

The rules governing product orders and purchases vary depending on the nature of the product ordered.

PRODUCTS NOT STRICTLY CONTROLLED

Drugs not subject to strict control can be ordered according to typical business procedures: a pharmacy staff person places the order by whatever means (phone, fax, email, mail), and the shipment arrives and is placed into inventory. There are no special signing requirements. Appropriate inventory records should be kept, but these are kept for purposes of the pharmacy's own inventory management.

REPORTABLE NARCOTIC AND CONTROLLED DRUGS

Certain narcotic products and other controlled drugs require special reporting at the time of purchase from a supplier. With respect to narcotics, the products that require special reporting:

- have a narcotic as a single ingredient, or one of two ingredients; and/or
- the narcotic component exceeds recognized therapeutic dose; and/or
- are for parenteral use (injection); and/or
- contain heroin, methadone, hydrocodone, oxycodone, or pentazocine.

Non-narcotic controlled drugs that require special reporting are those listed in schedules I, II, or III to Part G of the *Food and Drug Regulations*. These **reportable drugs** include amphetamines, barbiturates, anabolic steroids, and others.

Any purchase of a reportable narcotic or a controlled drug, as defined by O. Reg. 551, must be recorded in a "Narcotic and Controlled Drug Register." This form, developed by Health and Welfare Canada, is reproduced in Appendix C.

All pharmacy orders for reportable narcotics or controlled drugs must be either in writing or submitted electronically via approved electronic technologies. Written orders must be signed by a pharmacist. The order must be submitted to the distributor or manufacturer within five working days after the pharmacist signs it.

Electronic orders must be submitted using a computer or other device (for example, a handheld device). The device must be equipped with a program that marks orders with an identification number specific to a pharmacist who is legally permitted to order controlled drugs. The computer or system used must be in the care and control of the pharmacist. When orders are placed via this method, the pharmacist must submit to the distributor a signed receipt for the drugs within five days of receiving them.

An exception is made to the signed receipt requirement when the ordering technology uses a digital signature system for verification. An explanation of digital

reportable drug
a drug the details of purchase or sale of which must be recorded to permit reporting to a regulatory agency

signatures is beyond the scope of this textbook (interested readers can see the summary on the website of GS1 Canada: https://certificate.gs1ca.org/cpdn/narcotics-process-guide.php#b). Pharmacy technicians working in retail or clinical settings can simply inquire about the system used in their setting for ordering controlled drugs. Knowing which system is in place will help the pharmacy technician understand whether or not written and signed orders, signed receipts, or neither are required in their workplace.

Again, these topics may soon be covered not in O. Reg. 551, but in a new regulation, recently ratified by Council, that has been designed to replace it.

TARGETED SUBSTANCES

Upon receipt of a substance governed by the *Benzodiazepines and Other Targeted Substances Regulations*, pharmacy staff must make a record of the following information:

> (a) the brand name of the targeted substance received or, if the targeted substance does not have a brand name, the specified name;
> (b) the quantity and strength per unit of the targeted substance received, the number of units per package and the number of packages;
> (c) the name and address of the licensed dealer, pharmacist or hospital that supplied it; and
> (d) the date on which it was received. (s. 50)

EMERGENCY ORDERS

Occasionally, a pharmacy requires drug products for a patient immediately, and the usual supplier is unable to deliver an order in the necessary time frame. In this case the pharmacy can purchase drugs, including narcotics and other controlled or targeted drugs, from another pharmacy. If the emergency order is for a drug that would require special reporting if it were ordered from a supplier, it should be recorded in these circumstances as well.

Storing Controlled and Targeted Substances

All pharmaceutical products must be stored in an environment that preserves their quality and efficacy. Usually, this means low humidity, moderate temperatures, and darkness (opaque packaging is used for light-sensitive drugs).

Pharmaceutical products not for self-selection—in other words, prescription drugs, and certain non-prescription drugs that merit patient counselling—must be stored in an area where the public cannot access them.

Most drugs may be kept behind the counter, which must be continually staffed. Certain drugs more vulnerable to abuse, however, may require more secure storage.

While Ontario has no specific legal requirement to store narcotics in a locked cabinet or safe, many pharmacies choose to do so, both for the protection of the public and to deter break-ins. In a retail setting that houses a pharmacy, if the store is open to the public while the pharmacist is not on duty, the drug storage area must be locked whenever the pharmacist leaves.

Storage of narcotics and other controlled drugs in locked cabinets is almost universal practice in hospitals and other clinical settings. The volume of staff and

---

BOX 4.3

Codeine-Containing Non-Prescription Drugs

The College has a policy for the management of codeine-containing non-prescription drugs. In a nutshell, the policy states that:

- these medications cannot be advertised;

- they cannot be displayed, and must be stored behind the counter;

- the pharmacist must either personally decide whether or not to sell these products to a customer, or must supervise a pharmacy intern or registered pharmacy student while he or she consults with the customer and decides whether to sell the product;

- any time the pharmacist suspects that the customer intends to use the drugs for an inappropriate purpose, he or she must decline to sell them;

- pharmacists cannot import or export these products (for example, through a mail-order Internet-based site). ◈

---

patient traffic in these settings raises the potential for diversion of controlled drugs, and hospitals are required to address this risk through appropriate procedures. For example, where drugs are stored in locked cabinets, there should be clear rules about who can have the key, how to transfer keys, and how to record the removal of drugs from the cabinets. Drugs with a high risk for abuse (for example, oxycodone) should never be set out and left unattended in trays or carts destined for patient wards.

The *Benzodiazepines and Other Targeted Substances Regulations* list specific rules for the storage and management of targeted substances. These substances must be stored in an area without public access, and pharmacy staff must keep them secure. Any loss or theft of a targeted substance must be reported to the Minister of Health within 10 days of discovery.

Recording Consumer Sales

PRESCRIPTION EXPIRY

The DPRA requires that a prescription, to be eligible for filling, must be dated by the prescriber. However, there is no legal rule that prevents a pharmacy from filling the prescription at any particular time—unless the prescription advises to the contrary, it does not "expire."

However, if a patient presents a prescription long after the date it was written, professional judgment may prompt the pharmacist to ask questions. Some medications are prescribed on a "just in case" basis (for example, antibiotics for people travelling to developing countries). More usually, the physician intends the patient to begin therapy promptly. Depending on the nature of the drug prescribed, the pharmacist may deem it prudent to call the prescriber if a prescription is presented more than a few days after it is written.

In some cases, a prescriber may include a date beyond which refills are *not* to be permitted. This date must be respected.

CONSUMER SALES OF NARCOTIC AND CONTROLLED DRUGS

Certain sales of drugs to consumers must be reported on the Narcotic and Controlled Drug Register. Reportable drugs include narcotics and "controlled drugs" as defined by O. Reg. 551 under the DPRA ("a substance referred to in Part I, II or III of the schedule to Part G of the Food and Drug Regulations"). When recording a sale of a reportable drug, the following information must be entered on the register:

- the date of the sale;
- the name, strength where applicable, and quantity of the drug;
- the name and address of the purchaser or person named in the prescription;
- the name and address of the prescriber; and
- the identification number on the prescription.

Most pharmacies use an electronic (computerized) prescription-entry system that automatically generates the necessary record whenever a prescription for a reportable drug is entered. If a prescription lists more than one drug, one of which is a reportable drug, the reportable and non-reportable portions of the prescription are cross-referenced. These records must be kept for a minimum of six years.

SPECIAL SALES TRANSACTIONS

A pharmacist may sometimes be asked to dispense a controlled substance to a recipient other than a patient. Pharmacies are allowed, in emergencies, to sell narcotics or other controlled substances to other pharmacies. These sales must be documented on the Narcotic and Controlled Drug Register.

FACTS AND TRENDS   BOX 4.4

Can a Physician Self-Prescribe a Narcotic or Controlled Drug, or Prescribe One for a Family Member?

The College of Physicians and Surgeons of Ontario makes it clear that physicians should avoid diagnosing and treating themselves and their family members. Doing so can compromise objectivity, or lead to other ethical problems. The College has the following to say about self-prescribing or prescribing to family members:

> … Physicians should never write a prescription for themselves or family members for narcotics, controlled drugs, psychotropic drugs, or any drugs that are addicting or habituating, even when another physician is in charge of managing those medications.
>
> Physicians who prescribe narcotics or controlled drugs to themselves or to family members may have their narcotic or controlled drug prescribing privileges revoked by the federal government, and may also be subject to allegations of professional misconduct.

Source: Ontario College of Physicians and Surgeons, Policy Number 7-06, "Treating Self and Family Members." ◈

FACTS AND TRENDS   BOX 4.5

Medication Samples

In some cases, pharmacists receive medication samples free of charge from suppliers. If pharmacists wish to pass these samples along to the public, the College provides guidelines that must be followed. Narcotics must never be provided to consumers without a prescription. For more information, see "Policy Respecting the Distribution of Medication Samples" (OCP, n.d.). ◇

Pharmacies may also fill prescriptions for drugs intended for emergency use in a physician's office or in another clinical setting. For example, a physician may wish to keep on hand a supply of anti-anxiety medication (such as lorazepam) for patients who present with acute panic reactions. Prescriptions "for office use" must also be documented on the Narcotic and Controlled Drug Register.

Because electronic prescription management systems are not generally designed to record such sales transactions, manual entries on the register may be required.

The rules with respect to recording sales are contained in the new proposed regulation scheduled to replace O. Reg. 551.

Prescription and Refill Transfers

DRUGS NOT SUBJECT TO STRICT CONTROL

For the convenience of patients, pharmacies may transfer prescriptions from one pharmacy to another. If the prescription in question is for a substance not subject to strict control, transfer is perfectly acceptable as long as the sending pharmacy provides correct and sufficient prescribing information.

CONTROLLED AND TARGETED SUBSTANCES

Written and verbal prescriptions for narcotics cannot specify refills. Although it is possible, in some cases, to "part-fill" these prescriptions, no portion of the prescription can be transferred to another pharmacy. While pharmacists may, in some cases, provide refills for drugs controlled under Schedule I to Part G of the FDA, these refills cannot be transferred.

Prescriptions for substances targeted under the *Benzodiazepines and Other Targeted Substances Regulations* can be transferred as long as the transfer procedures set out in the regulations are followed.

Managing Refills and Part-Fills

REFILLS

As noted above, O. Reg. 551 under the DPRA prohibits refills or "repeats" on written or verbal prescriptions for narcotics. If additional medicine is needed, the patient must obtain a new prescription.

A pharmacy can refill a prescription for drugs controlled under Schedule I to Part G of the FDA or drugs targeted under the *Benzodiazepines and Other Targeted Substances Regulations* only if certain details about refills are provided, in writing, on the original prescription. The number of refills must be indicated, as must be either specified intervals (for example, 30 days) or specified refill dates.

For all other drugs, refills are permitted providing appropriate records are kept. The details of the information that must be recorded are listed in O. Reg. 551 under the DPRA.

PART-FILLS

A pharmacy may sometimes dispense only part of the quantity of a substance prescribed. One reason for a part-fill might be that the pharmacy lacks a sufficient inventory of the medication; in this case, the patient may be asked to return after a few days to obtain the unfilled portion.

In other cases, a prescriber may direct part-fills, subject to the pharmacist's professional discretion. Deliberate part-fills are done for the patient's protection, for example if there is concern that the patient may exceed the recommended dose. When prescribing part-fills, the prescriber does not always specify a fill interval; the pharmacist can use his or her discretion to determine whether the interval that has elapsed is reasonable. However, in all cases, the prescriber must stipulate the maximum quantity of drugs to be dispensed. Without this information, a new prescription is required to dispense additional medication.

Part-fills must always be recorded as such (including on the narcotics register), and remaining parts cannot be transferred to another pharmacy.

Sometimes determining whether a part-fill is authorized by the wording of a prescription is difficult. In 2006, the College issued a detailed guideline, "Prescription Part-Fills—An Update." This guideline includes useful examples of prescription formats that provide for (or fail to provide for) legal part-fills.

The rules with respect to managing refills, part-fills, and refill transfers are contained in the new proposed regulation scheduled to replace O. Reg. 551.

Disposing of Controlled Substances

INTRODUCTION

All drugs should be disposed of with care. The buildup of drug residues in our environment poses long-term threats to the health of all species. Careless disposal of drugs can also pose an immediate risk if those drugs are discovered and ingested by individuals for whom they have not been prescribed.

When the substance in question is a narcotic or other reportable drug, there are special rules governing disposal.

RETURNS

A pharmacy may sometimes choose to return non-expired drug stock to the manufacturer or distributor. This may be necessary in cases where the pharmacy is closing, or where an excessive quantity has been ordered.

There are no special rules for the return of non-reportable drugs; however, all medications must be shipped securely using methods that allow packages to be tracked. If drugs have been returned to manufacturers owing to the closing of a pharmacy, the details of these returns must be reported in a pharmacy-closing report and filed with the Registrar of the Ontario College of Pharmacists.

Before a narcotic or reportable controlled substance can be returned to the manufacturer, the pharmacy must obtain written permission from the manufacturer to ship it back. A notation explaining what was done with the drug must be made on the Narcotic and Controlled Drugs Register.

Returning expired or otherwise unneeded drugs to the manufacturer is the most desirable practice, because manufacturers generally have disposal systems that comply with environmental laws.

While a pharmacy may sometimes return *undispensed* stock to the manufacturer, a pharmacy employee must never return drugs that have been dispensed to a consumer back into inventory. Doing so is an act of professional misconduct as defined in section 140 of the DPRA.

DISPOSAL

If returning a product to the manufacturer is not possible or practical, a pharmacy may need to destroy the drug or otherwise dispose of it.

The rules for the disposal of substances vary from municipality to municipality. Most drugs should be treated as hazardous waste, and should be transported (following laws related to such transport) to a waste management facility.

In rare cases, a pharmacy may need to destroy drugs. This must be done with care and with knowledge of the process. Some drugs can be incinerated; others can be mixed with additives that denature them. Before taking any action, pharmacy staff must inquire about local environmental laws and comply with them.

Narcotics can be destroyed only with permission from Health Canada, and only in the presence of another pharmacist, pharmacy intern, or other appropriate professional as witness. For permission to destroy narcotics, pharmacies should contact the Office of Controlled Substances (see Appendix A(3)).

There are special rules, reproduced in the *Benzodiazepines and Other Targeted Substances Regulations*, for the destruction of targeted substances. As in the case of narcotics, a witness is necessary. The substances must be destroyed in accordance with local environmental laws in a manner that ensures they are denatured or unlikely to be abused. A record must be kept of the type and quantity of drugs destroyed and the date of destruction, and a joint statement confirming the destruction must be prepared and signed by both the person who destroyed the drugs and the witness.

KEY TERMS

controlled substance
delisting
reportable drug
schedule
targeted substance

REFERENCES

Benzodiazepines and Other Targeted Substances Regulations. 2000. SOR 2000-217.

Controlled Drugs and Substances Act. 1996. SC 1996, c. 19.

Drug and Pharmacies Regulation Act. 1990. RSO 1990, c. H.4.

Drug Interchangeability and Dispensing Fee Act. 1990. RSO 1990, c. P.23.

Excise Act, 2001. 2002. SC 2002, c. 22.

Food and Drug Regulations. CRC, c. 870.

Food and Drugs Act. 1985. RSC 1985, c. F-27.

Medical Devices Regulations. 1998. SOR 98-282.

Narcotic Control Regulations. CRC, c. 1041.

Natural Health Product Regulations. 2003. SOR 2003-196.

Ontario College of Pharmacists (OCP). (n.d.). Policy respecting the distribution of medication samples. Retrieved May 15, 2010 from http://www.ocpinfo.com/client/ocp/OCPHome.nsf/web/Policy+Respecting+the+Distribution+of+Medication+Samples.

Ontario College of Pharmacists (OCP). (2006, July–August). Policy for dispensing methadone. Retrieved May 15, 2010 from http://www.ocpinfo.com/client/ocp/OCPHome.nsf/object/Methadone_Policy_06/$file/Methadone_Policy_06.pdf.

Ontario College of Pharmacists (OCP). (2006). Prescription part-fills—an update. Retrieved May 15, 2010 from http://www.ocpinfo.com/client/ocp/OCPHome.nsf/web/Prescription+Part-fills+-+An+Update.

Ontario College of Physicians and Surgeons. (2007, February). Policy number 7-06: Treating self and family members. Retrieved May 15, 2010 from http://www.cpso.on.ca/uploadedFiles/policies/policies/policyitems/treating_self.pdf.

Ontario Drug Benefit Act. 1990. RSO 1990, c. O.10.

Precursor Control Regulations 2002. SOR 2002-359.

REVIEW EXERCISES

Discussion Question

These days, many of the legally mandated requirements with respect to government-controlled drugs—including purchase and sales reporting, refill management, and disposal tracking—are managed electronically. Some pharmacy information technology programs automatically create the forms required by law when they detect that the drug entered into the prescription system is a reportable drug. With such technology available, why is it still important for pharmacy technicians to understand the basics of controlled drug management?

Review Questions

1. Which tier of government—the federal government or the provincial governments—regulates drugs that merit strict control?

2. List two federal statutes that govern controlled substances.

3. What is the NAPRA National Drug Schedule, and is it part of Ontario law?

4. What should pharmacy technicians know about the *Excise Act, 2001*?

5. What must the manufacturer of a natural health product do before it can sell the product to retail stores for resale?

6. Which legislative instrument governs targeted substances, and to what kinds of substances does it apply?

7. Can any pharmacy employee independently place an order for narcotics?

8. Is it a legal requirement that narcotics be stored in a locked cabinet in the dispensary?

9. Summarize, in point form, the basics of Class A precursor management rules for pharmacies.

10. Must records be kept of sales of narcotics to consumers? If so, where should they be kept?

11. Which prescription detail is the most essential element of a legal part-fill prescription order?

12. What must a pharmacist do in order to destroy targeted substances legally?

CHAPTER 5

Insurance Coverage for Drugs in the Private and Public Sectors

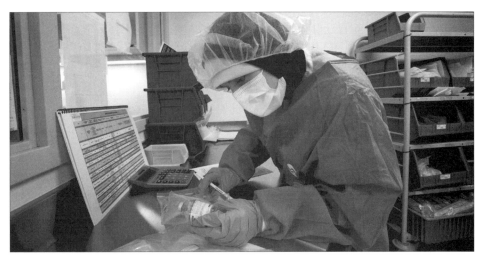

A hospital pharmacy technician prepares chemotherapy drugs wearing protective clothing because of the drugs' toxicity.

LEARNING OBJECTIVES

After completing this chapter, you should be able to:

- Explain what is meant by private drug insurance coverage.

- Understand some of the parameters of private drug coverage (deductibles, co-payments, restricted formularies).

- Describe common methods and systems for reimbursing the recipients of private drug coverage.

- List at least four Ontario programs for public drug benefit coverage, and one federal program.

- Understand the basic criteria for eligibility for drug coverage under the Ontario Drug Benefit Program.

- Explain how pharmacy staff can obtain both general and client-specific information about public drug benefit coverage.

INTRODUCTION

Because of the research and testing required to develop them, expensive source ingredients, and costs related to processing, quality control, and regulation, drugs are a costly commodity. Most people do not expect to become sick, and so many of us do not factor the cost of medicines into our budgets.

An individual's chance of becoming sick and needing drugs in any given year is a contingency—an unpredictable event. In a modern commercial economy, insurance is usually available to help people manage the costs associated with many kinds of contingencies: car accidents, house fires, job loss, and more.

Individual purchase of drug cost insurance is much less widespread in Ontario than the purchase of home or automobile insurance. One common reason is that medicine costs are less likely to have a catastrophic financial impact than the costs associated with a house fire, flood, or serious car accident. Nevertheless, if a person becomes seriously ill, or is ill for a long time, the costs can quickly escalate.

private insurance
insurance provided by a
third-party company

Many employers offer group drug insurance as a benefit to employees and their families. Such insurance, provided by a third-party company, is commonly known as **private insurance**. Private insurance through an employer is not available to all Canadians. Not all employers offer it, and not all individuals are employed—many Canadians are too old or too young to work, are self-employed, or are out of the workforce for other reasons.

For humanitarian reasons—based on the notion that no one should be denied access to essential drug therapy because of personal financial circumstances—the government of Ontario (and all other provincial and territorial governments) offers limited access to government-funded public drug insurance. The Ontario public drug insurance system consists of five different drug benefit programs with different eligibility rules.

Because pharmacy technicians are often involved with dispensing and billing decisions that require consideration of the patient's access to drug coverage, they need a general understanding of both private and public drug insurance plans. The ability to manage drug benefit tasks and questions is mentioned in the Ontario College of Pharmacists' proposed standards under Operational Component 3.1.5, which reads:

> The pharmacy technician determines patient preferences, applies knowledge about available forms of the pharmaceutical product, and applies knowledge of third-party insurance plan coverage to enter the pharmaceutical product/compound that meets the requirements of the prescription.

A more detailed expression of a pharmacy technician's responsibilities with respect to drug benefit plans appears in NAPRA (National Association of Pharmacy Regulatory Authorities) Competency 8.3:

8.3   Manage financial elements associated with the processing of prescriptions.

Competency Elements

8.3.1   Initiate billing, verify, and assist in the adjudication for payment.

8.3.2   Resolve billing/adjudication issues encountered in the processing of prescriptions, apply knowledge of formularies and their policies, benefit lists, generic substitutions, deductible limits, and quantity limits.

   i. apply knowledge of formularies and their policies, benefit lists, generic substitutions, deductible limits, and quantity limits.

  ii. assist patients in understanding the scope, limitations and exceptions to their third-party insurance plan coverage.

 iii. assist other health care team members in understanding the limitations and exceptions to an organization's formulary or of a third-party insurance plan coverage of medications and medication devices.

This chapter gives a general overview of both private and public drug coverage, and of the steps that a pharmacy technician should take to:

- understand individual patients' coverage;
- minimize out-of-pocket costs to patients;
- support the pharmacy's access to appropriate reimbursement from private insurers or government programs; and
- comply with applicable legislation, regulations, and policies.

PRIVATE INSURANCE PLANS

Prevalence

This chapter uses the terms **private drug insurance plan** and **private drug benefit plan** interchangeably to describe plans that do not rely on or benefit from government funding.

private drug insurance plan/private drug benefit plan
drug coverage plan that does not rely on government funds

Statistics suggest that approximately 60 percent of Ontarians enjoy private drug insurance as part of an employment benefits program. This figure includes not only the covered employees, but also their family members who qualify for coverage as dependents. Benefits are typically paid for either by the employer or by a labour union. Sometimes employees are required to make a financial contribution to the plans by paying premiums.

Another small percentage of Ontarians purchase private drug benefit insurance coverage directly, as individuals. Such coverage is unusual because it is often not cost-effective unless the purchaser has a chronic illness with high medication costs, and individuals in those circumstances are often eligible for publicly funded drug coverage (or partial coverage) anyway.

Coverage Terms

The terms of private drug insurance plans can vary widely with respect to several factors:

- the percentage of drug cost covered (some plans cover 100 percent of costs, while others cover a percentage);
- whether the dispensing fee is covered or partially covered;
- whether there is a per-prescription deductible (for example, the patient must pay five dollars out of pocket for each prescription);
- the list of drugs covered under the plan (often these lists are called "formularies");

- rules with respect to the class of drug covered—for example, most plans limit coverage to drugs that require a prescription;
- whether generic drugs are covered—in some cases, *only* generics, when they exist, are covered, although there may be terms in place to accommodate specific no-substitution instructions from prescribers;
- whether there are coverage limits relating to the amount of medication dispensed at one time;
- whether there are "caps" on the total coverage within a specific time period—for example, within a year—and whether the percentage of costs covered changes after a specified threshold is met; and
- how the plan member is reimbursed—for example, some plan members must pay the pharmacy for the full cost of the prescription and then submit a request for reimbursement to the insurer; however, most systems are designed to allow the insurer to reimburse the pharmacy instead.

Pharmacy staff often need to know the terms of a patient's private drug coverage. However, the patient may not be familiar with all of the various plan details. To allow pharmacists quick access to the information they need, most insurance providers ("plan sponsors") provide plan and client identification numbers that can be entered online to retrieve plan details. These numbers are sometimes written on or encoded into drug plan cards that patients carry with them when shopping for prescriptions.

Once retrieved from the plan sponsor, drug insurance plan details should be incorporated into the patient's health record. Each time the patient presents the pharmacy with a new prescription, the staff person receiving it should ask whether there have been any changes to the patient's coverage. Even if the patient says no, the plan data should be retrieved anew; some plans are subject to frequent change (for example, some have formularies that allow new drugs to be added as they are approved for sale in Canada or reviewed by the plan sponsor).

Benefit Management Companies

pharmacy benefit manager (PBM)
a company contracted by insurers and government programs to manage pharmacy networks, drug-use trends, patient outcomes, and disease protocols with the aim of saving money

Drug benefit plans are often offered by general insurance companies (Sun Life, Manulife, and others) as part of a larger package of employee benefits. Because it would be inefficient for each of these plan administrators to develop the expertise necessary to design drug benefits, many insurers use the services of **pharmacy benefit managers (PBMs)** to design and administer the drug insurance aspects of the plan. These companies offer a range of benefits to plan administrators and insurers, including tools to help track benefit usage trends, and tools to detect fraud.

Often the PBM, and not the insurer, handles the pharmacy's reimbursement claims. PBMs typically handle drug benefit administration for a number of different insurers who provide benefit plan packages to many employers. Working with a few PBMs—rather than a long list of employers or insurers—can simplify reimbursement for pharmacies. For an example of a PBM, see the website of ESI Canada (http://esi-canada.com).

open access plan
a drug benefit plan that covers any drug approved by Health Canada and prescribed by a physician

Formularies

While some Canadian drug benefit plans are **open access**—they cover any drug approved by Health Canada and prescribed by a physician—many other plans refer to a **formulary**—list of drugs—that is covered under the plan. Private sector formularies are usually more inclusive than those used by publicly funded plans; in other words, private plans typically cover a wider range of drugs.

There are several kinds of formularies. The simplest is a list of drugs that are chosen for therapeutic efficacy and cost-effectiveness. All drugs on the list are covered at the same rate—for example, 100 percent reimbursement or 80 percent reimbursement. Periodically (annually, or less often, for the simplest formularies), a review of available drugs takes place and some new drugs are added while others are removed from the list, according to a standard set of formulary criteria. When using this kind of formulary, pharmacy staff need only ensure that they have the most up-to-date list, and check to see whether the drug and preparation prescribed are on it.

Other formularies are more dynamic, adding new drugs as soon as they are approved for sale in Canada, or at least at frequent intervals (for example, every three months). Some formularies have more complicated rules with respect to coverage, co-payment, and access to particular drugs. For example, some formularies reimburse patients for generic drugs only, where these are available. Others use a reference-based system to determine maximum reimbursement. Still others create a tiered system for co-payments, in which some drugs are subject to greater co-payment than others. Each of these variations is discussed below.

Finally, some formularies create a class of drugs that require "prior authorization." A patient who wishes to be reimbursed for such a drug must first meet certain clinical criteria, as certified by a physician. An example of a drug requiring prior authorization is Humira, sometimes prescribed for arthritis and Crohn's disease, but which has a high potential for side effects. Another example is Sativex, which can help multiple sclerosis sufferers but is cannabis-based. A third example is Botox, a drug typically prescribed for cosmetic, rather than health, purposes.

formulary
a list of prescription drugs covered by a particular drug benefit plan

Cost Control Strategies

INTRODUCTION

Inflation—the rate of increase of prices for goods and services—has been quite low in Canada in recent years; however, pharmaceutical prices have been a notable exception to the trend. At the same time, spending on pharmaceuticals per average person has increased dramatically in the last 25 years: *Benefits Canada*, a publication serving the benefits industry, has reported that prescription drug spending in Canada increased 600 percent over the 22 years between 1986 and 2008. Researchers offer many possible explanations for this trend: our population is aging, and the elderly tend to take more prescription drugs than the young; new, effective, and expensive pharmaceuticals have emerged for many diseases; and there has been an increase in the marketing of pharmaceuticals to the public directly, a factor that may drive patient requests for prescriptions.

These trends have had a significant impact on the costs of employee benefit plans. In an article published in the *Report Card on Cancer in Canada, 2008–2009*, insurance specialist Chris Bonnett noted that the average cost, to employers, of providing drug benefits doubled between 2000 and 2007. In recent years, the cost of the drug coverage portion of these plans has seen steady increases. *Benefits Canada* (at 39) reported in 2008 that this trend is likely to continue through 2010, projecting an annual increase in drug reimbursement costs for benefit plans of 8 percent per year.

Bonnett describes the current rate of growth of these costs to employers as "unsustainable." However, employers face significant pressure to maintain the benefits that they have in place for employees. As a result, a range of cost-saving initiatives have emerged. The most common of these are explained below.

DEDUCTIBLES—LUMP SUM AND PER PRESCRIPTION

deductible
a set fee that the patient must pay per prescription

A few plan sponsors have introduced an "overall" **deductible** for drug benefits. Under this system, employees receive no coverage for drugs until costs reach a certain threshold, either annually or monthly—for example, an employee may be eligible for reimbursement only after spending $20 in any month on prescription drugs.

The obvious disadvantage of this plan is that it penalizes those members who spend the least on pharmaceuticals. Also, a study by benefits consulting firm Morneau Sobeco showed that the costs savings from aggressive deductibles were actually offset by decreases in employee productivity, because some employees reacted to the deductibles by not filling their prescriptions, even for essentials, such as drugs to manage diabetes.

Another deductible option operates on a per-prescription basis—for example, the plan member is reimbursed costs over a certain fixed level, say, seven dollars. Employees tend to find this scheme, which works more like a co-payment scheme, more palatable.

CO-PAYMENT

co-payment
a percentage of the total drug cost that the patient must pay

The majority of Canadian private drug insurance plans now require some **co-payment** by plan members. A co-payment is generally structured as a percentage of the total drug cost. For example, in a plan with a 20 percent co-payment (a common figure), the employee pays 20 percent of the cost of a prescription—for example, $12 on the cost of a $60 prescription.

Some sophisticated co-payment plans use different co-payments for different drugs, often to encourage patients to choose cost-effective drugs when a range of treatment options is available for a particular condition.

REFERENCE-BASED COVERAGE

reference-based coverage
drug insurance that limits the amount reimbursed to the cost of a particular drug with proven effectiveness

Reference-based coverage limits the amount reimbursed to the cost of a particular drug therapy with proven effectiveness. Sometimes new drugs emerge in the same therapy class that are only marginally more effective—or no more effective—than their predecessors, but that are much more expensive. To encourage plan members to choose cost-effective drugs, these plans limit coverage to the cost of the less expensive drug. For example, if the standard treatment for a condition costs $50 for a one-month supply, and the patient chooses instead a newer drug that costs $80 per month, the plan will allow the pharmacy to dispense the chosen drug, but will reimburse only $50 of the cost.

NON-COVERAGE OF BRANDED DRUG WHERE GENERIC AVAILABLE

Many drug plans in both the private and public sectors limit coverage to the cost of generic versions of a drug if a generic is available. A pharmacy is obliged, in these cases, to dispense the generic version.

If a patient specifically requests the brand-name drug, the pharmacist may be allowed to dispense it, but should advise the patient beforehand that he or she will be required to pay the difference between the cost of the brand-name drug and the generic.

If a prescriber has specifically requested the brand name drug ("no substitutions permitted"), some drug plans will reimburse the cost of the brand-name drug.

RESTRICTIONS ON AMOUNT DISPENSED

Sometimes, when first prescribed a new drug, patients may develop side effects serious enough to cause them to stop taking the drug, discarding the balance of the prescription. In an effort to reduce such waste and the associated costs, some drug plans encourage "trial" prescriptions. These are generally for a small supply of the drug, for example, a week's worth. If at the end of the trial period the patient cannot tolerate the drug, the physician can write a different prescription. If the trial is successful, the patient simply obtains a refill for a longer treatment term.

The opposite strategy—large-amount prescriptions—has also been used by plan sponsors hoping to save money on dispensing fees. If a patient requires a drug over the long term and can safely take it without needing frequent medical reassessment, the drug plan requires the pharmacy to dispense a large-amount prescription (usually, enough for 100 days).

Dispensing Fees

Finally, some plans do not cover dispensing fees, or they impose a cap on covering them. This strategy encourages patients to "shop around" for a pharmacy that offers a low dispensing fee.

Reimbursement Systems

There are two basic kinds of reimbursement systems: the first requires the patient to pay for the prescription and dispensing fee out of pocket, and to submit—or require the pharmacy to submit—a claim to the plan sponsor. Based on the claim documentation, the plan sponsor then reimburses the patient, either by cheque, by direct deposit, or by adding the reimbursement to the employee's pay.

The far more common method requires the patient to pay only the deductible or co-payment amount. The pharmacy then submits a claim to the plan sponsor, and the plan sponsor reimburses the pharmacy directly.

Pharmacy Staff's Role in Explaining Benefits

Many members of employer- or union-sponsored drug benefit plans are unfamiliar with the details of their plans. Questions about coverage, drug choices, formularies, deductibles, and co-payments may arise for the first time when the plan member goes to the pharmacy with a new prescription. Thus, pharmacy staff must often educate clients about the details of their plan. Because rising benefit expenses have led to the cost-cutting strategies discussed above, patients sometimes react angrily when they learn the answer to a drug insurance question. The extra time required for these discussions, and the potential for aggravation, is a burden that pharmacy staff must bear. Good customer service demands that pharmacists and pharmacy technicians handle these conversations with courtesy, and with the patient's best interests and health in mind.

While pharmacy staff should do their best to answer clients' questions, if staff are themselves unclear about plan details, it is perfectly appropriate to suggest that the patient contact the insurer directly. The pharmacy can provide contact phone numbers for most insurers, and can even initiate such calls, from the pharmacy, if the patient requests this.

THE ONTARIO DRUG BENEFIT PROGRAMS

Introduction

Canada's commitment to public health care is internationally known. Most Canadians enjoy access to high-quality health care without cost (other than through the payment of taxes) through programs developed and administered by the individual provinces. While certain procedures, devices, accommodation, and services are not covered, our health-care system is based on the value that no person should be denied essential care because of economic hardship.

Public drug benefit programs—offered by each province and territory—are a natural extension of our public health system. However, these programs are not available to all residents. Healthy Canadians spend modestly on pharmaceuticals, mostly for non-catastrophic expenses that the government deems affordable even though they are not predictable.

A minority of Ontarians incur high pharmaceutical costs. Such individuals may be unable to afford the drugs they need for a variety of reasons:

- They are retired and on a fixed or limited income (also, elderly people tend to have higher drug costs than young people).
- They have a low family income due to unemployment, responsibility for dependents, disability, or other reasons.
- They suffer from acute or chronic conditions that require expensive treatment—for example, cancer, rheumatoid arthritis, diabetes, schizophrenia, or heart disease.

Ontario's public drug benefit scheme currently consists of five different programs:

- the Ontario Drug Benefit Program;
- the Trillium Drug Program;
- the Special Drugs Program;
- the Drug Funding Program for Cancer Care; and
- the Inherited Metabolic Diseases Program.

All five programs are explained below.

The Ontario Drug Benefit Program

INTRODUCTION AND ELIGIBILITY

The Ontario Drug Benefit Program (ODBP), established by the *Ontario Drug Benefit Act* (ODBA) embraces the following principles:

1. The public drug system aims to meet the needs of Ontarians, as patients, consumers and taxpayers.
2. The public drug system aims to involve consumers and patients in a meaningful way.
3. The public drug system aims to operate transparently to the extent possible for all persons with an interest in the system, including, without being limited to, patients, health care practitioners, consumers, manufacturers, wholesalers and pharmacies.
4. The public drug system aims to consistently achieve value-for-money and ensure the best use of resources at every level of the system.
5. Funding decisions for drugs are to be made on the best clinical and economic evidence available, and will be openly communicated in as timely a manner as possible. (s. 0.1)

The ODBP was created for the benefit of Ontarians whose access to prescription drugs is at risk for economic reasons. According to the website of the Ministry of Health and Long-Term Care (MOHLTC), the classes of individuals who may be eligible for benefits under the plan are:

- people 65 years of age and older;
- people on social assistance (Ontario Disability Support Program, Ontario Works, or both);
- residents of homes for special or long-term care;
- people receiving professional home-care services; and
- registrants in the Trillium Drug Program.

In order to become eligible to receive benefits under the program, people in these categories must apply to the MOHLTC. (An application form is available on the Ministry's website at www.health.gov.on.ca.) Pharmacy staff may, on occasion, hear from patients who do not have private coverage that the costs of prescription medications are not affordable. Staff should direct these patients to the MOHLTC, either via the website or by telephone, so that the patients can determine their eligibility for public drug benefit coverage.

The MOHLTC has a manual that explains the program and policies related to it. All pharmacies should have a copy of the manual available for consultation by staff.

THE ODBP FORMULARY

The ODBP maintains a non-exhaustive formulary of essential, proven effective, and commonly prescribed drugs. Not all drugs approved for sale in Canada are included in the formulary. The ODBA and the general regulation made under it (O. Reg. 201/96) set out a detailed scheme through which drug manufacturers or other parties can request inclusion of a particular drug or formulation in the formulary.

When determining whether to include a drug in the formulary, the executive officer of the ODBP may consult the Pharmacy Council, an advisory body established under section 1.4 of the ODBA. The role of the Council is defined in the legislation as follows:

> 1.4 (1) The Minister shall establish a Pharmacy Council that will ensure the involvement of pharmacists in the development of pharmaceutical and health policy and whose duties shall include, without being limited to, the provision of expert advice to the executive officer and the Minister, assisting in the definition and implementation of pharmacists' professional services, and identifying the necessary infrastructure and supports for the implementation of professional services.

There is also a Citizens' Council, established under section 1.5.

Besides creating a scheme for the inclusion of drugs in the formulary, the legislation also establishes guidelines for:

- removing a drug from the formulary (for example, because its manufacturer does not comply with the ODBP rules, or the drug has been determined to be unsafe);
- the maximum price at which the government will reimburse pharmacies dispensing the drug;
- whether and how benefit recipients can obtain coverage for drugs that are medically necessary but not in the formulary; preparations or dosages of drugs not in the formulary; and special compounds not in the formulary.

listed drug product
a drug listed in the Ontario Drug Benefit Program formulary

listed substance
a non-drug item, such as vitamins or nutritional supplements, listed in the Ontario Drug Benefit Program formulary

designated drug product
a drug listed in the Ontario Drug Benefit Program formulary for which the government offers reimbursement

Once a drug has been included in the formulary, it becomes a **listed drug product**. The formulary also includes non-drug items (for example, certain nutritional supplements, vitamins, and diabetic testing agents) that are eligible for coverage; these items, once included in the formulary, are known as **listed substances**. Listed drug products for which the government offers reimbursement become **designated drug products**.

Once a product is listed in the formulary, the manufacturer is required to comply strictly with ODBP rules, and with the Code of Conduct set out in Schedule 3 to the General Regulation. This Code of Conduct will be discussed below, as it has important implications for pharmacy staff.

The ODBA formulary is posted on the website of the MOHLTC and can be accessed by anyone (including pharmacy staff seeking to determine whether a particular drug or dosage strength is covered).

THE EXCEPTIONAL ACCESS PROGRAM

The MOHLTC offers an Exceptional Access Program that allows individuals in "exceptional clinical circumstances" to apply (through their physicians, who must prepare the application) to the Ministry for coverage of drugs not listed in the formulary. To obtain this coverage, a patient must prove that a formulary drug has been tried but was ineffective or intolerable (for example, because of allergy or side effects).

THE PHARMACY AND THE PATIENT/CLIENT

The ODBA establishes certain rules about how patients eligible under the ODBP must be served.

First, a pharmacist (or other pharmacy staff) cannot refuse to dispense a drug for a patient because the patient is a recipient of public drug benefits. There is one exception: if a pharmacist deems it necessary, based on professional judgment, to refuse to fill a prescription for therapeutic reasons (for example, if the patient is known to be allergic to the drug, or if there are reasonable grounds to believe that the patient will abuse the drug). In such cases, the pharmacist can request reimbursement for professional services (that is, for having considered the patient's case and refusing to dispense) in connection with the transaction. The pharmacist may *not* make a "therapeutic substitution" for an ODBP patient. A therapeutic substitution is the substitution of a drug that is not deemed to be interchangeable (under the *Drug Interchangeability and Dispensing Fee Act* [DIDFA]). For example, if a patient presents a prescription for prednisone for a skin rash, the pharmacist cannot instead supply an antihistamine—a totally different drug—even though the pharmacist may, in his or her professional judgment, believe an antihistamine is a safer and equally effective alternative.

In any case where:

- there exists a less expensive interchangeable drug (a generic) corresponding with the drug prescribed,
- the interchangeable drug is listed on the ODBP formulary,
- the interchangeable drug is available in inventory, and
- the prescriber has not made a notation ("no substitutions") prohibiting it on the prescription,

the pharmacist or pharmacy staff must dispense the least expensive interchangeable drug to the patient. In situations where a co-payment is required (the ODBP does not cover 100 percent of all costs in all cases), the pharmacy must charge the patient his or her share of the drug cost at the drug benefit price; the pharmacist cannot, for example, assume that by receiving a generic, the patient is already saving money, and so the pharmacist and the patient can "split the difference." Any form of overcharging—charging the patient more than the patient's co-payment for the lowest interchangeable drug price, charging the patient even though the patient has benefits, and so on—is an offence under section 15(2) of the ODBA. Fines for this offence range from $25,000 to $200,000 (depending upon whether the person charged is an individual or a corporation, and whether it's a first or subsequent offence). For individuals committing a section 15(2) offence, there is potential for a prison sentence of up to 12 months.

The ODBA and the regulations made under it establish a standard dispensing fee for prescriptions covered under the ODBP. In 2010, the dispensing fee was $7 (O. Reg. 201/96, s. 13(4)). The dispensing fee, like the drug cost, is not paid out of pocket by the patient; instead, it is reimbursed by the ODBP. However, the legislation allows for the charging of a co-payment of a maximum of $2 per prescription in most cases. If the patient is eligible for coverage solely by reason of being over age 65, a slightly higher co-payment may be required; the formula for calculating that co-payment is very complex, and is set out in section 20.2 of the regulation.

There is one exception to the rule against charging/overcharging ODBP recipients: when a person does not meet the clinical criteria for use of the drug. The executive officer of the ODBP establishes clinical criteria for the prescription of certain drugs, and to deny coverage of those drugs to patients who do not meet the criteria. Such criteria must be noted in the formulary, so that pharmacy staff are made aware of the special conditions. When a patient presents a prescription that requires clinical criteria to be met, if the physician has followed the regulations for establishing clinical criteria, the prescription will bear a special "reason for use" code. If this code is missing, pharmacy staff must advise the patient that the drug will not be covered under the ODBP, and that the patient will have to pay for it out of pocket.

The ODBA establishes detailed and complicated rules about the amount of a drug, dispensed at one time, that will be reimbursed by the ODBP. Although these rules will not be reproduced here, pharmacy staff should be aware of them, and avoid dispensing quantities higher than the reimbursement limits (usually a 30-day supply maximum; however, the rules differ for Ontario Works recipients, people who are going out of the country, and those who take the medication on a permanent or long-term basis—for example, insulin for diabetics). For details of these rules, pharmacy technicians should review section 18 of O. Reg. 201/96 made under the ODBA.

In order to manage dispensing fee costs, the ODBP states that unless special circumstances exist, pharmacy staff must dispense the lesser of (1) the maximum allowable dispensable amount, or (2) the whole prescription (for example, if the prescription is for a 10-day course of treatment). Special circumstances can justify the dispensing of lesser amounts; for example:

- The patient is a resident of a certain kind of long-term care facility.
- The pharmacist determines, *and the patient or patient's representative agrees*, that the patient's physical, cognitive, or sensory impairment makes medication management difficult. In this case, the pharmacist must write out and file the reasons for the decision, as well as obtain the written consent of the person who consented.

A pharmacy can seek reimbursement for no more than two dispensing fees per prescription per month, unless the prescription falls into one of the above two categories.

THE PHARMACY AND THE MANUFACTURER OR SUPPLIER

Once a drug has been listed in the ODBP formulary, the manufacturer and supplier become subject to the legislation. Several implications flow from this requirement.

First, the manufacturer must negotiate a "drug benefit price" for the drug. If the drug to be listed is an interchangeable product (generic), the drug benefit price must be equal to or less than half the price of the original or brand-name product. Where circumstances warrant—for example, if the cost of raw ingredients for the drug escalates dramatically—the manufacturer can apply to increase the drug benefit price.

Once the drug benefit price has been established, the manufacturer must supply the drug to pharmacies *for the purpose of dispensing under the Act*, at that price. A manufacturer that fails to do this is subject to a penalty to be calculated according to the regulations, or may be charged with an offence under section 15(2) (discussed above).

To avoid allegations of improper influence, manufacturers and suppliers who supply a designated drug in the formulary are not allowed to provide rebates to pharmacies. Considering that pharmacies often receive reimbursement from the government for the full cost (plus legislated mark-up) for sales of designated drugs to eligible individuals, receiving a rebate as well from the supplier would enable the pharmacy to earn a significant additional profit, and provide an incentive to favour one drug over another. This situation would not be in the best interest of the public. For this reason, rebates are prohibited under the ODBA.

Appropriate standards of conduct between pharmacies and their suppliers are described more fully in the Code of Conduct that appears as Schedule 3 of the General Regulation made under the ODBA. The Code of Conduct states that while pharmacies cannot receive rebates from suppliers, they can receive professional allowances. A professional allowance is defined in the regulation as a "benefit, in the form of currency, services or educational materials that are provided by a manufacturer to ... [wholesalers, operators of pharmacies, or companies that own, operate or franchise pharmacies or to their directors, officers, employees or agents] ... for the purposes of direct patient care" (ODBA, ss. 1(8) and 11.5(1)).

The definition of professional allowance goes on to describe in detail the kinds of benefits that qualify as direct patient care. These include:

- certain kinds of continuing education programs for pharmacists and pharmacy staff;
- the costs of "clinic days," educational days, or monitoring clinics—for example, flu shot clinics, asthma management education clinics, blood pressure testing clinics, or other educational initiatives for the general public, whether held in the pharmacy or elsewhere;
- compliance packaging for drugs;
- funding for the creation of patient counselling areas in the pharmacy; and
- special services offered to hospital in-patients or residents of long-term care homes, for example, medication reconciliation consulting.

For further clarity, the Code of Conduct lists activities and purposes for which professional allowances must never be used. For example, a pharmacy cannot use a professional allowance to:

- prepare advertising materials for the pharmacy or for drugs;
- pay for meals and entertainment for personnel, including personnel involved in staffing the permitted clinic or education days;
- pay taxes or penalties; and
- pay for pharmacy fixtures or renovations, with the exception of a private patient counselling area.

Generally speaking, anything that benefits the pharmacy or its staff without benefiting the patient very directly would fall afoul of the Code of Conduct.

Some critics believe that abuses have occurred under the professional allowances system. In 2009, the Ontario government proposed changes to the *Ontario Drug Benefit Act*, including the Code of Conduct. One such change that attracted media attention was the proposed abolition of professional allowances. This proposal led to protests from some pharmacies—for example, in the form of reductions in operating hours. In response to these protests, the Ontario College of Pharmacists published the following notice on its homepage in April 2010:

> Recent changes to Ontario's Public Drug System continue to attract much media attention.

Regardless of the business models under which pharmacists and pharmacies operate, the Ontario College of Pharmacists trusts that pharmacists will put the care of their patients first.

The College expects that the standards of practice for pharmacists will be maintained and that pharmacists will uphold their duty in providing quality care to patients in a manner that assures patient safety and protection.

The Code of Conduct also provides some general guidelines for the behaviour of pharmacy representatives. These read:

Pharmacy representatives shall conduct business ethically and in a manner that is in the best interest of their patients.

Pharmacies must not make procurement and purchasing decisions based solely on the provision of professional allowances.

Violation of the Code of Conduct by accepting a payment that does not meet the definition of professional allowance, or by misdirecting a professional allowance, is tantamount to accepting a rebate as prohibited by section 11.5(1). If a pharmacy or its representative is found to have accepted a rebate, the person or organization may be forced to forfeit the rebate amount to the executive officer (s. 11.5(12)).

THE PHARMACY AND THE MINISTRY OF HEALTH AND LONG-TERM CARE

Once a prescription has been dispensed to a patient, the pharmacy is eligible to file a claim for reimbursement with the executive officer of the ODBP within the MOHLTC.

Ontario pharmacies are expected to accomplish this task electronically, through a computer system referred to in the legislation as the Health Network. When a patient's information (including his or her status as eligible for coverage under the ODBP) is entered into the system along with the prescription information, the system generates a claim for forwarding to the executive officer.

Some pharmacies may not be connected to the Health Network (for example, one that has just opened or is having computer problems). In these cases, the pharmacy is required to submit paper-based claims; the procedures for these are set out in the regulation at sections 24 and 25. Paper claims may also be submitted in certain special cases—for example, if the pharmacy does not receive proof that a drug is for an eligible person until more than seven days after the drug is supplied. The other special cases are listed in section 24(2) of the regulation. Pharmacy technicians should learn how to prepare these paper-based claims. Assistance is available from the manual provided by the MOHLTC.

When submitting a claim, a pharmacy is allowed to add an 8 percent markup to the drug benefit cost of the drugs dispensed. This markup is intended to cover the costs that would normally be paid out of pharmacy profits: rent, staffing, and other normal costs of running a business.

BOX 5.1

CASES

Public Drug Benefits: Crime and Punishment

1. Mischaracterizing Methadone Scripts (*R v. Rands; R v. Wolsey*)

Because government drug insurance programs are for the public benefit, attempts to defraud the system are dealt with harshly. In the 2005 decision in *R v. Rands* and the 2008 decision in *R v. Wolsey*, two pharmacists defrauded the British Columbia PharmaCare public drug benefit system by billing methadone-for-maintenance prescriptions as "narcotics for pain control." The scheme was discovered by chance, when PharmaCare took steps to investigate the medical file of a patient who was suspected of abusing prescriptions. The patient revealed that the prescriptions in question were methadone for addiction management, not narcotics for pain control. The PharmaCare program then commenced an audit of two pharmacies (owned by one corporation) and discovered a pattern of fraud over a seven-month period.

Under the criminal law of fraud, pharmacist Rands, who pleaded guilty, was convicted and sentenced to prison for a term of two years less a day. Pharmacist Wolsey, who initiated the scheme (and intimidated Rands into participating), pleaded not guilty. At Wolsey's trial, the prosecution could not prove beyond a reasonable doubt that the fraud was intentional. Despite being the mastermind of the scheme, Wolsey was acquitted.

The government also launched a civil suit against the pharmacists. The suit was settled for $560,000, much of which the pharmacists repaid.

The scheme is only one of the allegations that has arisen in recent years against Gastown Pharmacy, located in Vancouver's notorious Downtown Eastside. For the second half of the Gastown Pharmacy story, see Box 8.1.

2. Illegal Discounts (*Siu v. College of Pharmacists of British Columbia*)

In this 1990 case, British Columbia pharmacists Gary Siu and Daniel Leung brought an administrative law case before the Supreme Court of British Columbia.

The two pharmacists were facing disciplinary proceedings for professional misconduct, brought against them by their provincial regulatory college. The College was relying on information about inappropriate billing practices that had surfaced in the course of a fraud investigation by PharmaCare, the BC public drug benefit program.

After receiving an anonymous tip, PharmaCare investigated the billing practices of Siu and Leung. Under the PharmaCare plan, elderly recipients of public drug benefits were required to pay 75 percent of the dispensing fee charged by their pharmacies. The pharmacies were entitled to bill PharmaCare for reimbursement of the remaining 25 percent.

However, Siu and Leung were offering elderly drug benefit recipients a discount on the dispensing fee, while still billing PharmaCare for 25 percent of the full fee—an illegal practice. The pharmacists claimed they did not know the practice was illegal, and made reimbursement to the plan of approximately $20,000. Their PharmaCare privileges were temporarily suspended, but after the parties settled, their privileges were reinstated. During the course of the investigation, PharmaCare kept the College advised of the situation and disclosed its evidence against the pharmacists.

After the PharmaCare proceedings were settled, the College brought disciplinary proceedings against the two pharmacists. The pharmacists took the position that the College's access to and reliance on the information from the PharmaCare investigation was counter to the principles of administrative law. According to the pharmacists (and their lawyers), the College's reliance on the PharmaCare findings of fact constituted improper delegation of the College's investigative function.

The court considered the "separate mandates" of PharmaCare and of the College, and found that it was unreasonable to prevent the College from "seeking help from informed sources" in conducting its investigations. The court dismissed the pharmacists' petition, and the College was permitted to use the PharmaCare evidence in the course of its proceeding. ▣

OTHER SOURCES OF DRUG COVERAGE IN THE PUBLIC SECTOR

Other Ontario Drug Benefit Programs

Besides the ODBP, the government of Ontario offers relief from the cost of pharmaceutical care to certain Ontarians who meet the criteria for help through one of four additional programs. These programs are summarized here.

THE TRILLIUM PROGRAM

The Trillium Program is designed to offer relief from excessive burden of pharmaceutical care costs for individuals who:

- do not qualify for coverage through the ODBP (that is, not aged 65 or over, not on social assistance, not receiving Home Care Services, and not a resident of a long-term or special-care home);
- do not have private drug insurance coverage, or have coverage insufficient to relieve financial hardship; and
- face high pharmaceutical costs because of health problems.

Ontarians who believe they meet these criteria can apply for coverage through the MOHLTC website. When coverage is awarded, it covers the cost of drugs in excess of a statutory deductible. The deductible is based on household income and is split into quarters. In order for a recipient to receive drug coverage in any quarter, his or her pharmaceutical expenses must first exceed 25 percent of the set deductible.

For example, an applicant may be assigned a deductible of $800 per year. If the applicant's household spends $200 out of pocket on drugs (drugs listed in the ODBP formulary, or available through the Special Access Program), the program will cover further drug spending for the household for that quarter, with a $2 co-payment per prescription applied. Should the household not spend the quarterly deductible, unspent amounts are added to the next quarter's deductible. In other words, if the household spends only $170 in the third quarter of a year, the deductible for the fourth quarter becomes $230. The rules for eligibility and calculation of deductibles are set out in detail in the General Regulation made under the ODBA.

SPECIAL DRUG PROGRAMS

Special programs exist to assist individuals who must undergo certain essential, expensive, long-term drug therapies.

If an Ontario resident eligible for OHIP coverage meets certain clinical criteria is under the care of an approved caregiver, and requires pharmaceutical treatment for any of the following conditions:

- HIV/AIDS;
- thalassemia;
- cystic fibrosis;
- end-stage renal (kidney) disease requiring treatment with erythropoietin (EPO);

- bone marrow or organ transplant requiring cyclosporine;
- childhood growth failure requiring human growth hormone;
- schizophrenia requiring clozapine treatment; or
- Gaucher's disease requiring alglucerase,

he or she can apply for coverage of these medications. The medications are usually available from special treatment centres located in hospitals or clinics, and the facilities generally assist the patient with applying for coverage and proving eligibility.

DRUG FUNDING FOR CANCER CARE

Traditionally, individual hospitals were responsible for acquiring all drugs required for inpatient cancer treatment, and for determining which drugs patients would receive. Inpatient pharmaceutical care was covered, for the most part, through OHIP.

However, as new and expensive intravenous cancer drugs have emerged, not all hospitals have had equal access to the funds necessary to obtain those drugs. To ensure uniformity in the quality of care available to individuals across the province, the government of Ontario began providing special funding for certain new cancer drugs.

Because this funding flows directly to hospitals, and is primarily for drugs for intravenous use, patients do not present at pharmacies with prescriptions covered under this program. For more information, interested pharmacy technicians can visit the website of Cancer Care Ontario (www.cancercare.on.ca).

THE INHERITED METABOLIC DISEASES PROGRAM

Some individuals who suffer from inherited metabolic diseases require special products and foods to manage their disorders. These conditions are typically diagnosed in infancy, and a range of special products exists for their management.

The government of Ontario covers the cost of some of these products when they are obtained through a special (usually hospital-based) centre established to help patients and their caregivers. The MOHLTC provides a comprehensive list of the conditions and products covered under this program on its website.

Federal Government Programs and Initiatives

Under the Canadian constitution, the administration of health care and commerce are primarily provincially regulated activities. However, the federal government does provide some drug benefit coverage to individuals whose circumstances bring them within the government's mandate.

MILITARY PERSONNEL AND VETERANS

Actively serving military personnel and certain members of the reserve forces are entitled to health-care benefits through the federal government. These include drug benefits. The benefits are for the serviceperson exclusively; there is typically no coverage for dependants. The drug benefit program is quite broad, covering:

1. drugs which normally require a prescription;
2. drugs which may not legally require a prescription, but which are only available for purchase at an accredited pharmacy and have known therapeutic value;
3. replacement therapeutic nutrients provided that there is no other nutritional alternative to support the life of the member;
4. injectable drugs, including injectable allergy serums and vaccines;
5. compounded prescriptions;
6. vitamins and minerals, which are prescribed for the treatment of a chronic disease when the use of such products is proven to have therapeutic value;
7. drug delivery devices, such as those used to deliver asthma medication, which are integral to the product;
8. nitrous oxide when administered by a licensed practitioner; and
9. recognized contraceptive devices including, but not limited to, IUDs, condoms, spermicides and diaphragms … . (National Defence and Canadian Forces 2008)

Members of the Canadian Forces who are entitled to drug benefits carry a health-care identification card, and information about eligibility is accessible using the data from the card. Pharmacy staff who have questions about the program can call the member information number listed on the patient's card.

The Canadian Forces are currently in the process of making changes to their health-care programs. For up-to-date information as changes become effective, pharmacy staff can visit the Canadian Forces website (www.forces.gc.ca).

Veterans Affairs Canada, a federal government agency, offers a range of health-care benefits to veterans through a scheme called Programs of Choice. There are 14 separate programs within the scheme, including a medical supplies program that reimburses the cost of equipment and supplies needed for outpatient care, an oxygen therapy program, a prostheses and orthoses program, and a prescription drugs program.

The prescription drugs program covers a wide range of prescription and non-prescription drugs and medical supplies. A special authorization component of the plan covers, after clinical criteria are established, certain less common therapies.

Veterans eligible for coverage under this program carry a special identification card. The card lists the programs by number (the prescription drug program is number 10); below the number, the card carrier's eligibility for that benefit is indicated by a letter. According to the information pamphlet provided by Veterans Affairs Canada, the letter indicators signify the following:

- If "A" appears under any of POCs 1 to 14 on the front of the card, approved benefits and/or services directly related to the conditions for which you hold VAC disability entitlement are covered under the VAC Health Care Benefits Program for which you have clearly demonstrated a health need.

- For "A" clients, POCs 2, 5, 6, and 10 appear on all VAC Health Identification cards regardless of the conditions for which you have VAC disability entitlement, however, benefits and/or services under these POCs must be related to disability granted conditions.

- If "B" appears under any of the POCs 1 to 14 on the front of the card, approved benefits and/or services for which you have a clearly demonstrated health need and, which are not covered by a provincial or private health plan, will be covered under the VAC Health Care Benefits Program.

- When both "A" and "B" appear under any of the POCs 1 to 14 on the front of the card, eligibility for benefits and/or services depends on your granted conditions, your overall health issues, the benefit or service requested and provincial or private health coverage.

- If neither "A" nor "B" are shown under the POC, you do not qualify for any benefits or services under that program … . (Veterans Affairs Canada, 2008)

Pharmacy staff who have questions about the coverage available through Veterans Affairs Canada can call the program office at 1-866-522-2122.

INMATES OF FEDERAL PENITENTIARIES

The *Corrections and Conditional Release Act* and Corrections Canada policy provide that all inmates of federal penitentiaries must have access to essential health-care services. Inmates may also be granted access to non-essential mental health care if that care would assist in their rehabilitation and eventual reintegration into the community. Health care in penitentiaries is provided through on-site clinics or with the help of on-call physicians and health professionals.

Pharmaceutical products for inmates are provided either through a penitentiary-based pharmacy or through a contract with a pharmacy in the community. In general, medications for inmates are not obtained by the inmate directly but by health-care professionals. If drugs are purchased through a contract, reimbursement comes directly from the penitentiary and is funded by the federal government.

MEMBERS OF CANADA'S FIRST NATIONS AND INUIT PEOPLES

Canada's First Nations and Inuit peoples have access to provincial health-care programs in their provinces and territories of residence. Like many other Canadians, some First Nations and Inuit persons have private drug benefit coverage through employers.

Nevertheless, and for a range of reasons, the health status of many First Nations and Inuit persons is significantly poorer than the Canadian average. In an attempt to improve the health status of these individuals, the government of Canada offers access, for those who are otherwise uninsured, to limited drug benefits under the Non-Insured Health Benefits (NIHB) program.

The NIHB program is administered by Health Canada's First Nations and Inuit Health Branch. In 2009, ESI Canada (the pharmacy benefit manager company mentioned earlier in this chapter) replaced First Canadian Health as the administrator for NIHB claims processing. Pharmacies serving people eligible for benefits under the NIHB must be registered as providers with ESI Canada before they can submit claims.

Two important resources available for providers of NIHB pharmacy care are:

- the *Pharmacy Claims Submission Kit*, published by ESI Canada; and
- Health Canada's *Provider Guide for Pharmacy Benefits*.

Both guides are available on the website of Health Canada (www.hc-sc.gc.ca). Pharmacy staff who serve First Nations or Inuit recipients of NIHB benefits should familiarize themselves with both guides.

Like many providers of drug benefits, Health Canada maintains a formulary of drugs for which benefits are available.

KEY TERMS

co-payment
deductible
designated drug product
formulary
listed drug product
listed substance
open access plan
pharmacy benefit manager (PBM)
private drug insurance plan/private drug benefit plan
private insurance
reference-based coverage

REFERENCES

Bonnett, C. (2009). Insurance: A primer on private health benefit plans. In *Report Card on Cancer in Canada, 2008–2009*. Toronto: Cancer Advocacy Coalition of Canada.

Corrections and Conditional Release Act. 1992. SC 1992, c. 20.

Drug Interchangeability and Dispensing Fee Act. 1990. RSO 1990, c. P.23.

ESI Canada. (2010, April 9). NIHB Pharmacy claims submission kit. Retrieved May 29, 2010 from http://www.provider.esicanada.ca/pdf/Pharmacy_English/NIHB_Pharmacy_Claims_Submission_Kit.pdf.

Health Canada. (2009, April). Provider guide for pharmacy benefits. Retrieved May 29, 2010 from http://www.hc-sc.gc.ca/fniah-spnia/pubs/nihb-ssna/_drug-med/2009-prov-fourn-guide/index-eng.php.

Martinez, Barbara; "Buyer Aware: Cost trends and Containment Strategies for Private drug Plans in Canada To Help Foster Consumerism in Health Care." *Benefits Canada*, June 2008.

National Defence and the Canadian Forces. (2008, July 21). Supplemental health care: Drug benefits. Retrieved May 29, 2010 from http://www.forces.gc.ca/health-sante/ps/guide/ben-eng.asp.

Ontario Drug Benefit Act. 1990. RSO 1990, c. O.10.

R v. Rands. 2005 CanLII 264 (BCPC).

R v. Wolsey. 2008 CanLII 159 (BCCA).

Siu v. College of Pharmacists of British Columbia. 1990 CanLII 1041 (BCSC).

Veterans Affairs Canada. (2008, April). A guide to access health care benefits and Veterans Independence Program. Retrieved May 29, 2010 from http://www. vac-acc.gc.ca/clients/sub.cfm?source=services/vip/vachealthvip.

REVIEW EXERCISES

Discussion Question

The last several years have seen a trend in health care toward reducing the duration of hospital stays. Patients recovering from surgery or learning to manage chronic health conditions have been encouraged to recover at home, with help from outpatient clinics and home health-care services. Discuss the real or potential impacts on the pharmaceutical industry of this trend. Do you believe that our public health-care system may need to change to accommodate this trend? If so, how?

Review Questions

1. What is the approximate percentage of Ontarians who have access to private drug benefit insurance? List at least three reasons why a person might not have access to such coverage.

2. List some of the reasons why private insurers have taken steps in recent years to limit drug benefits or to contain drug benefit costs.

3. What is a per-prescription deductible? What is a co-payment? What is the difference, and how would you explain it to a patient?

4. Plans with an "overall deductible" or annual deductible tend to be unpopular. Why?

5. What are the two main methods for reimbursing people who have private insurance for the cost of their prescriptions?

6. What are the conditions for eligibility for coverage under Ontario's public drug benefit programs?

7. What is a formulary, for insurance purposes, and why must pharmacy staff consult it before filling a prescription?

8. How should pharmacy staff handle patients' questions about their drug coverage?

9. List at least three classes of individuals who may have drug benefit coverage through the federal government.

CHAPTER 6

Preventing Errors

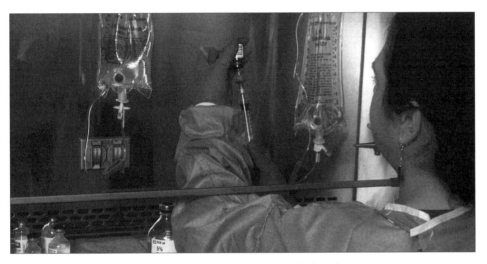

A hospital pharmacy technician prepares drugs under a sterile hood.

LEARNING OBJECTIVES

After completing this chapter, you should be able to:

- Explain why it is difficult and unrealistic to report statistics about medication errors.

- Explain the rationale for prevention or remediation rather than a punitive approach to practice errors.

- Describe the potential consequences to a patient of a medication error.

- Describe the potential personal and professional consequences to a pharmacy technician of making a practice error.

- Suggest strategies and best practices for avoiding practice errors.

- Describe the consequences of professional misconduct.

- Understand your responsibility, as a member of the pharmacy team, for preventing errors and for reporting misconduct.

INTRODUCTION

In discussing the issue of medication errors, the question naturally arises of how often these errors occur, and how often they cause harm to a patient. The Institute for Safe Medication Practices (ISMP) suggests that it is impossible to count these errors with any degree of accuracy.

One reason for this position is that a large percentage of medication errors are never detected. For example, an error occurs but the patient is not harmed, and no one ever knows it happened. The ISMP explains that having a system that permits the reporting of errors doesn't make error rates any more credible, for a number of reasons:

- There is no universally accepted definition of what constitutes a medication error.
- There is no accurate way to measure how often errors occur.
- There is little consistency in the diligence with which errors are reported.

In fact, relying on error reporting to estimate an "error rate" can create considerable distortion. As the ISMP explains: "It is very possible that an institution with a good reporting system, and thus what appears to be a high error 'rate,' may have a safer system" (ISMP, n.d.).

Despite these cautions, many sources continue to report "error rates." While it makes sense to treat these statistics with caution, the numbers are sobering. The range of error rates reported is wide and varies by setting; for example, error rates by non-pharmaceutical personnel working in hospitals tend to be higher than the rates reported for dispensing by a pharmacy. Reported error rates range from 3 to 24 percent, with most reports falling around the 10 percent mark. One study by the US Institute of Medicine's (IOM) Committee on Identifying and Preventing Medication Errors found that a hospitalized patient could be subjected to approximately one medication error per day during a typical stay (IOM, 2007)!

There are important differences among possible kinds of medication errors. What exactly constitutes a medication error is open to debate. Medication errors are sometimes categorized according to the following scheme:

- near-misses—medication errors that are discovered before the patient receives the medication;
- medication errors that do not cause harm to the patient; and
- adverse drug events (due to medication error) that do cause harm to the patient.

adverse drug event
an illness, injury, reaction, or the experience of serious symptoms resulting from the use of a medication

Fortunately, **adverse drug events** (errors causing harm) constitute a small minority of medication errors. For example, in clinical settings, the most common medication errors tend to be "missed-dose errors"—that is, the patient does not receive medication that has been prescribed.

More serious errors occur when a patient receives the wrong medication, or an excessive dose of medication. In the case of drugs administered via IV infusion, there is potential for very significant dosage errors. For example, one study (Parshuram, To, Seto, et al., 2008) asked physicians to prepare morphine for infusion according to instructions under simulated clinical conditions. The study found that nearly 35 percent of infusions prepared, when tested, deviated from the intended dose by more than 10 percent. More alarmingly, 1.2 percent of doses revealed 10-fold errors (the infusion was 10 times stronger than intended).

The Parshuram study concluded that, at least in the case of narcotics for infusion, the likelihood of a medication error resulting in an adverse drug event was approximately 1 in 100, and the likelihood that an individual patient would experience an adverse drug event while in hospital was 1 percent to 2 percent.

Medical and pharmaceutical community approaches to medication errors have varied over the years. Physicians' and pharmacists' serious medication errors have led, under some circumstances, to professional discipline, civil liability (lawsuits for damages), and even criminal charges.

While all these consequences are possible, the consensus about how to address medication errors has shifted somewhat. Many experts now recognize that disciplining "culprits" is not especially effective in reducing medication errors. Instead, efforts should be directed at practical strategies that counteract the inherent human tendency to make occasional mistakes. There are many different categories of error prevention strategies, and some of these are discussed below.

While the term "medication error" implies that any harm that may result to a patient is accidental, it is also possible for a patient to be placed at risk through the intentional or reckless actions of medical or pharmaceutical professionals, or for a patient to risk his or her own health through drug abuse or fraud. Besides explaining standards of professional competence, this chapter also explores the consequences of intentional violation of the law, disciplinary action, civil liability, and criminal liability.

STANDARDS OF PROFESSIONAL COMPETENCE

The Ontario College of Pharmacists' "Proposed Standards of Practice for Registered Pharmacy Technicians" (n.d. (f)) provide as follows:

Standard 5
The pharmacy technician, in collaboration with the pharmacist, designated manager, or hospital pharmacy manager, performs distributive and quality assurance functions to ensure safety, accuracy, and quality of supplied products.

The operational components expand on this directive by giving detailed instructions about how pharmacy technicians should organize their work to maximize safety and accuracy. For example, according to Operational Component 5.1, pharmacy technicians must:

- comply with all workplace procedures and policies—many of which are specifically designed to minimize errors;
- manage inventory effectively—well-organized inventory makes it more difficult to confuse drugs;
- participate in initiatives that evaluate the effectiveness of workplace policies at minimizing errors (often called quality control);
- employ effective time management, task prioritization, and work pattern evaluation; and

- select appropriate technology to assist in completing work tasks, and use the technology correctly. This includes following instructions for the use of automated dispensing technologies, evaluating the performance of these technologies (for example, by double-checking drugs dispensed), and ensuring that supplies are regularly replenished.

Operational Component 5.3 directly addresses the pharmacy technician's personal responsibility for preventing medication errors: "[t]he pharmacy technician individually and as a member of the pharmacy team takes appropriate action to prevent and reduce medication errors and medication discrepancies and implements measures to prevent recurrence."

Component 5.3 also makes it clear that a pharmacy technician is obliged to disclose all his or her medication errors, and to acknowledge his or her errors discovered by colleagues. The pharmacy technician must work with the pharmacy team to determine the causes of errors, and to put new procedures or technologies in place to avoid recurrence.

Finally, Operational Component 5.4 highlights the importance of professional independence as a safeguard against errors: "The pharmacy technician only practises under conditions, which do not compromise his or her professional independence or judgement."

The National Association of Pharmacy Regulatory Authorities' (NAPRA) "Professional Competencies for Canadian Pharmacy Technicians" are another source of guidance with respect to error prevention. Competency 9, "Quality Assurance," requires that pharmacy technicians "[c]ontribute to the creation and maintenance of a safe working environment and conditions," "[e]nsure the safety and integrity of pharmaceutical products," and "participate in quality assurance processes" to help promote the safety of both pharmacy personnel and pharmacy patients. With respect to quality assurance responsibilities, NAPRA provides that pharmacy technicians must:

9.1.1   Identify and respond to actual or potential problems within the drug distribution system.

  i.   acknowledge the problem.

  ii.   collaborate to assess and resolve problems.

  iii.   participate in the implementation of measures to prevent occurrences or reoccurrences.

  iv.   report and document problems and resolutions.

9.1.2   Contribute to organized initiatives to evaluate and improve the quality and safety of the medication use within the practice environment and the health care system.

Complying with these standards is a prerequisite for working at the fundamental level of competence expected of a pharmacy technician. Any pharmacy technician who does not understand these standards, or the workplace policies and procedures required by them, has a professional obligation to ask questions or request additional training. Working in pharmacy is a heavy responsibility, and pharmacy technicians are expected to assume full responsibility for their work. Counting on colleagues to double-check your work, or to discover and correct your errors because you are "just a pharmacy technician," is unacceptable practice in any setting.

Not only must you take responsibility for the accuracy of your own work, you must also commit, by being a member of the health-care team, to using your independent professional judgment to evaluate the accuracy of work done by others. This is a responsibility that you owe to each of your patients or clients.

PREVENTING UNINTENTIONAL ERRORS

Principles Essential to Safe Practice

Because of the potential impact on the health of their patients, pharmacy technicians must make safe practice their first professional priority.

Competent, responsible, and safe practice can be achieved only if individual practitioners and the profession as a whole abide by a set of basic but essential principles.

APPROPRIATE EDUCATION AND TRAINING

If you are reading this book, you are likely on your way to satisfying the first principle of safe practice: appropriate education and training. In preparation for the registration of the province's first complement of self-regulated, professional pharmacy technicians, the College has created a process for the accreditation of pharmacy technician education programs. As you learned in Chapter 2, for new Ontario practitioners, successful completion of a program of study at an accredited school is required before pharmacy technician students can move on to the next steps toward registration. Those steps include both written and practical entry-to-practice examinations.

For professionals, however, education and training do not end on the day graduates accept their diplomas. Registered pharmacy technicians are required to engage in continuing education activities over the course of their professional careers. These activities are designed to make practising professionals aware of new developments in the field, to refresh skills, and to provide opportunities to learn from peers.

FACTS AND TRENDS   BOX 6.1

What Is a Medication Error?

One of the most important obstacles to identifying the rate of medication errors in pharmacy practice is the lack of a consistent interpretation of what constitutes a "medication error." This chapter follows the definitions given in the "Proposed Standards of Practice for Registered Pharmacy Technicians," Operational Component 5.3:

"Medication Error"—(may also be referred to as a medication incident) is an event which involves the actual prescribing, dispensing, delivery or administration of a drug or the omission of a prescribed drug to a patient.

"**Medication Discrepancy**"—is an event that does not involve the actual administration of a drug to a patient, but where the error in the medication process has been detected and corrected before reaching the patient. ◇

medication discrepancy a medication error that is discovered before the medicine reaches the patient

Besides formal training programs, pharmacy technicians—and especially new hires—should expect to receive thorough and detailed on-the-job training specific to the settings in which they work.

Obtaining good on-the-job training can sometimes be a challenge. Often, employers hire new staff to address heavy workloads or staffing gaps, and despite best intentions end up tossing new employees "into the fray" to relieve pressure on other staff. While many employers are diligent about training, it's important for pharmacy technicians to be assertive about getting the training they need. Pharmacy technicians need to know, among other things:

- the safety, workflow, billing, quality control, and other procedures in place in the pharmacy;
- how to use technology in place in the pharmacy;
- how inventory is organized and replenished in the pharmacy;
- how records are kept in the pharmacy;
- how patient inquiries are managed in the pharmacy; and
- how to report concerns about staff or patient safety, medication errors, interpersonal conflicts, and other problems that may arise in the pharmacy.

A common error of new employees is believing that training is the employer's sole responsibility. While the employer is obliged to provide training, being well trained is a professional responsibility of the pharmacy technician also. Only you can decide whether or not you understand the procedures in place in your own workplace. You have a professional responsibility to keep asking for training until you are satisfied that you know everything you need to know to work effectively, efficiently, and safely, and to make a valuable contribution to the pharmacy team. Fears about "looking stupid" by asking questions are rarely founded. A hard-working, competent technician who is not afraid to ask questions when necessary is much more likely to inspire an employer's trust than a person who blunders along in silence, pretending she or he understands the job!

FACTS AND TRENDS   BOX 6.2

Your Continuing Education Obligation

Now that pharmacy technicians are eligible for registration in Ontario, those who choose to register will be subject to compulsory continuing education.

Continuing education, for the purpose of the College's requirements, involves participation in programs designed to enrich the practitioner's knowledge of the field in which he or she practises. The College maintains an up-to-date list on its website of opportunities for continuing education. There is currently no minimum obligation, in terms of hours of learning activities completed, that the College enforces; however, there is a general expectation that members will engage in learning activities every year throughout the course of their careers.

Registered pharmacy technicians will be required to maintain and update a document called a "learning portfolio" (OCP, n.d. (d)) in which they can record programs attended. Should a member become subject to a practice review, he or she will be asked to submit the learning portfolio for the College's review. ◈

SELF-ASSESSMENT AND WORKING WITHIN YOUR SKILLS AND EXPERIENCE

A safety principle closely related to education and training is learning to assess yourself, and to work within your skills and experience.

When you are new to a profession, it is useful to remember that even your most experienced colleagues were beginners once. Gaining skills and expertise is a gradual process. Having untested skills and limited experience is normal at the time of entry to a profession. As you complete tasks and observe others completing tasks, your skills and expertise will grow. Along the way, however, safety demands that you have an accurate understanding of your skills, your limitations, and your experience, and that you work within those parameters while seeking opportunities to expand your competence.

The general guideline for working within your competence is that the more competent you are at something, the less supervision you will need. For example, once you have restocked inventory with supervision several times, you may be confident doing it on your own, as long as someone is available to check your work. You are then ready to restock inventory without supervision.

However, you may never have completed an inventory review and restocking request for this pharmacy before. If you are asked to do this, and you use appropriate self-assessment (which is required of a professional), you will know that you must request supervision the first few times. Once you feel confident reviewing the pharmacy's inventory, you will be able to update your self-assessment, adding "capable of independently reviewing inventory" to your skill set. Your scope of safe, competent practice will have been safely expanded.

COMPETENT SUPERVISION

The third basic principle of safe practice is competent supervision. As a pharmacy technician, you will work under the direct supervision of a registered pharmacist (or more than one). Cultivating a good working relationship with this person is essential to practising safely. You will need to be comfortable approaching this person with your questions, referring patient inquiries to him or her, and reporting problems or concerns.

If you have concerns about the way in which you are supervised, it is almost always best to discuss these with your supervisor before you talk about them with anyone else. When raising a concern about supervision:

- Prepare first. Think about how you will explain your concern, and identify what you are requesting—for example, more training, more time to complete tasks, more clarity about your duties, or more respectful treatment.
- Choose an appropriate time—never approach your supervisor or colleague when she or he is dealing with a patient, customer, or supervisor.
- Be assertive, objective, calm, and fair.
- Listen carefully to your supervisor's response, and don't overreact— remember, people do not like being criticized. If you listen respectfully, your supervisor may take the time to think about your issue and provide a more measured response after he or she has had a chance to think about it.
- Write down a note about the conversation so that you can remember what was said.

- Give your supervisor a reasonable chance—if the concern doesn't involve patient safety or your own safety, a few days or shifts is reasonable.

- If your concern is not addressed, let your supervisor know that you will be communicating your issue to the person next highest in the chain of supervision (if there is such a person), and give your supervisor a chance to respond.

- If there is no one above your supervisor to whom you can communicate your concern, try talking it over with a trusted colleague. If the issue is important enough—for example, if it involves your safety, patient safety, or your human rights—you may wish to contact the College for advice about how to proceed further.

Addressing interpersonal problems in the workplace is discussed in greater detail in Chapter 7.

Developing positive working relationships with peers is your professional responsibility. In building your professional relationships, it is useful to remember that colleagues tend to like working with others who help lighten their workload, who help them look good to their own supervisors, or who make them feel like they are doing a good job as a supervisor or mentor. If you work hard and competently, take on additional tasks when you are asked, and show appreciation to those who help you, you will likely fit in well in your new workplace. For example, if a co-worker takes the time to explain a procedure to you, thank her for her time and attention! Your gratitude will make it more likely that she'll be responsive to your questions in the future.

MONITORING PRACTICE CONDITIONS

Some errors occur not because staff are not well trained, or because supervision is lacking, but because of problems in working conditions. Many workplace circumstances can contribute to the likelihood of errors. These include:

- lack of established workplace procedures (for example, finished prescriptions and prescriptions that are not completed—bottles have not been stickered, or a double-check has not been performed—are not kept in separate locations);

- poor organization of workflow (employees do not know which tasks they are responsible for);

- poor prioritization of work, especially in a busy pharmacy;

- interpersonal conflict or other problems with workplace relations;

- messiness or disorganization in the work space;

- time pressures or understaffing;

- employee fatigue due to overlong shifts, problems coping with shiftwork, or insufficient breaks or days off;

- personal or health problems affecting performance;

- unsafe or uncomfortable working conditions (the workspace is too hot, too cold, too cramped, etc.); and

- unsafe or inappropriate conditions for dispensing (problems with temperature or humidity, outdated or missing equipment, lack of supplies).

If any aspect of your workplace makes it difficult for you to do your job, it is also likely to affect the rate at which you make mistakes. It is your responsibility, as a professional, to bring these concerns to a supervisor. You cannot assume that "someone else will do it."

EXERCISING PROFESSIONAL JUDGMENT

The word "professional" appears often in this textbook. This emphasis is intentional.

Being a professional entails many responsibilities and privileges. One privilege is that your patients, your colleagues, and the public trust in your independent professional judgment. In relation to safety, an aspect of professionalism that requires special focus is independence.

Research has shown that no matter how competent prescribers, pharmacists, and pharmacy technicians may be, some medication errors will always occur. However, each layer of independent review that is added to a prescribing and dispensing task tends to reduce the chance that an error will pass undetected before reaching the patient. However, this is true only when reviewers apply both judgment and independence to the review task.

Using your judgment means applying your mental faculties to a task or to reviewing the work of others. Using your judgment independently means not allowing anyone else's influence to affect your own judgment.

Consider, for example, being asked to review this paragraph for spelling errors. Would you review it more attentively if you were given the paragraph scribbled on a napkin than you would if you read it in a published book?

You might. Seeing the paragraph in a published book, you might assume it had already been spell-checked by the author, and then reviewed by an editor, a proofreader, and maybe even a formatter. Your understanding of the publishing process might lead you to assume that the spellings in the paragraph are highly unlikely to be incorrect. This kind of assumption is sometimes called "confirmation bias." Confirmation bias, however, is the arch-enemy of independent professional judgment.

Even though you are likely to work with others more skilled and more experienced than you, they are not invulnerable to error. They are human just like you. Even the non-human technologies that you will work with may fail under particular circumstances. In order to discharge your professional duty to make a valuable contribution to quality control, you need to battle against confirmation bias by striving to notice, and speak up about, the errors that others have missed.

Best Practices for Safety Promotion

Although following the principles listed above will go a long way toward reducing errors, experience and research studies have shown that incorporating specific best practices into pharmacy tasks can further improve accuracy.

Best practices can take many forms. Some of the most effective have been part of pharmacy practice for so long that even pharmacy staff forget that safety was the original reason for their introduction.

For example, choosing characteristic shapes and colours for particular pills is an important safety feature. Sildenafil citrate is not naturally diamond-shaped and

BOX 6.3

CASES

Don't Make These Mistakes!

The following case summaries highlight four different errors, made in retail pharmacy settings, that led to complaints or lawsuits. As you read about them, consider strategies to avoid repeating these errors in your own work setting.

1. Wrong Dose (*Koczerzuk c. Pharmacie Jean Coutu*)

In 2004, a patient of a large chain pharmacy in Quebec brought a small-claims court lawsuit against a pharmacy and its staff after receiving (and taking, for nearly two months) Wellbutrin 150 milligrams instead of Wellbutrin 100 milligrams, which was the patient's prescribed and usual dose. The plaintiff suffered some minor symptoms, including hand tremors and loss of appetite. The court awarded the patient $5,000 for her pain and suffering.

2. Sticker Woes (*Boggia c. Chamard*)

In 2008, the Quebec small-claims court awarded a patient $2,500 in damages after she was given the wrong drug—Apo-Nitrazepam—instead of Apo-Metoclop. The pharmacist who was charged with checking prepared prescriptions discovered and corrected the initial mis-substitution after reviewing the bottle of pills; however, the pharmacist was never given the sticker (bearing the wrong drug name) that was created for the erroneous prescription. Because the sticker was neither used nor destroyed, it was discovered by another pharmacist. That pharmacist filled a pill bottle based on the sticker, and gave it to the patient. After taking the Apo-Nitrazepam, the patient suffered symptoms including nausea, dizziness, and stomach pain. She went to hospital, where the error was discovered.

3. Double-Bagged (*Fauteux c. Garneau*)

In another Quebec case, a patient sued a pharmacy for more than $400,000 after taking three drugs intended for other patients. The plaintiff presented three prescriptions (an antibiotic, a sleep aid, and an antidepressant) at a pharmacy. After explaining the dosages and purposes for the prescriptions, the pharmacist instructed the patient to sit and wait while the prescriptions were filled. When they were ready, the cashier called the patient to the cash register. The patient grabbed and took home not only his own package, containing his three medications, but also a package (containing another three medications) intended for a different customer. The patient—not noticing that he had three more bottles of pills than expected (of which three were labelled with a different person's name)—took all six drugs. After a few days, he became sleepy and confused. His brother took him to hospital, where he was admitted voluntarily to the psychiatric ward for 30 days. (The high damages claim was based in large part upon this detail—the plaintiff described the psychiatric ward stay as equivalent to wrongful imprisonment.)

(Continued on the next page.)

BOX 6.3

Luckily for the pharmacy, the court did not find that the cashier was at fault for placing the second patient's package within reach of the first patient, or for not following up with the first patient after she discovered that the second patient's package had disappeared. Instead, the court found that the first patient's hospitalization was not connected to the cashier's actions, and that he took the three additional prescriptions through his own fault. The court awarded no damages to the plaintiff.

4. Phenol Fears (*Sant v. Jack Andrews Kirkfield Pharmacy Ltd.*)

In a case brought in 2001 in Manitoba, a courier and his sister sued a pharmacy that was a client of the courier for damages associated with a phenol leak. While transporting a package from the defendant pharmacy, the courier noticed a strong smell in the car and developed a headache. Upon looking in the hatch, he noticed that a pink chemical had leaked out of the package. Opening the package, he found a bottle with the bottom disintegrated. He called the pharmacist, who advised that the liquid was phenol and that he should be careful not to get any on his hands.

The courier washed his hands, but the phenol smell lingered in the car, where it had spilled on the carpet. He tried to clean it himself but felt ill. After a car wash failed to remove the smell, he bought a new car. He transferred some items, including a plastic tool box, from the old car to the new.

A few days later, while riding in the new car, the courier's sister developed a tingling sensation in her arms and legs. Over the next seven years, she suffered symptoms ranging from dark-coloured urine to paralyzing leg pains, sensitivity to heat and cold, heart palpitations, dizziness, pain in her jaw, kidney and liver pain, peeling scalp, yellowed teeth, and memory loss. She attributed these symptoms to exposure to phenol vapours which she believed had been absorbed by the plastic toolbox and thus transferred to the second car.

The court found some medical evidence to support a connection between the patient's possible brief exposure to a small quantity of phenol vapours and the possibility of symptoms, especially if she was unusually sensitive to phenol. It also found, however, that it was highly unlikely that she actually suffered such exposure from the toolbox. There was also evidence to support the possibility that many of the plaintiff's symptoms were psychosomatic. The court concluded that the plaintiff's suffering was likely due not to the phenol but to post-traumatic stress disorder (PTSD) related to fear of the phenol. It awarded the plaintiff approximately $100,000 in damages for medical, loss-of-earnings, and other costs associated with the incident and the PTSD, finding that the pharmacist was negligent in failing to package the phenol properly. ◙

blue, of course; but as Viagra, it is widely identifiable, on first glance, by the public. Acetaminophen is usually white; ibuprofen usually has a rust-red coating. Some drugs even come in different shapes and colours depending on dosage, a strategy designed to assist both the dispenser and the patient in ensuring that the pills dispensed are the correct dose. Shape and colour are so important, from a safety perspective, that patient handouts often advise the patient to check with a pharmacist if the pills in a refill bottle differ in any way from the patient's expectations (based on previous experience with the drug).

Drug colour and shape is an example of a best practice that comes "built in" to pharmacy stock and supplies. Special labelling—for example, using large type to display the concentration of a clear liquid drug on its ampoule—is another such example.

Other best practices need to be "built in" to pharmacy and pharmacy technician graduates. For example, a properly trained graduate is expected to be familiar with "standard" doses of commonly prescribed medications. For example, the standard dose of ranitidine, a medication for ulcers, is 300 milligrams per day, often dispensed in a divided dose of 150 milligrams twice daily. A pharmacy technician who is familiar with this typical dosage and who receives a prescription that specifies two 150-milligram tablets every four hours should consider contacting the prescribing physician to ensure that the doctor truly intends the patient to take six times the standard daily dose. Developing a working familiarity with standard doses is therefore an important best practice. Another best practice that is often introduced through pharmacy education involves teaching pharmacy and pharmacy technician students about which medications are most likely to be confused with each other, often because they have similar-looking or similar-sounding names: consider, for example, Lanvis (an antineoplastic cancer drug) and Lantus, a form of insulin.

Another class of best practices are those that are built in to pharmacy procedures. For example, pharmacy staff who practise safely generally establish set locations within the workspace for completing specific dispensing tasks (and for storing the products of those tasks). For example, there should be a specific location for:

- prescription forms that have been accepted from clients but that have not been processed in any way;
- prescription forms for which the necessary information has been entered into the patient database, and that have been safety-checked against the patient's file and judged safe (for example, checked against a list of allergies, or compared with other active prescriptions to identify drug interactions);
- prescription forms that, upon review, either raise an issue on their face (for example, the prescription looks like it might be forged, specifies a very high dose, or does not state the drug name clearly enough), or that, after comparison with the patient's file, raise an issue;
- prescription forms entered into the system, safety-checked, approved by the pharmacist, and ready for dispensing;
- labels, safety stickers, and drug information handouts that have been printed;
- labels, safety stickers, and drug information that have been checked for accuracy;
- drugs, equipment, supplies, and materials that are "in use" for dispensing activities, but that do not represent finished prepared products;

- drug products ready for safety-check; and
- packaged and safety-checked drug products ready for distribution to the public.

Careful organization of the workspace permits all employees to quickly identify the status of prescription forms, work in progress, and finished pharmacy products. It also enables staff to understand which work is complete and which tasks remain outstanding; which work has been reviewed for safety and which has not; and which products are safe to distribute to the public.

An important procedure-based best practice that has been specifically included in the NAPRA competencies is the **independent double-check**. Before any pharmacy product is given to a patient, the finished product *must* be independently double-checked by a peer. That peer must, when checking the product, exercise his or her independent professional judgment. NAPRA describes this obligation as follows:

independent double-check
a best practice in which any product dispensed must be independently verified by a peer

Independent Double Check
An independent double check is a process in which a second authorized individual conducts a verification. Such verification can be performed in the presence or absence of the first authorized individual. In either case, the most critical aspect is to maximize the independence of the double check by ensuring that the first authorized individual does not communicate what he or she expects the second authorized individual to see, which would create bias and reduce the visibility of an error. (adapted from Institute for Safe Medications Practices Canada, 2005) (NAPRA, 2007, 10)

Finally, some best practices have been developed in response to research about medication errors and are designed to eliminate the human-error factor completely. Automated drug dispensing machines are an example of a technology that replaces functions (calculation and pill-counting) previously completed by humans. Another strategy that is designed to make common calculation errors nearly impossible is described as follows:

"Forcing functions" are safety design features that completely eliminate the possibility of a specific error. In the study by Parshuram and colleagues, the use of a concentrated morphine solution (10 mg/mL) was strongly associated with serious errors (2- and 10-fold errors). One potential forcing function would be to remove 10 mg/mL morphine solutions from pediatric areas and to use 2 mg/mL solutions exclusively. This simple manoeuvre would not change the rate of error, but it would change the rate of serious error. The Institute for Safe Medication Practice recommends the removal of 10 mg/mL morphine solutions from pediatric care areas. Despite this recommendation, a 2004/05 survey found that up to 25% of pediatric care centres in Ontario continue to stock the concentrated solution. (Etchells, Juurlink, and Levinson, 2008)

The same article recommends some other very basic and simple error-reduction solutions—for example, placing calculators in locations where people who will prepare infusions are working (to prevent calculation errors), and requiring that all narcotic infusions be prepared in the pharmacy instead of in treatment areas (to control the circumstances under which these infusions are prepared).

Many resources are available that can provide further information about pharmacy best practices. A good place to start is the website of the Institute for Safe

Medication Practices (www.ismp.org) and its Canadian branch, the Institute for Safe Medication Practices Canada (www.ismp-canada.org).

By incorporating the pharmacy best practices developed in other pharmacies and health-care facilities, pharmacy staff ensure that they are not "reinventing the wheel" when it comes to patient safety, but rather, learning from the cumulative experience of the profession as a whole. In addition, because every pharmacy work setting and patient base is different, every pharmacy has the potential to develop new best practices of its own. As a pharmacy technician new to practice, you may find yourself uniquely placed to notice situations or procedures that are confusing, or that create a potential for error. In thinking about how to correct these problems, you may very well develop a useful best practice of your own. Keep your eyes open!

Consequences of Unintentional Error

CONSEQUENCES TO THE PATIENT

Many medication errors occur with no consequences at all: the error is not discovered by pharmacy staff, health-care workers, or the patient, and the error is not sufficiently dangerous to injure the patient's health. Not all errors, however, are benign.

Other errors do cause harm—for example, unpleasant side effects or, in the case of underdosing or "wrong drug" errors, lack of relief from the condition that warranted the prescription—but are never reported to the pharmacy or to the patient's health-care professional.

The most serious medication errors cause side effects significant enough to lead to patient reporting or, in some cases, serious reactions or injuries that result in hospital admissions, permanent harm, or even death.

RECEIVING A REPORT FROM A PATIENT

No pharmacy, no matter how well run, can expect to operate for long without receiving a report from a patient about symptoms or a reaction that the patient believes to have been caused by a prescription drug. Handling these reports appropriately is of the utmost importance to patient health, and to the reputation of the pharmacy and its staff.

Patient reports of side effects, reactions, and suspected medication errors must be handled with sensitivity, professionalism, transparency, and in the spirit of care and cooperation. Taking a defensive approach to a patient report will only alienate the patient, and often has the effect of transferring the patient's discouragement with the drug to discouragement with the pharmacy.

When a patient telephones or arrives in the pharmacy to report a problem with a drug, the inquiry should be directed to a pharmacist. The pharmacist will typically review the patient's file, visually inspect the medication (if the patient has brought it to the pharmacy), and ask questions about the side effects or the patient's concerns. Usually, no medication error will be discovered—the patient will simply be suffering from one or more of the known side effects of the medication, or may have a sensitivity or allergy to it. The pharmacist uses professional judgment to advise whether the patient should discontinue the medication, or to suggest steps the patient can take to lessen side effects (for example, some medications are better tolerated when taken with food). In other cases, the pharmacist may recommend that the patient see the health-care provider for advice.

If a medication error is discovered, the pharmacist must immediately disclose the error (and the pharmacy's role in making it) to the patient. The pharmacist should, in all such cases, advise the patient to see his or her health-care provider promptly for a full assessment. It is also appropriate to offer a sincere apology to the patient. Should the patient's health-care provider contact the pharmacy, the pharmacist must provide a full and candid account of the medication error.

The pharmacist who discovered the error should document it in writing. Every pharmacy should adopt or develop a specific form for reporting medication errors, and these forms should be completed and kept on file to assist in external reporting, if appropriate, or internal review. Once the patient's safety has been addressed, the pharmacist should undertake, with the help of the pharmacy team, to determine the causes of the error. This activity is sometimes called a **root cause analysis (RCA)**.

root cause analysis (RCA) a process to identify and remedy problems with a view to avoiding recurrence

Finally, the pharmacist who discovered the error should disclose it to the rest of the pharmacy team, so that the team can learn from it and, if appropriate, adjust pharmacy procedures in an effort to avoid making the same error again.

FORMAL DISCLOSURE OBLIGATIONS

Although the Canadian Patient Safety Institute (CPSI), in its "Canadian Disclosure Guidelines," asserts that "[m]ost professional codes of conduct specifically require disclosure" of adverse events affecting a patient (for example, medication errors), the College's *Code of Ethics* (OCP, 2006), which applies to registered pharmacy technicians, does not mention disclosure.

It would be difficult to argue, however, that non-disclosure to a patient of a known medication error is consistent with the spirit of many of the principles expressed in the College's *Code of Ethics*. Principle One, for example, explains that "[t]he patient's well-being is at the centre of the member's professional and/or business practices." Principle Two requires that members exercise their professional judgment in the best interests of patients, and Principle Five requires that members act with honesty and integrity. Clearly, concealing a known medication error from a patient violates at least these three principles of professional ethics.

The College's "Standards of Practice for Pharmacists" (OCP, 2003) require that pharmacists "acknowledge" medication errors, which, in appropriate cases, means discussing errors with patients and their health-care providers (Operational Component 1.8).

However, although disclosing errors to patients helps preserve and rebuild patients' trust in their caregivers, it does nothing to help prevent the same error from occurring in other facilities. To support the development of safe medication practices, information about medication errors and near-misses must be collected and evaluated by an organization that has the capacity for a more general analysis.

There is currently no mandatory requirement, either in the province of Ontario or in Canada, for pharmacists, pharmacy technicians, or other health-care providers to report medication errors. In fact, many experts on the subject of medication adverse events suggest that a mandatory reporting system might in fact discourage reporting by motivating professionals to conceal their errors. For this reason, most error-reporting systems operate on a voluntary basis and permit reports to be made anonymously.

The most important collector of voluntary medication error reports in Canada is the Institute for Safe Medication Practices Canada (ISMP Canada). This agency encourages professionals who have become aware of medication errors and near-misses to report these using an online form available at https://www.ismp-canada.org/err_report.htm. ISMP Canada uses its analysis of the errors reported to support the development of policies, procedures, and guidelines for error reduction. Access to these resources is also available through the ISMP website.

ERRORS AND PROFESSIONAL DISCIPLINE

Although a pattern of repeated medication errors is likely to be viewed as evidence of competence problems in a pharmacy, a single medication error does not automatically warrant disciplinary action.

First, unless someone makes a formal complaint based on a medication error, the fact of the error is unlikely to come to the attention of the College.

If an error does lead to a complaint, the College conducts an investigation (this includes obtaining a statement of the member's position). The results of the investigation are then put before the Complaints Committee, not the Discipline Committee. The Complaints Committee can take one of a number of possible actions, including suggesting remediation if there is evidence that a practice problem lies at the root of the error.

If the complaint raises an allegation of professional misconduct or incompetence, the Complaints Committee may refer the matter to the Discipline Committee. Between 2003 and 2008, only 16 percent of complaints about medication errors were put before the Discipline Committee. The reason for this low percentage lies in the College's understanding that fault for medication errors can rarely be laid at the feet of a single individual. In a fact sheet about the relationship between medication errors and professional discipline, the College notes that:

> [t]he Complaints Committee in its deliberations recognizes that the cause of medication errors are [sic] often multi-factorial involving, but not limited to, prescription processing and dispensing procedures in place at the pharmacy, counselling issues, staff training and supervision. (OCP, n.d. (b))

Because many errors have multiple causes, the College generally prefers to take a remedial (helping) approach rather than a punitive (punishing) approach in dealing with these errors.

There are exceptions to this approach, however. If the evidence collected in the investigation of the complaint shows that the pharmacist or pharmacy technician, upon discovering the error, failed to take responsibility for it, failed to act quickly in the best interests of the patient, or failed to take steps to prevent a similar error from recurring, the issue becomes one of professional misconduct, and is likely to lead to discipline. The College summarizes its policy as follows:

> [A] medication error on its own does not result in a referral to the Discipline Committee. Rather it is the failure on the part of the Member, after he or she learns of the medication error, to demonstrate that he or she acted in a professional, accountable and ethical manner with an understanding that the needs of the patient are primary in a pharmacist–patient relationship that may result in a referral to the Discipline Committee. (OCP, n.d. (b))

Legal Liability for Errors

Although the chance of suffering professional discipline as a result of a medication error is fairly low, what about lawsuits?

A **lawsuit**—also described as litigation, a case, an action, a suit, or a claim—is a civil law (non-criminal) proceeding "brought" by a plaintiff (the person doing the suing) against a defendant (the person forced to defend the suit). Unlike a criminal case, the government is not a party to a civil lawsuit. For this reason, civil lawsuits are sometimes called "private law" (no public party involved).

There are many kinds of lawsuits based on many branches of the law. A lawsuit in which one person sues another for compensation for harm allegedly done by the other is said to be "based in tort." *Tort* is French for wrong, and tort law is the law of wrongs or harms.

There are a few different kinds of tort suits, but the most likely kind of tort that a pharmacy technician could be accused of is **negligence**. To prove negligence (and become entitled to a judgment, that is, an order for compensation), the plaintiff must prove certain things to the court (a judge, or a judge and jury). The plaintiff must prove that:

1. harm was done (the plaintiff will also need to put a dollar value on this harm);

2. the harm was sufficiently closely connected to an action—or the inappropriate inaction—of the defendant;

3. the defendant owed a duty of care to the plaintiff (pharmacy technicians almost always owe a duty of care to their patients, at least when undertaking normal pharmacy tasks);

4. a reasonable person in the defendant's position could have foreseen (predicted) that harm might be a consequence of the action or inaction; and

5. when the defendant acted—or failed to act—he or she took less care than is to be expected of a "reasonable" pharmacy technician.

Clearly, based on this list, a pharmacy technician's medication error could, under certain circumstances, meet all these criteria, and such a pharmacy technician could potentially be liable in a lawsuit even if the error was an accident.

Luckily, most medication errors do not result in harm serious or lasting enough to prompt a patient to bring a lawsuit. (Litigation can be very expensive.) When you consider the "statistics" and projections about the rate of medication errors, the number of such lawsuits brought in Canada is surprisingly low. Lawsuits are also more likely to result from errors made in clinical settings (for example, errors that result in the death of a newborn) than from errors made by community pharmacy staff.

Also, when a court compares the behaviour of the pharmacy technician to the standard of "a reasonable pharmacy technician," the court allows for the fact that "reasonable" is not the same as "perfect." It is possible to be diligent, competent, careful, and caring, and still make a mistake.

Nevertheless, any time a pharmacy technician completes a prescription (or checks a prescription) that will make its way to a patient, there is the potential for an error that could, conceivably, lead to significant legal liability.

lawsuit
a non-criminal proceeding brought by a plaintiff against a defendant to redress an alleged wrong

negligence
an act committed without intention to cause harm, but which a reasonable person would anticipate might cause harm

There are four ways, from the perspective of the pharmacy technician, to manage this risk. First, the pharmacy technician can accept that no matter how careful he is, perfection is an unrealistic goal, and professional liability insurance—which protects the technician financially should the unthinkable happen—is a good idea.

Second, pharmacy technicians should strive to work with care, keeping in mind that their highest professional responsibility is to the patient. While this statement stands to reason, in practice, pharmacy technicians face competing responsibilities, including a responsibility to their supervisors and employers. Time pressures, a poor work environment, or pressures to perform tasks in which the pharmacy technician does not yet feel competent can create situations in which errors are more likely. Pharmacy technicians must be conscious of these pressures, and must never allow them to affect their competence.

Third, pharmacy technicians must be careful always to practise within the legal limits of their roles. Doing work that falls outside the acceptable scope of practice is an easy way to fall short of the standard of a reasonable technician. One of the most serious ways in which a pharmacy technician can exceed his or her scope of responsibility is to work unsupervised. Being supervised means having the opportunity to ask questions and getting good-quality answers. It also means being assured that one's work is being independently double-checked by another person—preferably a pharmacist.

Finally, a pharmacy technician must act quickly and honestly, in the wake of an error, to communicate to colleagues and to the patient what has happened and the pharmacy technician's own role in the error. In its "Canadian Disclosure Guidelines," the CPSI explains that while many factors can influence a patient's decision to launch litigation in the wake of a medication error, "effective communication and appropriate provision of care after an adverse event are key factors influencing a patient's decision about whether to initiate legal action" (CPSI, 2008, 10).

The United States has seen a few litigated cases involving the work of pharmacy technicians in which the pharmacist (as the technician's supervisor) was sued and found liable for the harm. However, the pharmacy technicians in some of these cases were named as "co-actors" (not a term in common usage in Canada; a Canadian court might rule that the pharmacy technicians were "jointly liable"). Under US law, a person found liable in a lawsuit can sometimes sue co-actors for part or all of the damage award. In the Canadian context, it is more likely that if the facts of the case suggest a pharmacy technician might be responsible for the error, the court would encourage the plaintiff to add the pharmacy technician as a defendant in the case (by serving the technician with a copy of the statement of claim, forcing him or her to play a role in defending the lawsuit). If the pharmacist was responsible for supervising the pharmacy technician, however, and failed to do so competently, it is unlikely that the pharmacist would be able to shrug off all responsibility for the error onto the technician.

Professional Liability Insurance

Many professionals, including lawyers and physicians, must carry professional liability insurance as a prerequisite for registration. Such insurance is designed to provide funds to cover any claim if a client should ever suffer harm because of the professional's actions or inactions. In 2008, the College passed a bylaw making professional liability insurance coverage mandatory for Class A pharmacists and pharmacy interns (OCP, n.d. (e)).

The professional liability insurance requirement did not apply to pharmacy technicians at the time registration was extended to them. However, because pharmacy technicians perform work tasks that could cause harm to patients, they may well be required to carry such insurance in the future. It is worth noting that even before the College made professional liability insurance mandatory, some pharmacists arranged it on their own initiative. Pharmacy technicians can do the same.

Most pharmacies carry liability insurance, but because it is not personalized to individual practitioners, a pharmacy technician may not be covered under certain circumstances. In general, this kind of liability insurance covers actions by employees that fall only within the normal terms of their employment. Employees acting outside the terms of their employment who cause harm may not be covered. For example, a pharmacy technician who, contrary to the rules of practice, conducts dispensing activities completely unsupervised—that is, with no pharmacist on the premises, and no pharmacist available to consult by phone—would be acting outside the permissible terms of employment of a pharmacy technician and would therefore not be covered by the pharmacy's insurance.

Errors and the Criminal Law

Is it possible for an error to lead to a criminal conviction? This is highly unlikely, for two reasons.

First, with a few very narrow exceptions, the difference between an accident and a crime is intent to cause harm. While being reckless in the face of the possibility of harm is sometimes sufficient "intent," recklessness goes well beyond making an accidental error. A true error—one that did not involve serious negligence—is very unlikely to support a criminal charge.

The second reason a criminal conviction is unlikely is the standard of proof required to support a criminal charge. In a civil lawsuit (discussed above), the facts of the case need to be proved "on a balance of probabilities." That means that the plaintiff need only prove that there is more than a 50 percent chance that the defendant was responsible for the harm. In a criminal case, the standard of proof is much higher: to support a criminal conviction, the prosecution must prove all the elements of the crime (including intent) "beyond a reasonable doubt." If a defendant alleges an honest accident, the prosecution will likely have difficulty convincing the court, *beyond a reasonable doubt*, that the mistake was intentional.

Nevertheless, there have been a few instances in Canada of criminal charges being laid in circumstances where the defendant was alleged to have harmed someone by accident. The most famous case is that of Susan Nelles, a nurse who was charged with murder in the early 1980s in the wake of a number of baby deaths in hospital. Nelles was eventually exonerated.

In the unlikely event that you are ever charged with a criminal offence as a result of a professional error, you would need to obtain legal counsel immediately.

Addiction-Related Practice Problems

Although an isolated error is unlikely to result in professional discipline, an unusual frequency or pattern of errors or complaints would likely attract a practice review to determine whether a pharmacy staff person is competent to practise. The many possible causes of incompetence include poor or insufficient training, recklessness, poor organization of pharmacy workflow, understaffing, or physical or mental health problems affecting a staff member. Another potential cause of practice problems is addiction.

Pharmacists and pharmacy technicians, like the rest of the population, sometimes succumb to alcoholism or drug addiction. Should you find yourself suffering from an addiction, it is important to obtain treatment, even if you don't believe that the addiction has affected your fitness to practise. Impairment due to drugs or alcohol is absolutely incompatible with careful pharmacy practice.

If you suspect that a colleague's competence is being affected by an addiction, failing to act on your suspicions constitutes a failure to fulfill your own professional responsibilities. The safety of your patients is your first priority.

So, how do you take action?

If the addiction problem is your own, the first contact you might make is with your family physician. Your physician can discuss treatment options with you. Having taken this first step toward recovery can make you feel more comfortable, responsible, and in control when you approach your employer or your professional college.

The next step is to speak with your employer about getting the time off that you need to address your addiction. If you have a trusted supervisor, you can discuss the problem privately with him or her. Should you need to approach a more senior staff member to get time off, your supervisor may be able to support you in making that contact.

If you act quickly once you come to terms with your addiction and withdraw from professional practice while you recover, you may not be obliged to inform the College of your troubles (especially if you have made no serious errors and no complaints have been made about your work). The College does, however, recommend that professionals suffering from addiction make use of the Professionals' Health Program, offered by the Ontario Medical Association (OMA, 2009), which is designed to support health professionals suffering from addictions and psychiatric disorders.

If the problem is a colleague's addiction, the best first step almost always is to speak privately with the person. Sometimes, simply knowing that others have noticed the effects of an addiction can prompt the addict to take action. Knowing that your next step will be to speak with your supervisor may also motivate your colleague to obtain help.

If you have spoken with your troubled colleague and do not notice a prompt improvement, you have a duty to make an additional report. If your colleague has a supervisor, you should speak privately with him or her. If your colleague does not have a supervisor, and you believe that his or her addiction poses a risk to patients, you must file a report with the College.

You should avoid making an anonymous report, because the College will likely need information from you. For information about how to handle the difficult task of reporting a colleague's incapacity, consult the College's guideline on the matter, "Reporting Incapacity" (OCP, n.d. (g)).

AVOIDING AND PREVENTING FRAUD AND INTENTIONAL MALFEASANCE

Introduction

The foregoing sections of this chapter address accidental errors. Unfortunately, pharmacy staffers have occasionally committed intentional improper acts.

Intentional **malfeasance** on the part of pharmacists or pharmacy technicians generally takes the form of actions intended to generate or protect income in an illegal or improper way, for example, by overcharging patients or the government, by engaging in illegal commercial activities, or through tax evasion. Malfeasance motivated by financial gain often can, and does, hurt patients. For example, a pharmacy technician who steals oxycodone from inventory to sell on the street risks the health of every person who purchases the drugs. A pharmacist who runs an online pharmacy that does not require patients to prove that their prescriptions were written by a health-care provider after a proper medical assessment also puts patients at risk.

The professional standards and the laws that guide pharmacy practice in Canada exist for the protection of the public. Any action that falls afoul of those standards and rules carries the potential of harm either to the health of individual patients or to the health and viability of the health-care system as a whole. Professional misconduct also poses a threat to the careers and reputation of all those who become involved in it. The following sections address the issue of professional misconduct and its repercussions.

malfeasance
wrongful conduct by a professional who has a duty of care to the public

Fraud or Malfeasance by a Pharmacy Technician

RISKS

As a registered pharmacy technician, you will be expected to be aware of all standards and laws that apply to your professional activities. Any action you take that violates a professional standard may jeopardize your registered status, not to mention your job and your professional reputation. Violation of any law that applies to you specifically as a pharmacy technician, or even simply as a member of society, can lead to serious consequences, whether under a provincial statute (provincial offences) or under the *Criminal Code* of Canada.

In addition, acting outside the acceptable scope of professional practice can make you vulnerable to civil litigation and can render invalid any liability insurance coverage you may hold personally, or that your employer may hold on your behalf.

While all residents of Canada are subject to the criminal law and can suffer consequences from breaking it, people who hold professional designations (including that of registered pharmacy technician) face the additional risk of losing their designation—and often, the ability to make a living doing the work for which they were trained—as a result of a criminal conviction.

EXAMPLES OF IMPROPER OR ILLEGAL ACTIVITIES

Despite these consequences, some pharmacists and pharmacy technicians do choose to break the law, or to violate the standards of their profession. Some ways in which a pharmacy technician could get into trouble include:

- knowingly dispensing drugs to a patient in the absence of a valid prescription;
- knowingly dispensing drugs to a patient who is obtaining drugs in a manner not intended by his or her health-care providers (for example, a patient who is "**double doctoring**"—seeking duplicate or multiple prescriptions for a drug in order to abuse or resell the drug);
- intentionally dispensing the wrong drug (for example, so that the pharmacy technician can steal the drug listed on the prescription for the purpose of illegal resale);
- other intentional dispensing discrepancies (dispensing the wrong quantity or strength);
- stealing drugs from inventory for personal use or resale;
- falsifying inventory records;
- falsifying prescription or patient data records;
- making false statements of income, expenses, or deductions on tax forms;
- filing false claims for reimbursement with private or public insurers;
- falsifying records related to the loss or destruction of inventory; or
- assisting a colleague, or failing to report a colleague, who is involved in the above activities.

A pharmacy technician can also get into difficulty by working in a pharmacy that is not properly licensed, or that is involved in inappropriate dispensing activities. For example, online pharmacies are subject to important restrictions. Pharmacy technicians should not prepare drugs for dispensing to patients who have obtained their prescriptions through improper means—for example, without a diagnosis, or without seeing a health professional. There are also rules relating to the filling of prescriptions for overseas customers.

Finally, pharmacy technicians violate the standards of their profession when they engage in activities beyond their accepted scope of practice—for example, by dispensing drugs without supervision by a pharmacist, or by entering into an inappropriate relationship with a patient or colleague (for example, a sexually abusive or harassing relationship).

CONSEQUENCES OF MISCONDUCT

A pharmacy technician whose misconduct is discovered can expect one or more of the following consequences:

- termination for cause by the employer (which means no access to employment insurance benefits and no positive references);
- a complaint made to the College by the employer, a colleague, or a patient, which may result in a practice review, a recommendation for remediation, and/or discipline proceedings. Valid complaints based on professional misconduct nearly always result in a suspension from practice or the

---

double doctoring
A practice by which the patient obtains duplicate or multiple prescriptions for the same drug from different doctors, usually for illicit resale

permanent withdrawal of the practitioner's registration. Loss of registration in one province can sometimes preclude registration in other provinces;

- a lawsuit or other claim launched by an injured party (for example, a claim for reimbursement from the Ontario Drug Benefit Plan, if the pharmacy technician has falsified claims);

- being charged with an offence under a provincial statute (for example, the offence of engaging in a controlled act without authorization under the *Regulated Health Professions Act*, or an overcharging offence under the *Ontario Drug Benefit Act*;

- being charged with an offence under the federal *Controlled Drugs and Substances Act*; and/or

- being charged with an offence under the *Criminal Code* of Canada (for example, an offence based on theft, fraud, or sexual assault).

All these risks come with serious—sometimes irreversible—career consequences. Some can lead to imprisonment. Even if offences fail to "stick" (result in a conviction), damage to a professional's reputation from allegations of misconduct is almost inevitable. If you hope to have a long and successful career as a pharmacy technician, you must avoid becoming involved—even as a silent bystander—in any activity that does not fall squarely within the scope of your duties.

Should you find yourself facing a complaint or charge based on professional misconduct, you should obtain legal advice. No matter what the circumstances, you are entitled to be treated as innocent until proven guilty. Particularly if you believe that the allegations against you are false or inaccurate, you should seek support from the professional associations in which you are a member.

It is important to remember that the College of Pharmacists is, as a professional regulator, an advocate for the public. The College is responsible for ensuring that the public receives high-quality care from pharmacists and pharmacy technicians. In the event of a complaint against a pharmacy technician, the College cannot be counted on to "take your side" in a dispute; in fact, to be partisan in this way would violate the College's mandate. If you are looking for supporters and advocates, you should turn instead to your professional association and to your colleagues.

When You Suspect a Colleague of Malfeasance

Because your first priority, as a health-care professional, is the safety and welfare of your patients, you are obliged to take action if you suspect that a colleague is acting counter to the public interest. Specific details of this general obligation are set out in NAPRA's "Professional Competencies for Pharmacy Technicians" in Competency Element 1.2.2, which requires the pharmacy technician to:

1.2.2 Question, report, and assist in the resolution of potential and actual unsafe, illegal, unethical, or unprofessional actions or situations.

    i. identify, report, and correct errors, omissions, and unsafe practices or situations.

    ii. identify and report conduct that is illegal, unethical, or unprofessional to the appropriate authorities.

    iii. document the incident and actions taken.

BOX 6.4

CASES

Pharmacist Misconduct and Professional Discipline

The following case summaries involve disciplinary action against pharmacists, not pharmacy technicians. But they give an idea of the kinds of activities that result in professional consequences.

1. Dispensing Without Authority (*Murray Dale* Case)

In a 2004 case, an Oakville pharmacist was found guilty of professional misconduct after an investigation revealed that he dispensed Paxil to a patient without a prescription. The patient was the wife of the pharmacist's friend, and he dispensed the drug to her because he knew she was undergoing significant stress (her husband was dying). The pharmacist admitted his misconduct to the College and expressed remorse. He was reprimanded, suspended from practice for one month, and ordered to pay the College $2,000 in costs.

2. Fraud (*Christine Bolubash* Case)

In a 2009 case, the College found a pharmacist guilty of irregularities involving "dispensing" and claiming reimbursement payments for patients who had in fact moved away or died. The pharmacist was reprimanded, ordered to undergo remediation, prohibited from acting as a designated manager for three years, suspended for three months, and charged $2,500 in costs.

3. Covering Up a Dispensing Error (*Mark Haditaghi* Case)

In 2007, the College heard a case describing a dispensing error (patient given Apo-Azathioprine instead of methotrexate). The evidence showed that in the wake of the error, the responsible pharmacist amended records to cover it up, and failed to produce the patient's original prescription form when requested to do so by the College. While acknowledging that the dispensing pharmacist was under significant personal stress at the time of the error, the College found that he had shown insufficient regard for the patient's welfare and insufficient remorse for the harm he caused her. The College ordered discipline including a three-month suspension, remediation, and costs of $7,500.

4. Theft (*Babak Khazra* Case)

In a 2002 case, a pharmacist was made subject to discipline after he was convicted of theft of drugs worth more than $5,000 from his employer (a Zellers pharmacy). The drugs stolen were not narcotics for sale on the street, but rather drugs for high blood pressure and cholesterol control, and for cancer treatment. The pharmacist had allegedly stolen the drugs for illegal distribution to impoverished patients in Iran. The pharmacist was charged with misconduct, reprimanded, and suspended for six months.

5. Non-Supervision (*Marvin Turk* Case)

In a 2005 decision, the College found a pharmacy designated manager guilty of professional misconduct for allowing a grocery pharmacy to operate on two separate occasions with no pharmacist present. On one occasion, the on-duty pharmacist walked out after a dispute with a store manager; on the other occasion, no pharmacist ever arrived at work. On both occasions, pharmacy technicians (after telephoning the designated manager to report that no pharmacist was on premises) dispensed drugs to patients without supervision. The designated manager was reprimanded, prohibited from acting as a designated manager for three years, ordered to undergo remediation, and charged with $10,000 in costs.

Source: Ontario College of Pharmacists (n.d. (a)). ▣

Another specific aspect of your obligation is stated in the College's "Proposed Standards of Practice for Registered Pharmacy Technicians," which reads: "[t]he pharmacy technician responds appropriately to activities which would divert drugs from their intended legitimate use that come to his/her attention" (Operational Component 5.2).

Sometimes a new or junior employee encounters a situation at work that he or she does not fully understand, but that raises suspicions. If you are asked to do anything, or you observe anything that makes you uncomfortable, the best course of action is to speak up about your discomfort. Explaining your concerns in a non-confrontational way may lead to two possible responses. Hopefully, your supervisor or employer will respond with understanding and candour, and will explain the facts, legalities, or ethics of the situation in a way that helps you understand that what is going on is within the scope of acceptable practice. If your suspicions are warranted, however, your supervisor may be defensive or evasive, may tell you to mind your own business, or may admit to being involved in improper activities.

If a discussion with your supervisor confirms your suspicions, you have two new responsibilities: you must decline to participate in the misconduct, and you must report it.

Identifying the person to whom you should direct your report can be a challenge. The first factor to consider is the safety of your patients. If you suspect that a colleague's actions pose an immediate health risk to a patient—for example, your colleague is dispensing the wrong drug to a patient so that she can pocket the prescribed drug—you must act before the patient has a chance to consume the wrong drug. Speak to your colleague immediately, and let her know that unless the product to be dispensed is corrected, you will advise the patient of the error.

If there is no immediate risk to a patient, and you have already discussed your concerns with the person you suspect of misconduct, it is usually best to report the problem to your supervisor, your colleague's supervisor, or both. This may not be the end of the matter; if the supervisor is obliged, in turn, to file a report with the College or the police, you will most likely be asked to assist in filing it.

The College has issued a statement cautioning practitioners against going directly to the College with certain kinds of complaints when the matter could be better and more discreetly handled within the pharmacy. If the problem does not pose a direct safety risk to patients and is more of an interpersonal or work-style conflict (for example, a pharmacy staff person is late for shifts, is rude to others, or doesn't tidy up the work area promptly), staff should attempt to resolve the issue internally first.

If the misconduct is more serious—for example, it involves theft or fraud, or poses a risk to the public—a prompt complaint to the College is appropriate, because covering up for another staff member can endanger the professional reputation of the entire pharmacy staff.

In general, if the conduct involves theft, fraud, violence, or any other illegal conduct, it should be reported to the police. In rare cases, the conduct may be trivial enough that it can be handled internally—for example, a colleague who brings home pharmacy supplies (latex gloves, hand sanitizer, pens) should probably be warned not to do this again instead of reported to the police. However, if the employee were instead bringing home narcotics, it would be inappropriate *not* to make a police report. If you are uncertain about when to call police, it is best to consult with more experienced colleagues first. Treating the misconduct of colleagues seriously makes it less likely that you will be implicated in the improper or illegal activity.

Improper Prescribing Practices

Pharmacy technicians are not physicians. Under normal circumstances, a pharmacy technician is expected to defer to a patient's physician's judgment when it comes to which medicines should be prescribed (although good physicians often welcome pharmacists' advice about drug options). With experience, however, pharmacy technicians become familiar with typical dosages and other treatment parameters— for example, the typical duration of treatment with a particular drug.

With experience also comes the ability, on the part of pharmacy staff, to notice unusual prescriptions or patterns of prescribing. Not all physicians, unfortunately, are absolutely scrupulous. In rare cases, a physician may prescribe inappropriately— in a manner that poses a risk to patients. Examples of inappropriate prescribing may include:

- prescribing inappropriately high doses, or large prescriptions, of commonly abused medications (for example, tranquilizers or pain medications);
- prescribing a medication over the long term when long-term use is not warranted or is unsafe (for example, prescribing repeats of an addictive pain medication long after the patient is likely to be pain-free);
- prescribing drugs to a patient who is not suffering from the condition for which the drugs are approved (for example, prescribing a growth hormone to a patient who is not suffering from a growth disorder); or
- prescribing drugs commonly sold "on the street" to a patient who has a history of illegal trafficking in those drugs.

A more benign form of inappropriate prescribing occurs when a physician writes repeated new prescriptions without conducting periodic reassessments of the patient's condition.

If, as a pharmacy technician, you are asked to dispense a prescription that you believe to be inappropriate for some reason, you should bring the matter to the attention of your supervising pharmacist. If the pharmacist shares your concerns, he will likely telephone the physician to ask for clarification. In serious cases, the pharmacist may elect to refuse to serve the particular patient affected. This is a situation that should be handled with great sensitivity and caution; for more information about how to terminate the pharmacy–patient relationship, you can read the College's policy on the matter (OCP, n.d. (c)).

Fraud and Suspected Fraud by Patients

Finally, pharmacy technicians may develop suspicions about a patient's honesty. A written prescription may contain details that lead the pharmacy technician to believe that it is inauthentic (forged). If you have any reason to suspect that a patient's prescription is not authentic, you should ask your supervising pharmacist to telephone the prescriber for confirmation. Operational Component 2.1.2 made under Standard 2 of the College's "Proposed Standards of Practice for Registered Pharmacy Technicians" states:

2.1.2 The pharmacy technician checks for authenticity of the prescription.

- Determines whether the prescription meets all legal requirements, and where it does not, notifies the pharmacist, and follows up using applicable policies, effective communication, and discretion.
- Uses healthcare provider lists, where available, to determine current status of prescriber's privileges.

Another form of inappropriate conduct by patients is called "double doctoring." In an attempt to obtain greater quantities of a particular drug, the patient may visit several health-care practitioners to request multiple prescriptions for the same drug. Smart patients who engage in this activity rarely bring the duplicate prescriptions to the same pharmacy, but slip-ups can occur. If you suspect that a patient is engaged in double doctoring, you should report your suspicions to the pharmacist. The pharmacist can then contact (one of) the patient's physicians to alert him or her to the situation.

KEY TERMS

adverse drug event
double doctoring
independent double-check
lawsuit
malfeasance
medication discrepancy
negligence
root cause analysis (RCA)

REFERENCES

Boggia c. Chamard. 2008 CanLII 12616 (QCCQ).

Canadian Patient Safety Institute (CPSI). (2008, May). Canadian disclosure guidelines. Retrieved May 30, 2010 from http://www.patientsafetyinstitute. ca/English/toolsResources/disclosure/Documents/CPSI%20-%20 Canadian%20Disclosure%20Guidlines%20English.pdf.

Controlled Drugs and Substances Act. 1996. SC 1996, c. 19.

Criminal Code. 1985. RSC 1985, c. C-46.

Fauteux c. Garneau. 2006 CanLII 5279 (QCCS).

Etchells, E., D. Juurlink, and W. Levinson. (2008). Medication errors: The human factor. Commentary. *Canadian Medical Association Journal*, 178(1), 63–64.

Institute for Safe Medication Practices (ISMP). (n.d.). Frequently asked questions. Retrieved May 30, 2010 from http://www.ismp.org/faq.asp.

Institute of Medicine (IOM). (2007). *Preventing medication errors.* Washington, DC: National Academies Press.

Koczerzuk c. Pharmacie Jean Coutu. 2004 CanLII 45672 (QCCQ).

National Association of Pharmacy Regulatory Authorities (NAPRA). (2007, September). Professional competencies for Canadian pharmacy technicians at entry to practice. Retrieved May 11, 2010 from http://www.ocpinfo.com/ Client/ocp/OCPHome.nsf/object/Pharmacy+Technician+Competencies+Pr ofile/$file/PT_Competencies.pdf.

Ontario College of Pharmacists (OCP). (n.d. (a)). Discipline cases. Retrieved June 1, 2010 from http://www.ocpinfo.com/client/ocp/ocphome.nsf/ (DisciplineCasesDivided)?OpenView&T=1.

Ontario College of Pharmacists (OCP). (n.d. (b)). Do medication errors result in a referral to the Discipline Committee? Retrieved May 30, 2010 from http://www.ocpinfo.com/client/ocp/OCPHome.nsf/web/Medication+Errors+ Result+in+a+Referral+to+the+Discipline ?OpenDocument.

Ontario College of Pharmacists (OCP). (n.d. (c)). Ending the pharmacist patient relationship. Retrieved May 31, 2010 from http://www.ocpinfo.com/client/ ocp/OCPHome.nsf/web/Ending+the+Pharmacist+Patient+Relationship.

Ontario College of Pharmacists (OCP). (n.d. (d)). The learning portfolio and professional profile. Retrieved May 12, 2010 from http://www.ocpinfo.com/ client/ocp/OCPHome.nsf/d12550e436a1716585256ac90065aa1c/f7da1b2ce df4094e85256c32006f08e9?OpenDocument.

Ontario College of Pharmacists (OCP). (n.d. (e)). Professional liability insurance. Retrieved May 31, 2010 from http://www.ocpinfo.com/client/ocp/ OCPHome.nsf/d12550e436a1716585256ac90065aa1c/ 5478fd3ade008f54852572fe004c4064?OpenDocument.

Ontario College of Pharmacists (OCP). (n.d. (f)). Proposed standards of practice for registered pharmacy technicians. Retrieved May 11, 2010 from http:// www.ocpinfo.com/client/ocp/OCPHome.nsf/object/Proposed_For_ Techs/$file/Proposed_For_Techs.pdf.

Ontario College of Pharmacists (OCP). (n.d. (g)). Reporting incapacity. Retrieved May 31, 2010 from http://www.ocpinfo.com/client/ocp/OCPHome.nsf/web/ Reporting+Incapacity.

Ontario College of Pharmacists (OCP). (2003). Standards of practice. Retrieved May 30, 2010, from http://www.ocpinfo.com/client/ocp/OCPHome.nsf/ web/Standards+of+Practice.

Ontario College of Pharmacists (OCP). (2006, December). Code of ethics. Retrieved May 30, 2010, from http://www.ocpinfo.com/client/ocp/ OCPHome.nsf/d12550e436a1716585256ac90065aa1c/ fd4c299cfd1271cf852572eb0052aa67?OpenDocument.

Ontario Drug Benefit Act. 1990. RSO 1990, c. O.10.

Ontario Medical Association (OMA). (2009). Professionals' health program. Retrieved June 1, 2010 from http://www.phpoma.org/index.htm.

Parshuram, C.S, T. To, W. Seto, et al. (2008). Systematic evaluation of errors occurring during the preparation of intravenous medication. *Canadian Medical Association Journal*, 178(i), 42–48.

Regulated Health Professions Act. 1991. SO 1991, c. 18.

Sant v. Jack Andrews Kirkfield Pharmacy Ltd. 2001 CanLII 294 (MBQB).

REVIEW EXERCISES

Discussion Questions

Review the following scenarios and discuss the most appropriate actions that you, as a registered pharmacy technician, should take in response to them.

1. You are asked to check a prepared prescription for accuracy. The original prescription and the pill bottle specify Ativan 0.5 milligrams; however, the pills in the bottle are, upon inspection, Ativan 1 milligram, and there are half the number of pills dispensed than prescribed. You speak with the pharmacist, who advises that Ativan 0.5 milligrams is out of stock and that you should simply advise the patient to split the tablets in half before taking a half-tablet as required.

2. You are working as a pharmacy technician in a retail pharmacy under the supervision of a lone pharmacist. The pharmacist must, owing to a family emergency, leave the pharmacy for a couple of hours. He instructs you to carry on your work as usual (including dispensing tasks) and to call his cellphone if you have any questions.

3. While working as a pharmacy technician in a retail pharmacy, you observe a fellow pharmacy technician self-administer a prescription migraine headache drug from inventory. When you question your colleague, she advises that she has a prescription for the drug. Her personal supply has run out and she has left the prescription at home. She promises that she will bring in the prescription (and payment) the following day and "make things right."

Review Questions

1. Why is it difficult to collect reliable data about the rate of medication errors in Canada?

2. Which member of a pharmacy's staff is responsible for preventing and detecting errors?

3. List at least three high-quality sources of information about best practices for error prevention.

4. List the principles essential to safe practice.

5. Define a safety "best practice."

6. What is an independent double-check, and why is it important to patient safety?

7. List at least three problems, in a pharmacy work environment, that can lead to medication errors.

8. What should you do when a patient arrives at the pharmacy to report a suspected medication error?

9. What are the possible consequences, for a pharmacy technician, of making a serious medication error?

10. What should you do, while working as a pharmacy technician, if you observe another staff person doing something unethical, unprofessional, or illegal?

11. What should you do, as a pharmacy technician, if you suspect something improper about a prescriber's practices?

12. What should you do, as a pharmacy technician, if you suspect something improper about a patient's actions?

CHAPTER 7

Working Safely and Productively with Others

Pharmacists and pharmacy technicians must comply with health and safety regulations with regard to protective equipment and safety protocols.

LEARNING OBJECTIVES

After completing this chapter, you should be able to:

- Understand the importance of productive and respectful working relationships.

- Explain your role as a member of the pharmacy team.

- Describe the steps you should take to resolve a conflict with a colleague.

- Define "discrimination" and "harassment" and understand your right to work in an environment free of both.

- Describe the legislation that is in place to protect your physical safety on the job.

- Understand your role as a member of the occupational health and safety Internal Responsibility System.

INTRODUCTION

Many working adults spend more than 35 percent of their waking hours at work. Working in a comfortable, supportive, and rewarding environment is important to people's happiness, health, and overall quality of life.

When work involves caring for the health of others, a good working environment is even more important. As you have read in earlier chapters of this textbook, poor working conditions can lead to an increased error rate—an unacceptable consequence for professionals whose first priority must be the health and safety of patients.

Problems with the working environment can be caused by a variety of factors. Staff who are required to work together may develop poor interpersonal relationships that interfere with communication and collaboration. The conditions of employment (hours of work, staffing levels, job security, and availability of vacation and sick time) can be unsatisfactory. There may be interpersonal problems—such as discrimination or harassment—that go beyond poor communication. Finally, there can be problems with the physical environment, for example, safety hazards, that create an unacceptable risk of illness or injury for staff.

This chapter provides a brief overview of these issues.

WORKING RELATIONSHIPS

Introduction

Health care is delivered through the cooperation of many kinds of health professionals. Physicians, nurses, and pharmacists have worked together for centuries; in the last few decades, other professions have been added to the complement—including pharmacy technicians.

Research suggests that a team-based approach to health care fosters a consultative approach in which knowledge and experience are shared among experts. The key ingredient in team-based care is collaboration: each member of the team must do two things—first, take responsibility for his or her share of patient care, and second, communicate effectively with other team members.

The inclusion of pharmacy technicians in modern pharmacies has evolved from a need to balance professionalism and efficiency. As pharmacies become busier, pharmacists need more skilled help. Many pharmacy tasks go beyond basic customer service and retail management, especially where patient safety is concerned. Pharmacy technicians fill a special need for helpers who can manage a broad range of routine tasks, but who can also exercise professional judgment.

Pharmacy technicians who understand the importance of their role, and who strike the appropriate balance between working within their skill set and thinking independently, are an invaluable asset to a patient's health-care team, or "circle of care," as described in the National Association of Pharmacy Regulatory Authorities' "Professional Competencies for Canadian Pharmacy Technicians at Entry to Practice" (National Association of Pharmacy Regulatory Authorities [NAPRA], 2007).

The professional standards that apply to your profession can help you understand your role on your patients' health-care team.

Professional Standards

Several of the College's "Proposed Professional Standards for Registered Pharmacy Technicians" (Ontario College of Pharmacists [OCP], n.d.) touch on the management of interpersonal relationships in the pharmacy workplace. Issues addressed in the standards include:

- maintaining personal integrity;
- understanding staff roles;
- practising within the limits of one's role;
- taking responsibility for work and decisions;
- working collaboratively; and
- communication among the pharmacy team and referring patient inquiries.

Before you can work effectively with others, you need to understand and assume responsibility for your own role on the pharmacy care team. Operational Component 1.3 under Standard 1 states that a pharmacy technician must demonstrate both personal and professional integrity. Doing so includes complying with the following specific standards:

1.3.1 The pharmacy technician understands the roles, rights, and responsibilities of and collaborates with members of the pharmacy and healthcare teams to promote the patient's health and wellness.

1.3.2 The pharmacy technician recognizes and practises within the limits of his or her professional role and personal knowledge and expertise.

1.3.3 The pharmacy technician accepts responsibility for his or her decisions and actions.

One of the most important aspects of professionalism, for a pharmacy technician, is understanding when you can work independently and when you should ask for assistance or refer an issue to a pharmacist. For example, Operational Component 2.2.6 under the College's Standard 2 requires you to use your critical thinking and problem-solving skills to determine whether or not it's appropriate for you to receive an orally transmitted prescription independently:

2.2.6 The pharmacy technician when receiving orally transmitted prescriptions uses critical thinking and problem-solving skills to recognize the need for pharmacist intervention and to notify the pharmacist.

While independent work on the part of a pharmacy technician frees the pharmacist to handle other matters, it's important that you not overstep the bounds of your role, and that you learn to view your co-workers as a team. A pharmacy technician who is a good team player works collaboratively when collaboration is called for (see Operational Component 1.3.5). Some of the elements of collaborative work are described in NAPRA's "Professional Competencies for Canadian Pharmacy Technicians at Entry to Practice." NAPRA Competency 2 requires that pharmacy technicians "participate in the circle of care" and, more specifically:

2.1.3 Cooperate with and show respect for all members of the interprofessional team.
   i. make expertise available to others.
   ii. share relevant information.

      iii. contribute to achieving mutually determined goals and objectives.

      iv. support other professionals and accept their support to optimize health outcomes.

2.1.4 Refer patients to other health care professionals when required.

      i. determine if referral is necessary.

      ii. collaborate with the pharmacist to identify the most appropriate health care provider for referral.

      iii. recognize and refer situations requiring the knowledge, skills, and abilities of a pharmacist to the pharmacist.

      iv. work with other health care providers to achieve the desired health outcomes.

2.1.5 Understand, participate in, and promote patient safety initiatives.

2.1.6 Participate as a team member in organized initiatives for disaster and emergency preparedness.

The College's proposed Standard 4, which deals with responsibilities related to the preparation of pharmacy products, requires that pharmacy technicians actively pursue support from their colleagues by following preparation instructions and, where appropriate, requesting that the pharmacist (or in some cases, another pharmacy technician) check the accuracy of calculations.

Once the product is prepared, the pharmacy technician must actively ensure that it has been checked before being released to the patient. Operational Component 4.1 states:

> The pharmacy technician confirms that the pharmacist has had the opportunity to review the prescription and patient profile or health record, prior to the release of the pharmaceutical product.

Finally, Operational Component 5.1.2 reminds pharmacy technicians that not only are they responsible for following pharmacy policies and procedures, but that as members of the patient's health-care team, they are expected to play a role in developing and refining those policies, procedures, workflow patterns, and quality checks.

An important aspect of effective collaboration is communication. The College's proposed standards provide specific guidelines about many aspects of workplace communication. For example, Standard 6 states:

> The pharmacy technician, as a member of the pharmacy team, uses knowledge and skills and follows established policies and procedures to communicate with patients or their agents, pharmacists, and other healthcare providers.

The operational components associated with Standard 6 explain that effective interpersonal communication includes:

- communicating, within the pharmacy technician's role, to support the work of the pharmacy;
- referring all therapeutic inquiries to the pharmacist;
- using established communication policies, procedures, and protocols when communicating both with patients and with co-workers (for example, the pharmacy is likely to have a policy that should a pharmacy technician have

a question about a patient's confidential health information, she should speak with the pharmacist out of earshot of any other patients);

■ demonstrating a caring and professional attitude; and

■ maintaining patient confidentiality.

Standard 6 also states that whenever a pharmacy technician has direct contact with patients, he or she should ensure that patients know they are dealing with a pharmacy technician (and not a pharmacist) and, when appropriate, should explain the role of a pharmacy technician to the patient.

Direct contact with patients by pharmacy technicians poses an interesting professional challenge. Good pharmacy technicians are professional and knowledgeable, and may wear lab coats similar to those of pharmacists. Patients may understandably have trouble differentiating pharmacy technicians from pharmacists, and direct therapeutic questions to them. It is up to the pharmacy technician and the pharmacist to develop work patterns that allow the pharmacist to take over without delay when a patient's questions turn to therapeutic issues. For example, a patient is most likely to ask therapeutic questions when the prepared prescription is handed to him. If time permits, the pharmacy may opt to organize its work so that a pharmacy technician handles prescription intake, but the pharmacist hands the prepared prescription to the patient, creating a natural opportunity for therapeutic counselling. Should the patient ask questions at the intake stage, however, the pharmacist should be prepared to respond quickly to the pharmacy technician's signal for backup.

Therapeutic questions do not always come from patients; a question about the patient's health or health-care regimen may originate from a physician or other professional. In this case also, the pharmacy technician must refer the question to the pharmacist (OCP Standard 2, Operational Component 2.2.9).

As you can see, developing good working relationships with colleagues is not simply a matter of courtesy or a personal virtue. Because many aspects of teamwork and communication are incorporated into standards that apply to pharmacy technicians, working well with others is a core component of professionalism. And it's an essential part of your job.

EMPLOYMENT STANDARDS

Introduction

The contract between an Ontario employer and employees is not the only document that informs and shapes the employment relationship. Employment law—a distinct branch of the law that incorporates statute law, contract, and tort (civil) elements—influences many aspects of employment relationships. Several employment statutes, such as the Ontario *Employment Standards Act*, the Ontario *Labour Relations Act*, the *Canada Labour Code*, and provincial and federal human rights and anti-discrimination statutes, restrict and dictate the terms of private employment contracts, and "read in" certain rules that are not explicitly included in those contracts.

The Canadian and Ontario governments, through these statutes, attempt to ensure that employers treat their employees fairly and equitably. In fact, for employees covered by the *Employment Standards Act* (ESA), if there are differences between the benefits provided under an employee's employment contract and the benefits guaranteed under the legislation, the employee is entitled to the greater right or benefit offered—whether it's under the employment contract or under the legislation. Employers are not permitted to "contract out" of the ESA.

Employees who suspect that they are being denied an employment right can seek relief from a tribunal (decision-making panel) or a court.

Issues Covered Under Employment Law

A detailed discussion of employment law is beyond the scope of this textbook; however, you can learn more about the topic if the need arises. The nature of your employment will determine which employment laws apply to you. If you work for a private (non-governmental) employer, the *Employment Standards Act* likely applies to you. If you are represented by a union, the Ontario *Labour Relations Act* may determine some of the conditions of your employment, and you may need to settle employment problems through a labour relations grievance system. If you work for the federal government, the terms of your employment are governed by the *Canada Labour Code*.

There are a few other statutes that touch on general employment issues, including:

- the Ontario *Employers and Employees Act*, which can provide assistance in recovering wages or profit sharing owed to an employee;
- the Ontario *Pay Equity Act*, under which female employees can seek to have their pay adjusted so that they receive equal pay for work of equal value;
- the Ontario *Workplace Safety and Insurance Act*, which provides income replacement benefits to workers hurt on the job; and
- the federal *Employment Insurance Act*, which provides benefits to some job-seekers while they are searching for new employment.

Ontario's employment laws provide guidance on a wide range of issues, including:

- minimum wage;
- hours of work, overtime, and breaks;
- sick time;
- vacations and vacation pay;
- public holidays and holiday pay;
- employment benefits (these are not required by law, but if provided, cannot be provided in a manner that discriminates);
- leaves for pregnancy and parenting;
- personal emergency leave and family medical leave; and
- termination and notice.

For more information about specific standards, you may consult the employment or labour legislation that applies to you. Because this chapter is a basic overview, the only issue that will be discussed here is termination and notice.

Termination of Employment

INTRODUCTION

Contrary to what many people believe, employers are entitled to terminate employees at almost any time, and for almost any reason. However, the rights of the terminated employee, and the obligations of the terminating employer, vary depending on the circumstances.

PROBATION PERIOD

Many employers, when they first hire an employee, impose a probation period. Under the ESA, if an employee is terminated within three months of the date of hiring, the employer is not obliged to give notice or to pay termination pay or severance in lieu (instead of) notice.

LAYOFFS

Sometimes an employer may be forced to lay off one or more employees owing to lack of work. If the event is temporary, the employer is not immediately required to pay termination pay; however, if the layoff lasts longer than the statutory maximums (the rules are detailed; for example, a layoff can't last more than 13 weeks in any 20-week period), termination obligations are triggered.

While on layoff, many employees become eligible to collect employment insurance benefits.

If an employer purports to lay off an employee instead of firing him or her, but has no intention of ever returning the employee to work, a court can determine that the layoff is in fact a firing, and can order termination pay.

TERMINATION AFTER THE PROBATION PERIOD

Employees who have worked for an employer for longer than three months at the time of termination are generally entitled to notice of termination or pay in lieu of notice. If an employer chooses to give notice, the company must tell the employee ahead of time the date on which employment will cease, and permit the employee to work and continue to be paid in the interim.

In practice, giving working notice is uncommon, probably because employers worry that an employee who has been terminated will perform poorly or even sabotage the employer. Instead, many employers choose to give the employee **termination pay**—a lump sum that represents pay in lieu of termination notice. For example, if the employer believes that the appropriate notice period for a particular employee is six weeks, it may request that the employee leave work immediately after accepting a sum of money equal to six weeks' pay.

In general, an employee is entitled to one week of notice per year spent working for the employer. For example, an employee who has worked for an employer for seven years is entitled to seven weeks' termination pay. However, employees have sued employers on the basis that the notice provided was insufficient given the facts of the case. Finding a new job is easier for some employees than others—for example, highly specialized or very senior employees may need longer notice periods, and older employees may have a harder time finding work than younger ones. If you

termination pay
a lump sum required by law that represents pay in lieu of termination notice, typically one week's pay per year spent working for the employer

have reason to believe that the notice provided to you is unfair, you should speak with a lawyer for advice.

SEVERANCE PAY

severance pay
a lump sum negotiated between an employer and an employee on termination of the employment contract

Severance pay is not the same as termination pay. While termination pay is mandated by law, severance pay is typically negotiated in the employment contract between the parties, and is designed to reflect things like the loss of opportunities and loss of seniority associated with being forced out of a job earlier than expected.

TERMINATION FOR CAUSE

An important exception to the employer's termination obligations is termination for cause.

An employer who gives appropriate notice or termination pay is not required to give a reason for terminating an employee. In some cases, however, an employer may have a reason ("cause") that justifies ending the employment relationship with no pay obligation. "For cause" terminations that have stood up in court include terminations for:

- an employee's criminal conduct—for example, theft or fraud against the employer or against a client, or sexual harassment of a client;
- serious incompetence (usually, when the employee has been warned and has made no effort to improve, or when the employee's incompetence poses unacceptable risks to clients);
- an employee's serious harassment of other employees;
- serious insubordination (when the employee will not listen to or obey reasonable directives from superiors); or
- intentional violation of terms of the employment contract—for example, if the employee discloses proprietary information to competitors.

Should you be terminated and your employer alleges that the termination is "for cause," but you do not believe that the company has cause to terminate you, you should consult a lawyer about whether it may be appropriate to bring a lawsuit for wrongful dismissal.

CONSTRUCTIVE DISMISSAL

constructive dismissal
termination in which an employer provokes the employee to resign when he or she doesn't really want to leave the job

Constructive dismissal is a form of wrongful dismissal in which an employer does something that forces the employee to resign when she doesn't really want to leave the job. When an employee resigns instead of being fired, the employer is not required to pay termination pay or severance. For this reason, some unscrupulous employers would rather "encourage" an employee to quit than fire him outright.

Most constructive dismissal cases involve the employer making the employee's worklife intolerable—for example, by transferring the employee into a very undesirable position, demanding that he move to another city, demoting the employee, or otherwise creating an unpleasant work environment. If you feel you have been constructively dismissed, you should see a lawyer for advice.

BOX 7.1

CASE

Is a Reduction in Hours Constructive Dismissal?

The following summary is one example of the cases that come before the Ontario Labour Relations Board.

Constructive Dismissal

S&E Ghobrial Pharmacy Inc. v. Krasinska

In a 2002 case, the Ontario Labour Relations Board (OLRB) considered a constructive dismissal case brought by a pharmacist.

From 1995 to 2000, the pharmacist worked for a pharmacy owned by a company called I.K. Pharmacies Limited. In the spring of 2000, her regular hours of work were 31 hours one week and 38 hours the next. In June 2000, another corporation, S&E Ghobrial Pharmacy Inc., purchased the pharmacy. The new owners, as part of the sale, agreed to continue the pharmacist's employment with the same hours of work. Soon after the purchase, however, the pharmacist was informed that her hours would be cut to 31 hours every week. Although the pharmacist agreed to this, she later returned from vacation to find that her hours would be further cut to 26 hours per week (just above part-time level). She was unhappy about this cut. Her employer suggested she contact another pharmacy to see if she could make up additional hours there. When she contacted that pharmacy, she was offered a full-time job and went to work there.

Later, she brought an application before the OLRB, alleging that she had been constructively dismissed by S&E Ghobrial Pharmacy Inc. when her hours were cut.

The OLRB agreed that a cut in hours from an average of 34.5 hours per week to 26 hours per week ran contrary to the pharmacist's contract of employment, and amounted to constructive dismissal. It ordered S&E Ghobrial to pay the pharmacist five weeks' termination pay. S&E Ghobrial argued that the previous corporate owner of the pharmacy should be responsible for a portion of the termination pay because of the change in ownership, but the OLRB relied on a provision in the *Employment Standards Act*, which states:

> 13. (2) Where an employer sells a business to a purchaser who employs an employee of the employer, the employment of the employee shall not be terminated by the sale, and the period of employment of the employee with the employer shall be deemed to have been employment with the purchaser.

S&E Ghobrial Pharmacy Inc. was held liable for the pharmacist's full termination pay. ▣

SITUATIONS IN WHICH TERMINATION IS ILLEGAL

Although it is true that employers can fire workers for almost any reason, there is an important exception: an employer cannot fire employees for seeking to enforce their rights under the ESA (or under certain other statutes, such as Ontario's *Occupational Health and Safety Act* or the *Pay Equity Act*). The employer also cannot fire an employee for taking or requesting a statutorily created benefit, such as time off for public holidays or pregnancy leave. Terminating employees because they are exercising their employment law rights is called reprisal, and reprisals are illegal under the ESA and under many other statutes.

DISCRIMINATION AND HARASSMENT

Introduction

Earlier in this chapter, you read about the importance of effective communication and healthy working relationships to the safe practice of pharmacy. Two of the most important threats to working relationships are **discrimination** and **harassment**, which can often—but not always—occur together.

> "Discrimination" is not defined in the Ontario *Human Rights Code* ("the Code") … . Instead, the Code creates the right for all people to "equal treatment with respect to services, goods and facilities, without discrimination because of race, ancestry, place of origin, colour, ethnic origin, citizenship, creed, sex, sexual orientation, age, marital status, family status or disability. (s. 1)

On the basis of this provision, the essence of discrimination is unequal treatment that occurs because of a personal characteristic that falls into one of the named categories.

The term "harassment" does have a definition in the Code:

> "harassment" means engaging in a course of vexatious comment or conduct that is known or ought reasonably to be known to be unwelcome … . (s. 10(1))

Both discrimination and harassment are specifically prohibited in employment (s. 5), and "harassment because of sex" merits a special prohibition of its own:

> Every person who is an employee has a right to freedom from harassment in the workplace because of sex by his or her employer or agent of the employer or by another employee. (s. 7(2))

Although most workplace discrimination or harassment complaints are brought under provincial statutes like the Code, it is useful to know that there is also a federal human rights statute—the *Canadian Human Rights Act* (CHRA). The CHRA's anti-discrimination provisions are more detailed than those in the Code—for example, the federal Act includes a prohibition against discriminatory exclusion of employees from employee organizations (e.g., unions), and an explicit prohibition against payment of unequal wages based on sex.

The following sections provide a brief introduction to discrimination and harassment, including the steps you should take if you ever find yourself subject to either problem.

Discrimination

IN HIRING

One of the most commonly reported examples of discrimination is in hiring. As a pharmacy technician looking for work, you may encounter a situation in which you

---

discrimination
unequal treatment that occurs because of race, ancestry, place of origin, colour, ethnic origin, citizenship, creed, sex, sexual orientation, age, marital status, family status or disability

harassment
comments or conduct that may reasonably be predicted to be unwelcome

suspect that you were not given a job for which you applied because of a personal characteristic.

Proving discrimination in hiring is difficult—you might expect that an employer eager to disprove a discrimination charge would simply claim that another applicant was more qualified. Also, you might conclude, and perhaps reasonably, that you wouldn't want to work for an employer who is prejudiced against people with your personal characteristics. However, if every person who experienced discrimination in hiring failed to contest the employer, the offending practices would continue unabated.

Although a full-blown complaint before the Ontario Human Rights Tribunal is an extreme option, you can speak with a lawyer for advice or get in touch with the Human Rights Legal Support Centre (www.hrlsc.on.ca) to discuss your concerns. You may also want to ask around, within your personal network, to determine whether others have had similar experiences with this same employer.

ON THE JOB

It is also possible to experience discrimination after hiring, once you are on the job. Any instance of unequal treatment that you believe relates to one of the enumerated grounds for discrimination (race, ancestry, place of origin, colour, ethnic origin, citizenship, creed, sex, sexual orientation, age, marital status, family status, or disability) is, potentially, discrimination. For example, an employer might discriminate by:

- paying women less than men for the same work;
- consistently assigning a pharmacy technician who is not a native English speaker to duties that do not involve direct contact with patients;
- consistently scheduling an employee (for example, a mother of young children) to more desirable shifts while requiring others to work less desirable shifts;
- failing to promote or transfer an employee because that person is disabled; or
- avoiding scheduling two particular employees together because one of the two is gay and the other has expressed an unwillingness to work with a gay colleague.

There are many other possible scenarios.

The experience of discrimination is inherently isolating and discourages good communication. However, it is a good idea, at the outset, to handle this problem the same way you would any other workplace issue: by addressing your concerns directly to the offender.

You may discover that the supervisor, manager, or employer who has been acting in a discriminatory way is not even conscious of these actions, or has a well-meaning, though inappropriate, motive for the behaviour. In more difficult cases, the offender may be aware of the discrimination but denies it, or refuses to make changes.

If the offender is a supervisor or manager and has a supervisor of her own, your next step is to approach that person with your concerns. Before you do so, it is useful to be prepared. You may want to have a list of specific instances of discrimination, and a well thought out set of requests for specific changes. It is easier for the employer to take action on specific requests than to develop an original plan for addressing a vague complaint. Also, when your requests are specific, it is easier to determine whether progress has been made on trying to improve the situation—and, should you need to bring a formal complaint, it will be easier to establish the fact that your requests were refused or ignored.

In the event that your problem turns into a formal complaint, it is a good idea to make written notes about the discriminatory incidents, your reactions to them, and the reactions of your supervisor or employer to your attempts to overcome the problem. Keep copies of any documents (including email) that relate to the situation, and make note of any co-workers who have witnessed it.

If the discrimination persists and your attempts to resolve it are unsuccessful, you may decide to apply to the Human Rights Tribunal of Ontario (HRTO) for relief. That process is discussed below.

Harassment

Harassment goes beyond discrimination. While discrimination involves the denial of opportunities, harassment typically takes the form of unwanted attention. It can make you feel conspicuous, or even like a target.

Harassment, by definition, is done purposefully. The usual purpose is to provoke emotions or a reaction in the target. While one instance of "vexatious comment or conduct" can be enough to make you uncomfortable, harassers tend to escalate their conduct over time, and it is this persistence and escalation that have the greatest potential to poison your working environment.

Some harassment is easy to identify: the harasser makes disparaging comments about you, including one of the prohibited grounds for discrimination. These comments may be made directly to you, or they may be made to others, within your earshot or not. Comments need not be direct to constitute harassment.

Harassment need not be verbal. A person can commit harassment by mimicry—for example, by mimicking an unusual gait or other disability. A person can harass you by moving or touching your belongings, or by bringing something into the workplace (for example, a food that your culture or religion prohibits you from consuming) and leaving it at your workstation. A person can harass you by putting up a poster or other decoration that is intended to make you feel uncomfortable.

Harassers can also use body language. For example, a harasser may stand too close to you to make you uncomfortable, or may block a walkway so that you have to squeeze past. Or, he or she may avoid you in an exaggerated way, as if to suggest that your presence is repulsive.

A harasser may also touch you in an unwelcome way, for example, by putting his palm on the seat of your chair as you are about to sit (this may be construed as a sexual assault), or by hitting you "accidentally" with garbage thrown in the direction of a wastebasket (potentially a non-sexual assault).

Finally, some harassers (especially sexual harassers) are skilled at disguising their harassment as acceptable behaviour; for example, a harasser who continually comments on your appearance may later argue that he is simply being friendly or complimentary.

The best time to act on workplace harassment is immediately. You may be tempted to ignore the behaviour, either because it seems too trivial to report or in the hope that it will go away. Unfortunately, because the goal of most harassers is to provoke a reaction, ignoring the behaviour will often cause it to escalate, not abate. As soon as you realize that a co-worker's behaviour is making you uncomfortable, you should take the steps discussed above in relation to discrimination: talk to the offender directly, then, if necessary, talk to his or her supervisor, your own supervisor, or the employer.

If the employer is the harasser, or if your first steps fail to solve the problem, you should file a complaint with the HRTO.

Filing a Complaint with the Human Rights Tribunal of Ontario

In 2008, the human rights complaints system in Ontario underwent a major change. Previously, the Ontario Human Rights Commission received complaints from the public, and referred some of these to the HRTO for adjudication. However, since June 30, 2008, all complaints must now be filed directly with the HRTO.

If you are contemplating or ready to make a complaint to the HRTO, there are at least three places you can go for help. The HRTO's website provides detailed information about the tribunal's rules and process, and you can obtain an application form there.

If you need help with your complaint application—and if you are in a situation in which you stand to lose significant money, face the loss of opportunities, or suffer other significant consequences because of discrimination or harassment—you should seek personalized advice.

You can obtain advice about your human rights complaint from a qualified lawyer in private practice or from the Human Rights Legal Support Centre (see Appendix A of this textbook), which can also provide representation if you are in financial need. Alternatively, you may be eligible for representation by a lawyer from a community legal aid clinic.

When you are ready to complete your application, you will need to fill in details about the respondent (the person whom you are alleging discriminated against you or harassed you), the circumstances of the discrimination, the identity of witnesses who can help support your case, the effects of the discrimination on you, and the remedy that you are seeking from the tribunal. Some applicants seek financial compensation as a remedy, others seek different kinds of orders—for example, an order forcing your employer to reconsider you for a promotion that you were denied. The tribunal can also make orders requiring the employer to change its policies and practices to avoid discrimination in the future.

The complaint application allows you to request **mediation** in an attempt to resolve a complaint without a formal hearing. If you agree to mediation, the tribunal will, through the work of trained mediators, support you in trying to resolve your problem informally and by agreement. In cases where you would like to keep your job, agreeing to mediation instead of proceeding directly to a hearing can help preserve the relationship between you and the respondent—an important factor if the two of you must work together later. The parties to a mediated agreement are less likely to come away from the process feeling as though one party was the "winner" and the other the "loser." Instead, both parties will at minimum feel they have been heard, and at best, that the resolution was mutually acceptable.

If you and the respondent are unable to resolve your differences through mediation, you will need to proceed to a hearing before the tribunal. Once the HRTO has

mediation
a process in which a neutral third party attempts to help parties in a dispute reach an agreement

set a date for your hearing, it will send a notice of the date and time, and you will be asked to file additional documents—including witness statement summaries—with it. The witness statements may be shared with the opposing party to help him or her prepare for the hearing.

In an attempt to streamline the case, the HRTO may prepare and send out a "case assessment direction," which is an analysis of the case with instructions about the witnesses from whom the tribunal will wish to hear, the matters that can be dealt with as preliminary issues, and whether additional information from any party is required. There may also be a conference call in which you will need to participate.

At the hearing, which might alternatively be called a "case resolution conference," there will be formal procedures. You will need to present witnesses, question the other parties' witnesses, present physical evidence (objects related to the case, if any) and make legal arguments. Most hearing participants rely on formal legal representation (a lawyer) to assist in this process.

At the conclusion of the hearing (sometimes in writing, a few days after the hearing), the HRTO adjudicator who heard the case will enter a decision either dismissing the application if it is not supported by evidence or by law, or ordering a remedy if the applicant is successful.

If the respondent in your complaint is the federal government or a federal government agency (for example, if your complaint is against your employer, and your employer is the Canadian Forces), you will need to bring your complaint before the Canadian Human Rights Commission (CHRC) instead (see Appendix A).

In some cases, a person who has suffered discrimination or harassment elects, instead of bringing a human rights complaint, to bring a civil lawsuit instead. Whether or not you should do this is a decision you can make with the help of your lawyer. Civil litigation can be more complicated than the human rights complaints process, but if you have suffered significant harm—especially economic harm—it may be the right choice for you. Even if the person who harassed you does not have the money to pay your claim, you may be able to establish that the person's employer (who could also be your employer or former employer) is vicariously liable for the harm that was done to you. Bear in mind that if you have a civil lawsuit under way, you will not be allowed to lodge a human rights complaint based on the same facts.

Finally, in serious cases, it may be appropriate to report an act of harassment to the police. The police may elect to charge the harasser with assault or sexual assault, or make the charge under hate-crime legislation.

When *You* Are the Discriminator or Harasser

The preceding sections dealt with discrimination and harassment complaints from the perspective of the victim; however, it is possible for a pharmacy technician to be accused of perpetrating such activities.

As a registered pharmacy technician, you are expected to be professional, to show respect for your colleagues, and to obey all laws and policies that apply to you—including human rights laws. If you engage in discrimination or harassment while on the job, you will automatically be acting outside the limits of your role and violating the standards of your profession. You will also be breaking the law.

Employers have low tolerance for employees who discriminate against or harass others, because the employer is ultimately responsible for the conditions of employment for all staff. An employer who allows staff to harass one another is likely to face

---

BOX 7.2

CASE

Harassment Grievances Under Labour Relations Law

Zehrmart Limited v. United Food & Commercial Workers International Union, Locals 175/633

Some pharmacy technicians are employed in unionized workplaces. If you are represented by a union, any disputes you may have with your employer will be handled somewhat differently than if you lacked union representation. As a union member, the conditions of your employment will be covered by a collective agreement (a group contract)—although the terms of your employment still must, generally, be equal to or better than those guaranteed under the ESA.

If you believe that your employer has violated the collective agreement or violated your rights in some other way, your first formal avenue to relief would be to bring a grievance (a complaint) against your employer. You would likely be eligible to have your union (and its lawyers) support you in bringing your grievance, which would be heard by a labour arbitrator at the Ontario Labour Relations Board (OLRB).

In 2005 and 2006, the OLRB heard evidence in a grievance brought by a pharmacy technician (the grievor) against her employer, Zehrs Markets Inc. The employer grocery chain operated pharmacies in some of its grocery stores, and the grievor was employed at one of these.

The grievor's troubles began when the employer hired a new pharmacist to work in her workplace. According to the grievor, over a period of more than two years, the new pharmacist harassed her on the basis of age and sex. She alleged that he told her that she was old enough and had enough savings to retire, and that he wanted her job for his wife. She alleged that he drove past her home, because he had made a comment about its market value. She also alleged that he once yelled at her, "What kind of hormones are you taking?" and that on several occasions the pharmacist made comments that she was not doing her job well enough—for example, that she didn't help with data entry tasks. Finally, she alleged that the pharmacist had threatened her by saying, "A narcotics count can always be arranged."

The employer gave evidence suggesting that after the grievor complained of the conduct, it had conducted a thorough investigation of the allegations. Although it had found no merit in them, it offered the grievor a different position in the company, which she declined.

After considering all the evidence, the arbitrator came to the conclusion that the grievor's case for harassment was not supported by the facts for two reasons. First, her evidence was plagued by credibility problems. The grievor had in many ways falsified her evidence: by lying about many of the dates given for the instances of alleged harassment, by lying about and minimizing the steps the employer had taken to accommodate her, by minimizing the apologies the pharmacist had made to her about his tone of voice, by lying about having seen the pharmacist driving around her house, and by refusing to answer questions.

Second, although the arbitrator found that the pharmacist did in fact make some of the comments complained of by the grievor, many of those—for example, the comment that he would be speaking with head office about her—related to his concerns with the grievor's job performance. These concerns, which were shared by others in the employer company, did not amount to discrimination on the basis of age or sex, but were legitimate requests for improvement in job performance. The arbitrator found that the employer's attempts to respond to the grievor's concerns were adequate, especially in light of the fact that there was no credible evidence of harassment.

The arbitrator dismissed the grievance. ◙

human rights or civil law proceedings. For this reason, even one clear-cut act of discrimination or harassment may be enough to get you fired for cause.

Even if you are not fired, you may find yourself subject to a human rights complaint, a complaint to your regulatory College, or both. Such complaints can result in the loss of the privilege to practise your profession for a period of time, and potentially the loss of your reputation forever.

Finally, serious acts of harassment can lead to a lawsuit for civil damages that will not be covered by your employer's malpractice insurance, or to a criminal charge that could result in imprisonment and a permanent criminal record.

OCCUPATIONAL HEALTH AND SAFETY

Introduction

Like most other jobs, working in a pharmacy comes with certain risks. Because you work with liquids, there is a risk of slipping because of spills. Working with equipment that has sharp points or blades creates a risk of punctures or cuts. Flammables create a risk of burns. Standing for long periods can cause back or leg strain; working at a computer can cause wrist or eyestrain. There are also some risks that are elevated in your workplace compared with others: many of the chemicals you work with are toxic, and if not handled properly, pose special health risks.

No work comes completely free of risk, but you are entitled to be reasonably safe on the job; to have protective equipment, guards, and other technologies in place to shield you from harm; and to refuse work that entails an unreasonable level of risk.

These entitlements have not always existed. For centuries, workers have accepted jobs "at their own risk" because they needed to make a living. As civilization has evolved, however, we have come to understand that the willingness of employees to take risks to earn a living comes with a benefit to employers, in the form of profits.

Protecting employees often comes at a cost, and so, without laws in place to shape their behaviour, unscrupulous employers might be tempted to skimp on protective equipment and safety protocols to increase profits. For this reason, many jurisdictions around the world—including all provinces and territories in Canada—have introduced laws that enforce occupational health and safety practices. In Ontario, the main such statute is the *Occupational Health and Safety Act* (OHSA).

The OHSA details a blueprint for creating workplace programs for the promotion of occupational health and safety. While the statute establishes certain important employee rights, such as the right to refuse unsafe work, it emphasizes that creating a safe workplace is the shared responsibility of all workplace parties, including employers, supervisors, and employees themselves.

The OHSA is a long and detailed statute, and a discussion of all of its components is beyond the scope of this textbook. However, you should be aware of the issues covered by the Act. These include:

- the role of the Ministry of Labour in administering the Act by, for example,
  ◇ appointing health and safety inspectors and conducting workplace inspections;

   ◇ investigating reports of accidents and injuries in the workplace;

   ◇ compelling employers to take steps to remedy health and safety problems in the workplace; and

   ◇ resolving disputes over employee work refusals, and other safety-related conflicts in the workplace;

- the workplace safety Internal Responsibility System, and the roles of the parties within it;

- the appointment of a Health and Safety Representative or Joint Health and Safety Committee to administer the health and safety program in the workplace;

- the employer's responsibility to provide a safe workplace and to address safety hazards promptly when they arise;

- employees' safety rights, including the right to refuse unsafe work;

- guidelines for reporting accidents and injuries in the workplace;

- consequences for workplaces with poor safety records; and

- requirements for compliance with specific safety strategies, including the provision of personal protective equipment and compliance with the Workplace Hazardous Materials Information System (WHMIS).

Pharmacy technicians who wish more information about occupational health and safety than is provided in this chapter can review the OHSA and the regulations made under it. You can also consult the following sources:

- the Ontario Ministry of Labour (http://labour.gov.on.ca);

- the Canadian Centre for Occupational Health and Safety (http://ccohs.ca);

- the Ontario Workplace Safety and Insurance Board (http://wsib.on.ca); and

- the Workers Health and Safety Centre (http://whsc.on.ca).

The Internal Responsibility System

Because research suggests that safety promotion works best when all workplace parties cooperate, the OHSA creates an **internal responsibility system** that imposes safety obligations on all workplace parties.

Because the employer has the greatest control over the workplace, it has a significant obligation to provide a safe place to work. Because workplaces differ, the content of this obligation varies widely. In a retail pharmacy, it would include such environmental concerns as having a workspace with adequate heating, lighting, ventilation, exits, and room to move around. Facilities for handwashing would need to be readily available, and equipment for dealing with spills, sharps, and fires would need to be provided.

The employer is also required to provide up-to-date personal protective equipment where such equipment exists. In a pharmacy setting, personal protective equipment may include lab coats, masks, gloves, and eye protection.

Finally, if a hazard develops or is discovered in the workplace, the employer is responsible to take immediate steps to remedy it or to protect the employees from it.

internal responsibility system
a system created by the Ontario *Occupational Health and Safety Act* that imposes role-specific workplace safety duties on all workplace parties

The responsibilities of supervisors overlap in some respects with those of the employer—they are responsible for protecting those who report to them, and for addressing safety hazards. However, supervisors are also responsible for monitoring work, for identifying and correcting unsafe work patterns, and for communicating problems to management.

Workers have the most to gain from safety initiatives. However, they are not free from responsibilities of their own. The OHSA requires you, as a worker, to:

- work safely within your capabilities, following all workplace instructions, policies, and procedures, and using equipment as it was meant to be used (no shortcuts, no modifying of safety equipment);
- wear personal protective equipment when it is provided, and use provided safety equipment (for example, dedicated sharps containers); and
- promptly report to a supervisor or manager any hazards you may encounter or create while on the job.

Besides the employer, supervisors, and workers, the OHSA creates another key workplace party with duties in the Internal Responsibility System: the health and safety representative or Joint Health and Safety Committee.

Depending on the size of the workplace, the employer is usually required either to appoint a single health and safety representative (for most workplaces with between six and 19 workers), or a Joint Health and Safety Committee (for larger workplaces). (Very small workplaces need not have either, because the management tends to be fairly readily accessible and attuned to workers.) A Joint Health and Safety Committee (JHSC) is a committee composed of both management members and "worker members"—staff who do not hold senior management positions. Some, but not all, of the members of a JHSC are expected to obtain special training in workplace safety and risk management.

The health and safety representative or the JHSC provides support and expertise in the event of a safety problem, and helps support communications between the employer, the workers, and the Ministry of Labour. If you work in a workplace that has a health and safety representative or a JHSC, you are encouraged to approach them (as well as your supervisor) if you detect a safety problem at work.

Your Right to Refuse Unsafe Work

One of the most important rights created by the OHSA is the right of workers to refuse to undertake or to continue doing work that the worker considers unsafe.

In general, you cannot refuse to do work that is a normal, everyday job function simply on the basis that it comes with risks. If no employees ever did risky work, we would have no firefighters, no police, no farmers, no dog groomers, and no pharmacy technicians, just to cite a few examples. The right to refuse work under the OHSA is meant to allow you to speak up about unusual or excessive risks that are not a normal part of your job functions.

For example, as a pharmacy technician, you cannot refuse to handle acetone simply because it produces unpleasant fumes. But if a short in the electrical supply to the cash register causes you to receive an electric shock whenever you touch the register, you would likely be entitled to refuse to use it until it was repaired.

If you refuse to undertake or to continue unsafe work and your supervisor disagrees with your assessment of the danger, the two of you should speak with your health and safety representative. Your employer is required to investigate the problem, and to take action to remedy any risks. Regardless of the outcome of the investigation, however, if the safety problem is not remedied to your satisfaction, you are entitled to continue to refuse to do the dangerous task until an inspector from the Ministry of Labour has assessed the problem work area and declared it safe. If the delay between your refusal to work and the repair of the problem is long, you may be assigned to other work in the meantime.

Never hesitate to speak up about risks in the workplace; as in the case of ESA rights, your employer is not entitled to make reprisals (for example, to fire you) for exercising a right you have under the OHSA.

The Workplace Hazardous Materials Information System

Pharmacy settings, like many other workplaces, have materials on site that could pose a danger to human health if handled improperly. Employers, as part of their duty to protect the health and safety of workers, are required to store these materials properly and to provide employees with adequate training in how to handle them.

To support this employer duty, and to promote the development of accurate and consistent labelling and safety guidelines for hazardous materials, the federal and provincial governments collaborated to create the **Workplace Hazardous Materials Information System (WHMIS)**. The WHMIS is supported by legislation and regulations at both the federal and provincial levels. The federal *Hazardous Products Act* (HPA) and the *Hazardous Materials Information Review Act* (HMIRA) create a scheme for identifying hazardous materials, classifying them, and assessing the risks that they pose to health. At the provincial level, provisions in the OHSA and the WHMIS regulation made under it incorporate the system into the provincial occupational health and safety program.

To comply with WHMIS, employers who store hazardous materials in the workplace must ensure that they are labelled with specific information relating to properties, risks, and appropriate handling. This information must be provided by manufacturers, who generally supply the labels with their products. Along with written information, WHMIS-compliant labels bear standardized symbols designed to permit workers to spot risks quickly—for example, poisonous or infectious materials may carry a "skull and crossbones" symbol on the label. Employers must also ensure that more detailed information is available in the workplace, in the form of material safety data sheets (MSDS). These sheets must be kept in a location accessible to all workers. Finally, employers must provide materials handling and general health and safety training to employees sufficient to protect them from workplace risks.

When handling hazardous materials, workers must follow appropriate procedures and wear proper protective gear.

Workplace Hazardous Materials Information System (WHMIS)
a Canada-wide system designed to inform employers and workers about hazardous materials used in the workplace—for example, via labels, material safety data sheets, and educational programs

Compensation for Injured Workers

Despite the OHSA and employers' and workers' best efforts, workplace accidents do happen, and employees are sometimes rendered ill as a result of workplace expo-

FACTS AND TRENDS   **BOX 7.3**

Needle Stick Surveillance Program

The WSIB's needle stick surveillance policy is of particular interest to pharmacy staff. While the injury from an accidental needle stick is generally trifling, the worker may be at risk for infection. Workers who accidentally get stuck with used needles are encouraged to report the incident to their employers, because the employer is expected to report needle sticks to the WSIB.

   The only exception to this policy is when a surveillance program is already in place. If the worker has been tested by a health-care provider to determine the presence or absence of infection, the employer must report the needle stick accident only if the worker tests positive for infection. ◇

sures. Should an injury or illness that you suffer on the job leave you unable to work, the *Workplace Safety and Insurance Act* can, in some cases, provide income replacement benefits while you recover.

   In general, workers are eligible for benefits if:

- they received health-care treatment for the accident or illness beyond basic on-the-job first aid;
- they were away from work beyond the day of the accident due to their injury or illness; and/or
- upon returning to work, they were able to work only reduced hours.

   If you believe that you may be entitled to benefits, you will need to file a claim with the Workplace Safety and Insurance Board (WSIB) within six months of the accident (or of discovering the work-related illness).

   To file a claim, the worker must fill in a Form 6 and file it with the WSIB. The worker must also consent to the disclosure, by his or her health-care provider, of information about the worker's functional abilities (the kinds of work the worker can and cannot do). The employer is also required to file documentation of its own. The WSIB then makes a decision about benefits payable to the worker.

   WSIB benefits do not replace 100 percent of the worker's pay, and so most workers are eager to get back on the job as soon as possible. The WSIB promotes the principle of an "early and safe return to work" and requires the worker and the employer to cooperate toward this goal as early as possible, even if this means that the worker's disabilities must be accommodated—for example, by allowing the employee to do a different type of work from the original job.

KEY TERMS

constructive dismissal
discrimination
harassment
internal responsibility system
mediation
severance pay
termination pay
Workplace Hazardous Materials Information System (WHMIS)

REFERENCES

Canada Labour Code. 1985. RSC 1985, c. L-2.

Canadian Human Rights Act. 1985. RSC 1985, c. H-6.

Employers and Employees Act. 1990. RSO 1990, c. E.12.

Employment Insurance Act. 1996. SC 1996, c. 23.

Employment Standards Act. 2000. SO 2000, c. 41.

Hazardous Materials Information Review Act. 1985. RSC 1985, c. 24 (3rd Supp.).

Hazardous Products Act. 1985. RSC 1985, c. H-3.

Human Rights Code. 1990. SO 1990, c. H.19.

Labour Relations Act. 1995. SO 1995, c. 1.

National Association of Pharmacy Regulatory Authorities (NAPRA). (2007, September). Professional competencies for Canadian pharmacy technicians at entry to practice. Retrieved May 11, 2010 from http://www.ocpinfo.com/Client/ocp/OCPHome.nsf/object/Pharmacy+Technician+Competencies+Profile/$file/PT_Competencies.pdf.

Occupational Health and Safety Act. 1990. RSO 1990, c. O.1.

Ontario College of Pharmacists (OCP). (n.d.). Proposed standards of practice for registered pharmacy technicians. Retrieved May 11, 2010 from http://www.ocpinfo.com/client/ocp/OCPHome.nsf/object/Proposed_For_Techs/$file/Proposed_For_Techs.pdf.

Ontario Ministry of Labour. (2008, August). *Workplace hazardous materials information system: A guide to the legislation*. Retrieved June 1, 2010 from http://www.labour.gov.on.ca/english/hs/pdf/whmis.pdf.

Pay Equity Act. 1990. RSO 1990, c. P.7.

S&E Ghobrial Pharmacy Inc. v. Krasinska. 2002 CanLII 22038 (ONLRB).

Workplace Safety and Insurance Act. 1997. SO 1997, c. 16.

Zehrmart Limited v. United Food & Commercial Workers International Union, Locals 175/633. 2007 CanLII 71646 (ONLA).

REVIEW EXERCISES

Discussion Questions

Review the following scenarios and discuss the steps you would take in response to each of them.

1. You are a pharmacy technician working in a retail pharmacy. You work with a pharmacist who, instead of putting away supply bottles and other equipment after he has finished dispensing, expects you to clean up after him. While you can do this during slow business periods, when the pharmacy is busy you can't keep up. Then you have trouble finding clear counter space for your own dispensing, and you often cannot locate a product in inventory because the pharmacist has left it out. You are concerned that the chaotic workspace may lead you to make errors, and at the end of each shift, the pharmacy looks like a disaster area.

2. You are a pharmacy technician working in a large pharmacy. On three separate occasions, you have observed patients coming in to complain that their prescription bottles contain a few less pills than indicated on the label. In all three cases, the missing pills were the same type of narcotic. You happen to know that all three prescriptions were prepared by the same colleague—another pharmacy technician. You suspect that the pill counts were purposely short, to allow the pharmacy technician to pocket a few pills.

3. While working as a pharmacy technician, you notice that many of the pills in a supply bottle containing metformin seem to be crumbly and in poor condition. When you ask the pharmacist if you should continue dispensing these or if they should be disposed of and reordered, she tells you that you are "getting too big for your britches" and that you should stop "trying to run the place and just do your job."

Review Questions

1. List at least three reasons why it is important to strive for positive working relationships with your pharmacy colleagues.

2. What does it take to make a real contribution to a patient's health-care team?

3. If you have a conflict with a co-worker, and you have spoken directly with the co-worker about your concerns, how long should you wait for relations to improve before you speak to a supervisor about the problem?

4. If you had a question about your entitlement to vacation pay, where might you look for the answer?

5. If your employer tells you that you are being laid off permanently, are you entitled to termination pay?

6. List at least five of the personal characteristics or attributes based on which it is illegal to discriminate under the Ontario *Human Rights Code*.

7. Imagine that while working as a pharmacy technician, your co-worker—a person from who you had been subjected to a six-month campaign of rude comments—calls out, "Wet t-shirt contest!" and dumps a bottle of water on the front of your lab coat, causing you to slip on the wet floor, break your hip, cancel your winter holiday trip, and miss six weeks of work. List three different possible proceedings you could pursue against this co-worker.

8. Who, in the workplace, is responsible for protecting the safety of workers?

9. If you feel that you have been asked to do a task in your workplace that is hazardous to your health or safety, what should you do?

10. If you are asked to work with an unfamiliar material in the workplace and you would like to know more about the material—for example, whether it is safe, or how it should be handled—where can you go for information?

CHAPTER 8

Professional Ethics for Pharmacy Technicians

A pharmacy technician checks labels on drugs to be shipped from Winnipeg-based Canadadrugs.com, one of Canada's largest online pharmacies.

LEARNING OBJECTIVES

After completing this chapter, you should be able to:

- Provide definitions for the terms *ethics*, *morals*, and *professional ethics*.

- Demonstrate familiarity with the College's *Code of Ethics* for members.

- Explain how the principles in the *Code of Ethics* might apply to situations you encounter in the course of your work.

- Identify professional standards relating to ethical practice that apply to you.

- Explain the importance of having a specific goal or outcome in mind when conducting ethical reasoning.

- Describe strategies for choosing ethical responses to practice situations.

INTRODUCTION

ethics
principles of right and wrong conduct

The term **ethics** generally refers to principles relating to right and wrong conduct. "Doing the right thing," in one's job and in life, is a goal to strive for; it enhances self-esteem and wins the respect of others. However, the right thing is not always the easiest thing. There are many motivations for failing to do the right thing: monetary or other personal gain, or avoidance of social discomfort or conflict.

The news is full of stories of businesspeople who have done things for the sake of profit that were later judged unethical. Such people often defend their actions, asserting that profit, not virtue, is what business is all about. For many workers, the need to work ethically—while it may be an expectation or a preference held by many employers—is not an expressed job requirement.

For health professionals, however, the situation is different. Health professionals enjoy the privilege of their patients' trust. They are expected to honour that trust by practising their professions with special care and integrity. Acting ethically and being guided by professional ethics in every situation is a central feature of that expectation. Like many other professionals, registered pharmacy technicians in Ontario are subject to an explicit (articulated and written down) code of ethics. Violation of the Ontario College of Pharmacists' *Code of Ethics* by a registered pharmacy technician could lead to professional discipline or even the loss of professional designation.

The College's *Code of Ethics* ("the Code"), which applies to all College members, is a relatively brief document (reproduced in this textbook as Appendix E). The Code's brevity is misleading, because each of the principles is written in very general language and can be subject to broad interpretation. Stating ethical principles in this broad fashion is common in such documents for two reasons. First, being overly specific (for example, "Members may not deny access to birth control pills to a client on the basis of the member's religion") limits the application of the Code and can encourage members to find ways to act unethically while complying with the letter, not the spirit, of the principles. Second, it is impossible to anticipate all ways in which a professional could act unethically, and a detailed Code would inevitably be full of omissions and loopholes.

Very general ethics wording poses a challenge in terms of compliance, because it is not always immediately clear whether a particular decision or course of action complies with a code's ethical obligations. For this reason, it is important to develop not only a familiarity with the particular code of ethics that applies to you, but also a more general understanding of the process of ethical decision making. This chapter provides an introduction to both.

WHAT ARE PROFESSIONAL ETHICS?

morals
principles, values, convictions, or beliefs, held by individuals or shared by groups, that influence perceptions of the rightness or wrongness of actions

Ethics are related to but are not synonymous with morals. **Morals** may be defined as principles, values, convictions, or beliefs, held by individuals or shared by groups, that influence perceptions of the rightness or wrongness of actions.

Moral absolutists believe that there is only one true morality, that it is a truth that can be discerned and known, and that it is the same for everybody. Many moral absolutists believe that God and God's intentions for humankind are the source of morality; however, not all moral absolutists are religious—it is possible to believe that absolute morality resides in human reason and can be discerned, perhaps through self-reflection.

Moral relativists deny that there is a single true morality. They view morality as individual or cultural, and they do not believe that it is possible to learn or discover one true and absolute moral code.

Whether you are a moral absolutist, a moral relativist, or somewhere in between, you almost certainly have a moral code, and you may also have learned and internalized the moral code of the culture in which you live. You almost certainly take morals into account when you make decisions that require you think about right and wrong.

While the reasons for reflecting on one's morality vary from person to person, most people can identify at least two central motivations: first, so that we can "be good people" and lead a good life (however we may define that). Second, we consult our morals because we have an obligation toward others to interfere as little as possible with their right to lead a good life. Sometimes, the process of consulting our morals is unconscious, like breathing.

The point at which we become conscious of the process of examining our morals is the point where ethics comes in. Ethics is the *conscious* process of turning morals (which are fairly passive and innate, like a norm or a personality trait) into an active tool for guiding behaviour. Most ethicists (people who study ethics) view ethics as a form of analysis: a person who is faced with an ethical issue or problem analyzes the problem in relation to his or her morals in an effort to produce a result. The result of ethical analysis is usually a decision about how to behave.

In summary, morals are something that we have, while ethics are something that we do.

Adding the term "professional" to "ethics" helps narrow the definition further. **Professional ethics** is the analytical application of morals to problems in a specific way that enables compliance with professional duties.

The term "professionalism" generally implies an especially high standard of moral compliance. Professionals are expected to act with special integrity, partly because they are charged with maintaining the reputation and status (and trustworthiness) of their profession.

Health-care professionals have a higher duty still because of their fiduciary duties. A fiduciary is a person who is entrusted with an aspect of the care of another person. The aspect relevant to health professionals is, of course, health care. As fiduciaries, health-care professionals are required to ensure that their actions are always consistent with compliance with their duty to care for the health of patients.

Health-care professional ethics, then, can be described as the analytical application of morals to decisions that are consistent with a fiduciary duty of care for the health of patients.

professional ethics
the analytical application of morals to problems that enables compliance with professional duties

THE COLLEGE'S CODE OF ETHICS AND OTHER RELATED PROFESSIONAL STANDARDS

The Ontario College of Pharmacists' Code of Ethics

Like many other professional self-regulatory bodies, the College has a *Code of Ethics* that applies to all members: pharmacists, pharmacy students, pharmacy interns, and registered pharmacy technicians.

The Code begins with a preamble (introduction). In a formal document like the Code, the preamble is intended to summarize the intent of the document and assist with interpretation of its terms. It reads:

> All members of the College have moral obligations in return for the trust given them by society. They are obliged to act in the best interest of and advocate for the patient, observe the law, uphold the dignity and honour of the profession, and practice in accordance with ethical principles and their respective standards of practice.

The preamble urges College members to view ethical practice as a reciprocal obligation: society places its trust in pharmacy technicians, and in return, pharmacy technicians must do six things:

- assume "moral obligations" toward society (in this case, society is represented by patients, potential patients, and colleagues);
- act in the best interest of patients;
- advocate for patients (advocacy can be defined as "speaking up for" or "standing up for");
- observe the law;
- uphold the dignity and honour of the profession; and
- practise in accordance with ethical principles and their respective standards of practice (that is, the respective standards of each class of members).

In complying with the specific principles of the Code, pharmacy technicians are required to keep these six separate obligations in mind.

The following paragraphs introduce each of the eight Code principles, and what they might mean in the context of your particular duties as a pharmacy technician.

PRINCIPLE ONE

> The patient's well-being is at the centre of the member's professional and/or business practices. Each member develops a professional relationship with each patient at a level that is consistent with his or her scope of practice. Patients have the right to self-determination and are encouraged to participate in decisions about their health.

The first two obligations created by this principle—patient well-being and scope of practice—are discussed earlier in this textbook. You have read that your first priority is your patient's interests—not your own interests, and not the business interests of your employer. You have also seen that your interactions with patients must be consistent with your scope of practice.

In practical terms, this means that you must maintain a clear understanding of what you can do for your patients, and what aspects of patient service you must refer to the pharmacist. Principle One also requires that your relationship with your patients be professional. A great deal can be read into that word, including your status as a fiduciary, and your need to distinguish the requirements and limits of a professional relationship from those of personal relationships. While you are encouraged to be friendly and pleasant to clients, your professional ethics require that you not permit the boundaries of your personal and professional relationships to blur—for example, by entering into a sexual relationship with a patient, or by providing unauthorized discounts for friends.

The third requirement created by Principle One is your obligation to support the patient's self-determination. Self-determination, in the health-care context, means the exercise of choice. Where your work permits choices to be made, you must allow patients to participate fully in those choices. For example, in October 2009 there was a shortage in Ontario of pediatric Tamiflu, a medicine for influenza. Some patients who presented a prescription for pediatric Tamiflu liquid were advised by their pharmacists that no product was in stock; however, there was a supply of adult Tamiflu in capsule form. Although the Tamiflu capsules could be broken to produce a dose low enough for a child, the process of partial dosing of capsule contents requires some judgment, and comes with a risk of parents making dosage mistakes.

When the pediatric Tamiflu shortage first arose, individual pharmacies and pharmacists (ideally with the input of pharmacy technicians, who are expected to have a share in pharmacy policy making) had to decide whether to supply adult Tamiflu capsules to parents who wished to cut them to create pediatric doses. The decision was an ethical one: should a pharmacy decline to dispense adult Tamiflu for pediatric patients, potentially leaving families without a source of the medication prescribed by their physicians? Or should the pharmacy dispense the adult capsules, knowing that there was some risk that parents would make dosing errors?

Principle One demands that, in conducting an ethical analysis of the pediatric Tamiflu shortage, pharmacy professionals take into account the patients' right to self-determination (or in this case, the patients' representatives' right). That might mean considering the option of leaving the decision up to the parents themselves. What finally happened was that Health Canada developed a procedure for the emergency compounding of a liquid Tamiflu product using the contents of adult capsules and Ora-Sweet pediatric syrup. Having a pharmacist create this compound (though not an exact substitute for the pediatric version) transferred the responsibility for dosing to the pharmacist, an approach that would improve safety.

PRINCIPLE TWO

> Each member exercises professional judgment in the best interest of the patient, at a level consistent with his or her scope of practice to ensure that patient needs are met.

The requirement to exercise professional judgment means that you must make your own practical and ethical judgments rather than automatically defer to the judgment of others. While you need to be mindful of the appropriate scope of your work, you cannot make a meaningful contribution to the pharmacy team unless you take the time to think for yourself.

PRINCIPLE THREE

> Each member preserves the confidentiality of patient information acquired in the course of his or her professional practice and does not divulge this information except where authorized by the patient, required by law, or where there is a compelling need to share information in order to protect the patient or another person from harm.

The task of managing confidentiality will sometimes engage your ethical reasoning skills.

Consider, for example, the third exception cited: you must maintain confidentiality except "where there is a compelling need … to protect the patient or another person from harm." As you might imagine, you will need to exercise professional judgment (a) to determine whether there is a need to breach confidentiality to protect a patient, and (b) to determine whether that need is compelling. In most cases, such a decision is best left to the pharmacist; however, there is a remote possibility that an urgent situation may require you to disclose confidential information.

For example, assume that you are a pharmacy technician working in a retail pharmacy in a very small town, and you regularly encounter your patients in the community. While participating in a "fun run," you come across a patient (a fellow runner) sitting, slumped forward, on the curb. An EMS technician is asking the runner questions that relate to heart attack symptoms ("Do you have pain in your chest, do you have a history of heart disease," etc.). The patient is not answering the questions. You know that the patient has Type 1 diabetes, and her confusion and lethargy could well be related not to heart problems, but to acute hypoglycemia. Do you tell the EMS technician about the diabetes, even though to do so would compromise the patient's right to confidentiality? You probably should, in the interest of getting her prompt and appropriate treatment in a life-threatening situation.

PRINCIPLE FOUR

> Each member respects the autonomy, individuality and dignity of each patient and provides care with respect for human rights and without discrimination. No patient shall be deprived of access to pharmaceutical services because of the personal convictions or religious beliefs of a member. Where such circumstances occur, the member refers the patient to a pharmacist who can meet the patient's needs.

As you learned in Chapter 7, Canadian and Ontario law guarantees the right to be free from discrimination in the provision of services. Thus, your ethical obligation under the Code is backed up by a matching legal obligation. Not only is it unethical to discriminate against patients; it is also illegal. Health care is an essential need, and discriminatory treatment in the provision of health-care services is not tolerated by either your College or the Human Rights Tribunal of Ontario.

The second half of Principle Four suggests that some aspects of pharmacy practice may run counter to the personal convictions or religious beliefs of pharmacy staff. Frequently cited examples include the dispensing of birth control pills or devices, of emergency contraceptives like Plan B, or of abortifacient drugs. Some religions proscribe birth control and abortion, and some people are ethically opposed to abortion for non-religious reasons. If your convictions prevent you from dispensing any kind of product stocked by the pharmacy, you should disclose this limitation to your co-workers ahead of time. Because you are expected to work under supervision, it is unlikely that there will be no one in the pharmacy available to do such dispensing (unless the pharmacist is also opposed); but knowing about your convictions will assist the pharmacy manager in assigning your duties.

Occasionally, pharmacy staff may be tempted to discriminate against patients on the basis of patient traits that are not listed in the Ontario *Human Rights Code* (HRC). For example, section 1 of the HRC does not mention discrimination on the basis of body size. What if a patient whom you consider to be at an appropriate body weight brings in a prescription for a weight-loss drug? Are you justified in telling the patient that she doesn't need the prescription and that you won't fill it because you don't fill "vanity" prescriptions?

Unless you have good reason to believe that taking the prescribed medication poses a real and serious risk to the patient's health, you are ethically not justified in refusing to dispense it. If you are legitimately concerned about the appropriateness of the prescription, your most prudent action is to report your concerns to the pharmacist, who may choose to call the patient's prescriber to ensure that the prescription is appropriate. If the prescriber confirms the prescription, you are ethically required to dispense it. While it may not be illegal under the HRC to discriminate on the basis of body size, it is probably unethical under the College's *Code of Ethics*.

PRINCIPLE FIVE

Each member acts with honesty and integrity.

Although this principle is easy to understand, it is not always easy to comply with.

Not only is honesty expected of you—it can also help limit the consequences of any errors you may make. Nearly all professions impose more onerous penalties for misconduct on those members who attempt to evade the consequences of their errors or wrongdoing by lying and covering up. If you have made an error in judgment, taking responsibility for it shows integrity. It also helps re-establish the trust that your College and your patients had in you.

Being honest can even limit your legal liability: when health-care providers communicate openly with patients about mistakes, patients are less likely to sue.

PRINCIPLE SIX

Each member commits to continually improve his or her professional competence.

Besides being required to undertake professional development activities throughout the course of your career, you must also document those activities and provide a record for review by the College should you be subject to a performance review.

PRINCIPLE SEVEN

Each member collaborates with other health care professionals to achieve the best possible outcomes for the patient, understanding the individual roles and contributions of other health care providers and consulting with or referring to them as appropriate.

The importance of developing positive working relationships with your colleagues is discussed in Chapter 7.

PRINCIPLE EIGHT

Each member practices under conditions which neither compromise professional standards nor impose such conditions on others.

This is an interesting principle because it suggests, without describing, situations that do compromise professional standards. Several discipline cases in Canada have dealt with practice conditions that have hampered efforts of pharmacy staff to meet patients' needs. Examples of practices that have come under scrutiny include:

- Designated managers allowing pharmacies to remain open for business and to conduct dispensing activities while the pharmacist is not present (for example, if the pharmacist has left to attend to a family emergency). This situation has been found, not surprisingly, to violate the standards relating to the supervision of pharmacy technicians.

- The operation of online pharmacies that accept prescriptions written by caregivers who have not conducted an assessment of the patient's condition appropriate to the circumstances. For example, an online pharmacy that accepts prescriptions from prescribers who are available only by telephone or email to patients whom they have never seen in person would be non-compliant with the standards of practice for pharmacists.

- Remote dispensing, except as permitted by law—when a pharmacy technician dispenses drugs to patients while being supervised remotely (for example, by telephone) by a pharmacist. Remote dispensing is not currently permitted, but legislation and regulations designed to support it are expected to come into force in the near future.

- Dispensing of drugs (notably, methadone) to patients by non-pharmacists working in a clinic setting, where the pharmacist is not readily available to supervise each instance of dose preparation and dispensing.

- "Countersigning" of US prescriptions by Canadian prescribers who have never seen the patients, usually in order to permit the US patients to fill prescriptions online.

- Pharmacy practices that are designed to permit excessive billing to public or private insurers, without therapeutic reason. For example, a pharmacist might opt to dispense less than a full prescription, requiring a return visit by the patient, when there is no valid therapeutic reason for the practice (and for the multiple dispensing fees it generates).

Can you think of other situations that could potentially compromise your ability to comply with professional standards?

Ethical Obligations from Other Sources

The importance of ethical decision-making is reflected not only in the College's *Code of Ethics*, but also in its "Proposed Standards of Practice for Registered Pharmacy Technicians." The very first standard provides:

The pharmacy technician *practises within legal requirements and ethical principles*, demonstrates professional integrity, and acts to uphold professional standards of practice. [Emphasis added.]

Operational Component 1.2 expands upon the way in which you will need to bring ethics to bear upon your day-to-day work:

The pharmacy technician applies ethical principles and guidelines to practice.

1.2.1   The pharmacy technician acts in the best interest of the patient and the public by:

- Reflecting on personal values and attitudes and examining their influence on interactions with the patient, the patient's agent, members of the pharmacy team, and other healthcare providers

- Respecting diversity.

- Protecting patient rights to quality care, dignity, privacy, and confidentiality.

Also, many of the obligations reflected in the Code (maintaining integrity and gaining knowledge to maintain competence, to name two examples) are incorporated into the standards (Operational Components 1.3 and 1.4, respectively) and are supported with more detail to assist you in complying with them.

The exercise of professional ethics is also embraced by the National Association of Pharmacy Regulatory Authorities (NAPRA) "Professional Competencies for Canadian Pharmacy Technicians at Entry to Practice." Competency 1 requires pharmacy technicians to "meet legal, ethical and professional responsibilities in the performance of their practice," and Competency 1.2 provides specifics:

1.2   Uphold and act on ethical principles.

Competency Elements

1.1.1   Be accountable to patients.

  i.   advocate on behalf of patients.

  ii.   involve patients in decision making.

  iii. respect patients' rights to make their own choices.

  iv.   consider patient-specific circumstances.

1.2.2   Question, report, and assist in the resolution of potential and actual unsafe, illegal, unethical, or unprofessional actions or situations.

  i.   identify, report, and correct errors, omissions, and unsafe practices or situations.

  ii.   identify and report conduct that is illegal, unethical, or unprofessional to the appropriate authorities.

  iii. document the incident and actions taken.

1.2.3   Demonstrate personal and professional integrity.

  i.   accept responsibility and accountability for actions and decisions.

  ii.   show sensitivity to and respect for the patient's dignity, values and diversity.

  iii. maintain appropriate professional boundaries.

  iv.   practise within personal limits of knowledge, skills, and abilities.

While the specific actions described in these standards are a good starting point, the standards cannot possibly contemplate and address every potential ethical issue or problem that you might address in your practice, and so should not be viewed as an exhaustive list.

You will need to use professional judgment to determine whether a given situation falls within the ambit of a particular standard. For example, NAPRA Competency 1.2.2(ii) requires you to "identify and report conduct that is illegal, unethical, or unprofessional … ." Are you confident that you will be able, in every context and with the level of practical experience that you have now, to decide whether a colleague's actions are illegal, unethical, or unprofessional? Ethical reasoning is a skill, and developing it requires reflection, judgment, and practice.

ETHICAL DECISION MAKING AS A SKILL

Introduction

It's not uncommon to hear someone described as "ethical" (or "moral"). When a person is described in this way, the speaker seems to suggest that being ethical is a quality, trait, or virtue that some people have—like being detail-oriented, shy, or warm. It's true that certain people become known for their ethical behaviour: these people act (or appear to act) consistently with their own or society's morals a majority of the time. However, being ethical is not a trait that, like a sense of humour, "you either have or you don't."

Ethical behaviour, like many other kinds of behaviour, is a choice. It is also a skill, in the sense that the more you practise it, and the more experience you have with resolving ethical problems, the more consistent you will become at choosing action that meets your own—and society's—highest ethical standards.

Whether or not ethics can be taught—and whether it can be taught in the abstract, such as by reading books, instead of through actual experience—is a matter of debate. But it's almost certain that if you have the will and the motivation to improve your ethical reasoning skills (and having to comply with a professional code should be an important motivation), then you can indeed improve them.

Having Help

One important point to remember about developing good ethical reasoning is that you need not do it alone. When you are first starting out in your career, you will no doubt be surrounded by colleagues who have more experience than you. Do not hesitate to speak with them about your efforts to make ethical decisions; they may have faced similar situations, and they may have very useful insights about your options.

Pharmacy technicians who work in hospitals often have formal ethics committees that can advise on serious ethical problems. Ethical committees strive to analyze ethical issues with a view to recommending particular courses of action, or to developing policies to help guide others facing the same problem in the future. The existence of ethics committees is a testament to the fact that ethical reasoning need not be conducted in isolation, but that it can be a cooperative process.

Having a Goal

"Practising ethically," although a well-intentioned goal, is simply too broad to guide your ethical reasoning. So is "complying with the professional Code of Ethics." You will have a much easier time weighing the ethical merit of alternative courses of action if you define a goal in terms beyond those of simply being ethical or avoiding discipline. Rather, you must actively relate ethical choices to the work you do every day.

Ethicist Ruth Purtilo (2005) suggests that for health-care professionals, ethical practice must be tied to the ethic of care. She suggests framing ethical analysis by asking the question: "What does it mean to provide a caring response in this situation?"

Purtilo's question may, when applied to particular circumstances, lead to more than one possible answer; however, it will narrow the field to those choices that are consistent with the essential duty of care that lies at the heart of your professional responsibilities.

If you have trouble relating to Purtilo's question, you might develop a focus question of your own. Your question, and the kinds of answers that it provokes, should be in line with your personal morality and the College's *Code of Ethics*.

Using Strategies and a Process

The process of ethical reasoning starts long before you actually begin analyzing alternative courses of behaviour. Most ethicists believe that ethical reasoning begins at the point at which you start to feel **ethical distress**—the feeling that something going on in your environment is not quite right, or not consistent with your moral convictions. Ethical distress is a feeling that alerts you to the presence of an ethical issue that engages your morals and convictions and prompts you to perform an ethical "check-up" of the situation.

ethical distress
discomfort related to activities in a professional's environment that are inconsistent with his or her moral convictions

Ethical distress prompts a natural desire to relieve it. Ignoring the distress, or waiting for others to take action, are ineffective choices because inaction in the face of an ethical problem is, in itself, unethical. The best approach is to begin the work of identifying and considering the courses of action that would be consistent with your convictions, the moral values of your society, and your professional obligations.

In fortunate cases, a single course of action can be found that meets these criteria. In most situations, solutions are more complex, and there arises the need to choose between alternative possible courses of action.

When, as a registered pharmacy technician, you arrive at this problem-solving stage, it is time to reflect on your ethical goal(s) and the question or questions that help you narrow the choices to reach your goal(s).

When you have asked yourself "What does it mean to provide a caring response in this situation?" (or your own question) and you've arrived at more than one answer, how do you choose among the answers?

One approach is to measure each answer against the ethical principles that you value, as well as those that society believes should guide your judgment. Purtilo (2005) lists the following principles as relevant to the ethics debate for health-care practitioners:

BOX 8.1

CASES

Ethical Concerns

The following cases arose in pharmacy settings and involved ethical problems.

1. Attacks on Reputation as an Ethical Pitfall (*Duke v. Puts*)

In 2001, the Queen's Bench of Saskatchewan (Saskatchewan civil trial court) entered a decision in this case.

Duke was a pharmacist who had been practising for several years in the small community of Broadview, Saskatchewan. Puts was a physician who had recently arrived in the community. Shortly after Puts arrived in Broadview, he developed concerns about some aspects of Duke's practice. Notably, he disapproved of Duke's participation in a "medicine chest" program under which the pharmacy provided certain pharmacy supplies, free of charge, to the First Nations reserves in the area. (The practice of providing a medicine chest had its basis in a treaty between the Canadian government and the First Nations.) Many of the pharmacy supplies were items that were unavailable on a reimbursed prescription basis (not on the formulary) for non-Natives in the area.

Puts soon came to the conclusion that the medicine chest program, and the participation of Duke and Jones, the other local physician, in it, amounted to an illegal or unethical money-making conspiracy from which he was excluded. In reaction to this belief, Puts launched a smear campaign against Duke. He began spreading a rumour that Duke had offered him a bribe for his silence. He encouraged a rival pharmacy to set up shop across the street from Duke's. He contacted the Saskatchewan College of Physicians and Surgeons to "report" the "Duke/Jones conspiracy," and an investigation followed. Although Duke was absolved of any wrongdoing, his reputation in the community was damaged, and he felt forced to sell the pharmacy at a significant loss and leave town.

Eventually, Duke brought a civil lawsuit against Puts, claiming damages related to loss of reputation and to the sale of the pharmacy. The court awarded the holding company that sold the pharmacy $300,000 in damages for loss of value, and awarded Puts general and aggravated damages based on damage to reputation and loss of livelihood in the amount of $250,000.

2. Kickbacks and Threats Used to Retain Pharmacy's Methadone Clients (from Tomlinson, 2008)

In a September 9, 2008 online news story, the Canadian Broadcasting Corporation (CBC) reported that Gastown Pharmacy, a pharmacy in Vancouver's Downtown Eastside, was threatening certain patients with eviction unless they continued to have their prescriptions filled at Gastown.

A previous complaint against the pharmacy had led to disciplinary proceedings for irregular methadone prescribing practices (see Box 5.1). Despite that complaint, the CBC's 2008 investigation revealed that the pharmacy's staff were unrepentant, and that they were using unethical tactics to encourage methadone clients to bring their business to the pharmacy.

One strategy uncovered by the CBC was the pharmacy's practice of paying a $10 weekly kickback to methadone customers as a reward for bringing their lucrative methadone prescriptions to Gastown.

Another strategy was made possible because the owners of Gastown also owned a housing development called the Wonder Hotel. In their tenancy agreement, Wonder Hotel tenants were made to promise that they would fill their methadone prescriptions at Gastown. When tenants failed to do so, George Wolsey, a pharmacist at Gastown, would threaten them with eviction.

The CBC contacted the BC Ministry of Health, which confirmed that neither tactic was consistent with the Ministry's policy forbidding incentives to retain methadone patients. ▣

- the principles of non-maleficence (do no harm) and beneficence (do good);
- the principle of autonomy (decide for yourself, without undue influence and with self-determination; but also allow others—including your patient—the benefit of autonomy);
- the principle of fidelity—being faithful to the patient's reasonable expectations: what would a patient, thinking reasonably, expect from you?
- the principle of veracity (truthfulness);
- the principle of justice—is the course of action you're contemplating just and fair? If you put yourself in the patient's shoes, would you feel as though you had been treated fairly?

Comparing your potential actions against these principles can help you assess whether a particular course of action is ethical.

KEY TERMS

ethical distress
ethics
morals
professional ethics

REFERENCES

Duke v. Puts. 2001 CanLII 130 (SKQB).

Ontario College of Pharmacists (OCP). (2006, December). Code of ethics. Retrieved May 30, 2010, from http://www.ocpinfo.com/client/ocp/ OCPHome.nsf/d12550e436a1716585256ac90065aa1c/fd4c299cfd1271cf852 572eb0052aa67?OpenDocument.

Purtilo, R. (2005). *Ethical Dimensions in the Health Professions*, 4th ed. New York: W.B. Saunders.

Tomlinson, K. (2008, September 9). Pharmacy uses kickbacks and threat of eviction to keep methadone clients. *CBC News*. Retrieved June 1, 2010 from http://www.cbc.ca/canada/british-columbia/story/2008/09/09/bc-080909-peoples-pharmacy-evictions.html.

REVIEW EXERCISES

Discussion Questions

Consider the following scenarios and discuss possible ethical responses.

1. You are working as a pharmacy technician in a large retail pharmacy. You observe a co-worker dispense two Tylenol 3 tablets to himself from the

pharmacy's inventory and swallow them with a glass of water. When you ask him about the incident, he tells you he has his own prescription for the medication, which he takes for back pain, but that he forgot his pills at home and will replace the "borrowed" tablets tomorrow.

2. You are working as a pharmacy technician in a large retail pharmacy. You overhear the pharmacist counselling a patient about a Viagra prescription. The patient mentions to the pharmacist that the reason he goes through his prescription so quickly is that he gives half of the pills to his wife, who reports that they improve her libido. The pharmacist just laughs, and says nothing to the patient about the appropriateness of sharing his medication with a person for whom it was not prescribed.

3. While working in a small pharmacy, you are preparing documentation for submission to the Ontario Drug Benefits Program. A colleague joins you and asks you to change the coding you are using—"Methadone for Addiction Management"—to "Narcotic for Pain Control." When you ask why, the colleague explains that it's simpler, administratively, to claim for the prescription in this way. You notice, however, that the ODBP reimburses narcotics for pain control at nearly triple the amount available for methadone for addiction management.

Review Questions

1. Explain the difference between morals and ethics.

2. Explain how being a professional, and providing personal health care, can influence your ethical reasoning.

3. What is ethical distress, and how should a pharmacy technician react to it?

4. Explain what is meant by the patient's right to self-determination in health care.

5. What if your own personal ethics or convictions prevent you from dispensing certain pharmacy products?

6. Apart from the College's *Code of Ethics*, where else can you find statements of your ethical responsibilities?

7. Is being ethical a personality trait?

8. Where can you find help in learning how to make ethical decisions?

9. How can you make a choice between two different, and both apparently ethical, courses of behaviour?

Appendixes

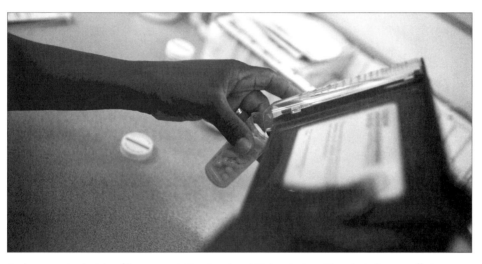

A pharmacy technician fills a prescription in a local Walmart store. The chain began offering low-priced generic drugs in its store-based pharmacies in 2006.

APPENDIX A

Some Useful Associations in Pharmacy

1. Regulatory Bodies and Public Advocates

Ontario College of Pharmacists (OCP)
483 Huron Street
Toronto ON
M5R 2R4
Phone: 416-962-4861
Website: www.ocpinfo.com

Pharmacy Examining Board of Canada (PEBC)
717 Church Street
Toronto ON
M4W 2M4
Phone: 416-979-2431
Fax: 416-599-9244
Website: www.pebc.ca
Email: pebcinfo@pebc.ca

National Association of Pharmacy Regulatory Authorities (NAPRA)
20 Laurier Avenue West, Suite 750
Ottawa ON
K1P 5Z9
Phone: 613-569-9658
Fax: 613-569-9659
Website: napra.ca
Email: info@napra.ca

Institute for Safe Medication Practices (Canada)
4711 Yonge Street, Suite 501
Toronto, Ontario
Canada M2N 6K8
Phone: 416-733-3131 (Toronto); 1-866-544-7672 (Toll-free)
http://www.ismp-canada.org/
Email: info@ismp-canada.org

2. Member Associations and Advocates for Pharmacy Professionals

Canadian Association of Pharmacy Technicians (CAPT)
15–6400 Millcreek Drive, Suite #164
Mississauga ON
L5N 3E7
Email: info@capt.ca
www.capt.ca

Canadian Pharmacists' Association (CPhA)
1785 Alta Vista Drive
Ottawa ON
K1G 3Y6
Phone: 1-800-917-9489 or 613-523-7877
Fax: 613-523-0445
Website: www.pharmacists.ca
Email: info@pharmacists.ca

Ontario Pharmacists' Association (OPA)
375 University Avenue, Suite 800
Toronto ON
M5G 2J5
Phone: 416-441-0788
Toll Free: 1-877-341-0788
Fax: 416-441-0791
Email: mail@opatoday.com
Website: www.opatoday.com

Canadian Society of Hospital Pharmacists (CSHP)
30 Concourse Gate, Unit 3
Ottawa ON
K2E 7V7
Phone: 613-736-9733
Fax: 613-736-5660
Email: info@cshp.ca
Website: www.cshp.ca

Canadian Association of Pharmacy Students and Interns (CAPSI)
PO Box 68552
360A Bloor Street West
Toronto ON
M5S 1X0
Website: www.capsi.ca
Email: Use online form

American Pharmacists' Association (APhA)
2215 Constitution Avenue NW
Washington, DC
20037
USA
Phone: 1-800-237-APhA (2742) or 202-628-4410
Fax: 202-783-2351
Email: infocenter@aphanet.org
Website: www.pharmacist.com

Canadian Association of Chain Drug Stores (CACDS)
45 Sheppard Avenue East, Suite 301
Toronto ON
M2N 5W9
Phone: 416-226-9100
Fax: 416-226-9185
Email: cacds@cacds.com
Website: www.cacds.com

3. Other

Office of Controlled Substances
Compliance, Monitoring and Liaison Division
Health Canada
Phone: 613-954-1541
Email: OCS-BSC@hc-sc.gc.ca

Human Rights Legal Support Centre
400 University Avenue, 7th Floor
Toronto ON
M7A 1T7
Phone: 416-314-6266
Toll-free: 1-866-625-5179
TTY: 416-314-6651
TTY Toll-free: 1-866-612-8627
Website: www.hrlsc.on.ca

Canadian Human Rights Commission
344 Slater Street, 8th Floor
Ottawa ON
K1A 1E1
Phone: 613-995-1151
Toll-free: 1-888-214-1090
TTY: 1-888-643-3304
Fax: 613-996-9661
(Also see the directory of regional offices at the CHRC's website)

Ontario Ministry of Labour (MOL)
(for occupational health and safety issues/emergencies;
and for employment standards inquiries)

Telephone contacts:

Occupational Health and Safety inquiries:
416-326-3835
1-800-268-8013 (Toll-free)

To report possible unsafe work practices:

1-877-202-0008

For Employment Standards inquiries:

Employment Standards Information Centre
416-326-7160
1-800-531-5551 (Toll-free)

Either section can be contacted by email using a form on this page:
www.labour.gov.on.ca/english/feedback/feedform.php?source=hs

Website: www.labour.gov.on.ca

Verified Internet Pharmacy Practice Sites (VIPPS) Criteria

The US National Association of Boards of Pharmacy has created a program for certifying "Verified Internet Pharmacy Practice Sites" (VIPPS). In Canada, VIPPS certification is administered by the National Association of Pharmacy Regulatory Authorities (NAPRA). The VIPPS seal is available to online pharmacies that meet the following criteria designed to protect the health of patients:

Licensure and Policy Maintenance

Qualifying VIPPS Pharmacies must:

1. Provide National Association of Boards of Pharmacy (NABP) with the information necessary to verify that the VIPPS pharmacy is licensed or registered in good standing to operate a pharmacy and/or engage in the practice of pharmacy with all applicable jurisdictions;

2. Provide NABP with the information necessary to verify that all persons affiliated with the site, including those affiliated through contractual or other responsible arrangements, engaging in the practice of pharmacy are appropriately licensed or registered and in good standing in all applicable jurisdictions;

3. Maintain and enforce a comprehensive policy and procedure that documents how the pharmacy's policies and procedures are organized, authorized for implementation, revised, retired, and archived; and

4. Comply with all applicable statutes and regulations governing the practice of pharmacy where licensed or registered, and comply with the more stringent law or regulation as determined by conflicts of law rules. VIPPS pharmacies must maintain and enforce policies and procedures that address conflicts of law issues that may arise between individual states or between state and federal laws and regulations. Said policies and procedures must assure compliance with applicable laws including generic substitution laws and regulations, and must prohibit unauthorized therapeutic substitution from occurring without necessary patient or prescriber authorization and outside of the conditions for participation in state or federal programs such as Medicaid.

Prescriptions

Qualifying VIPPS Pharmacies, in accordance with applicable state and federal laws and regulations, must:

5. Maintain and enforce policies and procedures that assure the integrity, legitimacy, and authenticity of the Prescription Drug Order and seek to prevent Prescription Drug Orders from being submitted, honored, and filled by multiple pharmacies. Maintain and enforce policies and procedures that assure that prescription medications are not prescribed or dispensed based upon telephonic, electronic, or online medical consultations without there being a pre-existing patient–prescriber relationship that has included an in-person physical examination.

Patient Information

Qualifying VIPPS Pharmacies, in accordance with applicable state and federal laws and regulations, must:

6. Maintain and enforce policies and procedures ensuring reasonable verification of the identity of the patient, prescriber, and, if appropriate, caregiver, in accordance with applicable state law;

7. Obtain and maintain in a readily accessible format, patient medication profiles and other related data in a manner that facilitates consultation with the prescriber, when applicable, and counsel the patient or caregiver;

8. Conduct a prospective drug use review (DUR) prior to the dispensing of a medication or device in accordance with applicable state law; and

9. Maintain and enforce policies and procedures to assure patient confidentiality and the protection of patient identity and patient-specific information from inappropriate or non-essential access, use, or distribution while such information is being transmitted via the Internet and while the pharmacy possesses such information. (Note: The NABP Guidelines for the Appropriate Use and Disclosure of Protected Health Information in Patient Compliance and Patient Intervention Programs can serve as a useful resource for addressing the confidentiality and security of patient data.)

Communication

Qualifying VIPPS Pharmacies, in accordance with applicable state and federal laws and regulations and VIPPS program criteria, must:

10. Maintain and enforce policies and procedures requiring pharmacists to offer interactive, meaningful consultation to the patient or caregiver;

11. Maintain and enforce policies and procedures establishing a mechanism for patients to report, and the VIPPS Pharmacy to take appropriate action regarding, suspected adverse drug reactions and errors;

12. Maintain and enforce policies and procedures that provide a mechanism to contact the patient and, if necessary, the prescriber, if an undue delay is encountered in delivering the prescribed drug or device. Undue delay is defined as an extension of the normal delivery cycle sufficient to jeopardize or alter the patient treatment plan;

13. Maintain and enforce policies and procedures establishing mechanisms to inform patients or caregivers about drug recalls; and

14. Maintain and enforce policies and procedures establishing mechanisms to educate patients and caregivers about the appropriate means to dispose of expired, damaged, and unusable medications.

Storage and Shipment

Qualifying VIPPS Pharmacies, in accordance with applicable state and federal laws and regulations and VIPPS program criteria, must:

15. Ship controlled substances to patients via a secure means that ensures proper delivery and seeks to prevent diversion; and

16. Assure that medications and devices are maintained within appropriate temperature, light, and humidity standards, as established by the United States Pharmacopeia (USP), during storage and shipment.

Over-the-Counter Products

Qualifying VIPPS Pharmacies must:

17. Comply with all applicable federal and state laws regarding the sale of Over-the-Counter Products identified as precursors to the manufacture or compounding of illegal drugs.

Quality Improvement Programs

Qualifying VIPPS Pharmacies must:

18. Maintain a Quality Assurance/Quality Improvement Program.

Reporting to NABP

Qualifying VIPPS Pharmacies must:

19. Notify NABP within thirty (30) days of any change of information provided as part of the verification process, including change in pharmacist-in-charge, or involving data displayed on the VIPPS website. VIPPS pharmacies shall notify NABP in writing within ten (10) days of ceasing operations. The written notification shall include the date the pharmacy will be closed, and an affirmation that all VIPPS Seals and references to the VIPPS program have been removed from the website and wherever else they are displayed.

Revised 5/31/05

APPENDIX C

Narcotic and Controlled Drug Register Form

The following is an example of the Narcotic and Controlled Drug Register Form from Health Canada that is to be used to record purchases and sales of certain controlled drugs.

 Ontario College of Pharmacists

Pharmacy Narcotic & Controlled Drug Register

Record of Receipts of Narcotics and Controlled Drugs
Registre des achats des stupéfiants et des drogues contrôlées

Date	Quantity Quantité	Name of Drug or Specialty Nom de la drogue ou spécialité	Received From Fournisseur

Date	Quantity Quantité	Name of Drug or Specialty Nom de la drogue ou spécialité	Received From Fournisseur

Proposed Standards of Practice for Registered Pharmacy Technicians*

Standard 1

The pharmacy technician practises within legal requirements and ethical principles, demonstrates professional integrity, and acts to uphold professional standards of practice.

Refer: Operational Components 1.1–1.4

OPERATIONAL COMPONENT 1.1

The pharmacy technician complies with federal and provincial regulatory by-laws, standards of practice, policies and guidelines, practice expectations, and where provided, workplace policies and procedures.

1.1.1   The pharmacy technician keeps current with and applies knowledge of legal requirements, professional standards, and where provided, workplace policies and procedures.

1.1.2   The pharmacy technician recognizes the right, role, and responsibility of regulatory bodies to establish and monitor professional standards, ethical guidelines, and practice expectations.

---

*   As explained in Chapter 3, the College has expressed an intention to adopt, in place of its own draft standards, a document currently titled "Professional Competencies for Canadian Pharmacy Technicians at Entry to Practice" prepared by the National Association of Pharmacy Regulatory Agencies (NAPRA), once that agency, in turn, has released the revised version of that document. In the meantime, the College's standards—which are similar to the NAPRA competencies in many respects—remain a useful guideline for pharmacy technicians, especially when considered in conjunction with the NAPRA competencies in their current form.

OPERATIONAL COMPONENT 1.2

The pharmacy technician applies ethical principles and guidelines to practice.

1.2.1   The pharmacy technician acts in the best interest of the patient and the public by:

- Reflecting on personal values and attitudes and examining their influence on interactions with the patient, the patient's agent, members of the pharmacy team, and other healthcare providers
- Respecting diversity
- Protecting patient rights to quality care, dignity, privacy, and confidentiality

OPERATIONAL COMPONENT 1.3

The pharmacy technician demonstrates personal and professional integrity.

1.3.1   The pharmacy technician understands the roles, rights, and responsibilities of and collaborates with members of the pharmacy and healthcare teams to promote the patient's health and wellness

1.3.2   The pharmacy technician recognizes and practises within the limits of his or her professional role and personal knowledge and expertise.

1.3.3   The pharmacy technician accepts responsibility for his or her decisions and actions.

1.3.4   The pharmacy technician shows respect for the dignity of the patient.

1.3.5   The pharmacy technician collaborates with the pharmacist in enabling the patient to achieve his or her healthcare goals and to support optimal patient care.

OPERATIONAL COMPONENT 1.4

The pharmacy technician continuously strives to gain knowledge and maintain professional competence.

1.4.1   The pharmacy technician identifies learning needs and seeks, evaluates, and participates in learning opportunities to meet these needs to enhance practice through education and experiential learning.

1.4.2   The pharmacy technician seeks out and incorporates into his or her practice information, guidance and constructive feedback from the pharmacist and/or, if required, from other healthcare providers.

Standard 2

The pharmacy technician, as a member of the pharmacy team and in compliance with relevant legislation and established policies and procedures, uses knowledge and skills to receive, renew, and transfer/copy prescriptions and to document.
Refer: Operational Components 2.1–2.3

OPERATIONAL COMPONENT 2.1

The pharmacy technician receives a new prescription or a request to renew a prescription from patients and/or patients' agents.

2.1.1   The pharmacy technician having obtained the patient's or patient's agent's consent where required and while ensuring patient privacy and confidentiality, gathers information to create and maintain a patient profile* or health record.

> *   A profile shall include demographic information about the patient as articulated under the Drug and Pharmacies Regulation Act and Regulations or the CSHP Standards of Practice and may also include where appropriate other information that is considered important for the continuity of care and achievement of optimal therapeutic outcome. This profile could include known patient risk factors for adverse drug reactions, drug allergies, or sensitivities, known contraindications to prescription drugs, non-prescription drugs, natural health products and complementary and alternative medicines, and other medications or treatments the patient is currently taking that may contribute to their condition or interact with suggested therapy. (Source: Operational Component 1.2, Standards of Practice for Pharmacists, 2003)

2.1.2   The pharmacy technician checks for authenticity of the prescription.

- Determines whether the prescription meets all legal requirements, and where it does not, notifies the pharmacist, and follows up using applicable policies, effective communication, and discretion.
- Uses healthcare provider lists, where available, to determine current status of prescriber's privileges.

2.1.3   The pharmacy technician verifies accuracy and completeness of the demographic and prescription data.

- Checks the demographic and prescription data for accuracy and completeness
- Reviews the prescription for clarity of abbreviations, medical terminology, drug names, dosage forms, strengths, availability, schedule, route, and related information
- Notifies the pharmacist regarding known allergies, therapeutic considerations, and/or discrepancies

2.1.4   The pharmacy technician differentiates when there are changes in the drug and dosage, the patient profile or health record, and where provided, the diagnosis or medical condition; and notifies the pharmacist.

2.1.5   The pharmacy technician completes appropriate documentation.

OPERATIONAL COMPONENT 2.2

The pharmacy technician receives a prescription from healthcare providers.

2.2.1   The pharmacy technician complies with workplace policies and procedures to receive prescriptions.

2.2.2   The pharmacy technician uses effective communication skills and workplace policies and procedures to receive an orally transmitted prescription.

2.2.3   The pharmacy technician, while ensuring patient confidentiality, gathers information to create and maintain the patient profile or health record.

2.2.4   The pharmacy technician checks for authenticity of the prescription.

- Determines whether the prescription meets all legal requirements, and where it does not, notifies the pharmacist, and follows up using applicable policies, effective communication, and discretion.
- Uses healthcare provider lists, where available, to determine current status of prescriber's privileges

2.2.5   The pharmacy technician verifies accuracy and completeness of demographic and prescription data.

- Checks the demographic and prescription data for accuracy and completeness
- Reviews the prescription for clarity of abbreviations, medical terminology, drug names, dosage forms, strengths, availability, schedule, route, and related information
- Notifies the pharmacist regarding known allergies, therapeutic considerations, and/or discrepancies

2.2.6   The pharmacy technician when receiving orally transmitted prescriptions uses critical thinking and problem-solving skills to recognize the need for pharmacist intervention and to notify the pharmacist.

2.2.7   The pharmacy technician transcribes an orally transmitted prescription accurately and completely.

2.2.8   The pharmacy technician differentiates when there are changes in the drug and dosage, the patient profile or health record, and where provided, the diagnosis or medical condition and notifies the pharmacist.

2.2.9   The pharmacy technician refers to the pharmacist all therapeutic questions or queries made by other healthcare providers.

2.2.10   The pharmacy technician completes appropriate documentation.

OPERATIONAL COMPONENT 2.3

The pharmacy technician, in compliance with relevant legislation and, where provided, established policies and procedures, transfers prescriptions to other pharmacies, receives prescriptions from other pharmacies, and copies prescriptions for authorized recipients.

2.3.1   The pharmacy technician confirms that the patient or the patient's agent has consented to the transfer.

2.3.2   The pharmacy technician checks for authenticity and ensures accuracy and completeness of the demographic and prescription data before transferring to or receiving/transcribing a prescription from another pharmacy and when copying a prescription for an authorized recipient.

2.3.3   The pharmacy technician completes appropriate documentation.

Standard 3

The pharmacy technician, as a member of the pharmacy team, uses knowledge, skills, and established policies and procedures to enter demographic and prescription data into the patient profile or health record.
   Refer: Operational Component 3.1

OPERATIONAL COMPONENT 3.1

The pharmacy technician enters a prescription as part of the processes used to prepare pharmaceutical products for release and to keep records.

3.1.1   The pharmacy technician while ensuring patient privacy and confidentiality enters, updates, and verifies demographic information in the patient profile or health record.

3.1.2   The pharmacy technician enters prescription data into the patient profile or health record using correct format, terminology, symbols, and abbreviations and which prescription data and notes have been confirmed for accuracy, completeness, and authenticity. When entering prescription data, the pharmacy technician uses knowledge to recognize drug names and to associate these with common health conditions.

3.1.3   The pharmacy technician verifies entered prescription data and notes against information contained in the written prescription received, the electronically transmitted prescription, or the transcribed oral prescription.

3.1.4   The pharmacy technician notifies the pharmacist of any alerts or therapeutic issues.

   ■ Differentiates when there are changes in the drug and dosage, the patient profile or health record, and where provided, the diagnosis or medical condition
   ■ Identifies to the pharmacist all prescriptions received in that pharmacy for the first time
   ■ Reviews the patient profile or health record for alerts
   ■ Reviews the patient notes for patient preferences
   ■ Reviews current patient profile or health record and notes duplicate therapy and active prescriptions on file
   ■ Brings to the pharmacist's attention any changes and/or compliance issues
   ■ Contacts the patient or patient's agent to obtain relevant information or instructions

3.1.5 The pharmacy technician determines patient preferences, applies knowledge about available forms of the pharmaceutical product, and applies knowledge of third-party insurance plan coverage to enter the pharmaceutical product/compound that meets the requirements of the prescription.

Standard 4

The pharmacy technician, in collaboration with the pharmacist, designated manager, or hospital pharmacy manager, prepares pharmaceutical products for release and documents.

Refer: Operational Components 4.1–4.4

OPERATIONAL COMPONENT 4.1

The pharmacy technician confirms that the pharmacist has had the opportunity to review the prescription and patient profile or health record, prior to the release of the pharmaceutical product.

OPERATIONAL COMPONENT 4.2

The pharmacy technician, in collaboration with the pharmacist, prepares/compounds pharmaceutical products for release.

4.2.1 The pharmacy technician obtains a pharmaceutical product that meets the requirements for the prescription.

4.2.2 The pharmacy technician follows formulation instructions, calculates, and confirms calculations with another registered pharmacy team member, documents calculations, and uses proper techniques to prepare/compound sterile pharmaceutical products.

4.2.3 The pharmacy technician follows formulation instructions, calculates, and where necessary confirms calculations with another registered pharmacy team member, documents calculations, and uses proper techniques to prepare a non-sterile compound, a pre-packaged pharmaceutical product, or a reconstituted pharmaceutical product.

4.2.4 The pharmacy technician uses the appropriate container, labels pharmaceutical products including auxiliary labels, and where specified by the pharmacist, provides patient information materials.

4.2.5 The pharmacy technician performs quality control/assurance procedures.

OPERATIONAL COMPONENT 4.3

The pharmacy technician verifies the accuracy and completeness of pharmaceutical products prepared for release.

4.3.1 The pharmacy technician shall be permitted to check pharmaceutical products prepared by another registered pharmacy technician/unregistered pharmacy personnel.

4.3.2   The pharmacy technician, having prepared a pharmaceutical product, shall have it checked by a registered pharmacist/pharmacy intern or another registered pharmacy technician.

4.3.3   The pharmacy technician checks the accuracy and completeness of the demographic and prescription data for pharmaceutical products prepared for release.

4.3.4   The pharmacy technician confirms that the prescribed pharmaceutical products being released are the correct products, are properly labelled including auxiliary labels, and that patient materials have been provided.

4.3.5   The pharmacy technician confirms the accuracy and completeness of pharmaceutical products prepared for release and documents that verification.

4.3.6   The pharmacy technician confirms that a registered pharmacy team member has checked the accuracy and completeness of the pharmaceutical product and documents that check before releasing the product.

OPERATIONAL COMPONENT 4.4

The pharmacy technician collaborates with the pharmacist in the release of the pharmaceutical product to the correct patient or patient's agent.

Standard 5

The pharmacy technician, in collaboration with the pharmacist, designated manager, or hospital pharmacy manager, performs distributive and quality assurance functions to ensure safety, accuracy, and quality of supplied products.
   Refer: Operational Components 5.1-5.4

OPERATIONAL COMPONENT 5.1

The pharmacy technician participates in distributive and quality assurance functions in accordance with federal and provincial legislation, policies and guidelines, and/or workplace policies and the Canadian Society for Hospital Pharmacists (CSHP) Standards of Practice.

5.1.1   The pharmacy technician collaborates with the pharmacist in providing optimal patient care and pharmacy services through compliance with health and safety legislation, guidelines, and workplace policies and through efficient and effective inventory management.

5.1.2   The pharmacy technician collaborates with the pharmacist in the provision of adequate and appropriate staffing, development of efficient workflow patterns, and the development, implementation and evaluation of workplace policies and procedures and quality indicators.

5.1.3   The pharmacy technician follows established policies and procedures for ensuring proper location, storage, handling, preparation, distribution, removal, and disposal of drugs, in compliance with environmental requirements.

5.1.4   The pharmacy technician uses time management skills to prioritize workload demands, to establish and work within realistic time frames, and to evaluate and modify work patterns.

5.1.5   The pharmacy technician selects technology appropriate to the task and uses the technology correctly.

5.1.6   The pharmacy technician follows guidelines for safe and correct use of automated medication storage distribution devices and performs appropriate quality assurance measures on automated dispensing cabinet replenishment, packaging/repackaging of pharmaceutical products, bulk compounding products, and medication storage areas outside the dispensary.

OPERATIONAL COMPONENT 5.2

The pharmacy technician responds appropriately to activities, which would divert drugs from their intended legitimate use that come to his/her attention.

OPERATIONAL COMPONENT 5.3

The pharmacy technician individually and as a member of the pharmacy team takes appropriate action to prevent and reduce medication errors* and medication discrepancies** and implements measures to prevent recurrence.

> *   *"Medication Error"—(may also be referred to as a medication incident) is an event which involves the actual prescribing, dispensing, delivery or administration of a drug or the omission of a prescribed drug to a patient.*

> **   *"Medication Discrepancy"—is an event which does not involve the actual administration of a drug to a patient, but where the error in the medication process has been detected and corrected before reaching the patient.*

(Source: Operational Component 1.8, Standards of Practice for Pharmacists, 2003)

5.3.1   The pharmacy technician complies with workplace policies and procedures that have been established to prevent and reduce medication errors and medication discrepancies.

5.3.2   The pharmacy technician acknowledges and discusses his or her medication error or medication discrepancy with the pharmacist, pharmacy manager, or hospital pharmacy manager.

5.3.3   The pharmacy technician documents the medication error or medication discrepancy and completes appropriate procedures according to established workplace policies and procedures.

5.3.4   The pharmacy technician participates, as a member of the pharmacy team and/or a healthcare team, in the evaluation of medication errors and discrepancies.

OPERATIONAL COMPONENT 5.4

The pharmacy technician only practises under conditions, which do not compromise his or her professional independence or judgement.

Standard 6

The pharmacy technician, as a member of the pharmacy team, uses knowledge and skills and follows established policies and procedures to communicate with patients or their agents, pharmacists, and other healthcare providers.

Refer: Operational Components 6.1–6.2

OPERATIONAL COMPONENT 6.1

The pharmacy technician communicates within his or her professional role to support optimal patient care and pharmacy services.

6.1.1   The pharmacy technician clearly identifies self and is clearly identifiable as a registered pharmacy technician and when necessary describes the role and responsibilities accurately to the patient, the patient's agent, other healthcare providers, and others.

6.1.2   The pharmacy technician refers all therapeutic issues, questions, and queries to the pharmacist.

6.1.3   The pharmacy technician establishes and maintains positive working relationships with the patient, the patient's agent, members of the pharmacy team, and other healthcare providers:

- Listening, speaking and writing skills
- Sensitivity to nonverbal forms of communication
- Sensitivity to language barriers, and
- Sensitivity to diversity

6.1.4   The pharmacy technician uses established communication policies, procedures, or protocols within the pharmacy and when interacting with the patient, the patient's agent, and other healthcare providers.

6.1.5   The pharmacy technician demonstrates a caring and professional attitude.

6.1.6   The pharmacy technician maintains confidentiality of patient information.

6.1.7   The pharmacy technician documents demographic and prescription data, and other pharmacy related information in the patient profile or health record.

- Follows standards, policies, and procedures related to documentation and to the maintenance, security, and disposal of records
- Documents clearly, concisely, correctly, and in a timely manner

OPERATIONAL COMPONENT 6.2

The pharmacy technician communicates using effective and appropriate communication skills while respecting the patient's personal, cultural, and educational differences. When interacting with the patient/patient's agent the pharmacy technician demonstrates flexibility in recognizing the unique qualities of each patient/patient's agent to find workable communication solutions.

Ontario College of Pharmacists' Code of Ethics

Preamble

All members of the College have moral obligations in return for the trust given them by society. They are obliged to act in the best interest of and advocate for the patient, observe the law, uphold the dignity and honour of the profession, and practice in accordance with ethical principles and their respective standards of practice.

Principle One

The patient's well-being is at the centre of the member's professional and/or business practices. Each member develops a professional relationship with each patient at a level that is consistent with his or her scope of practice. Patients have the right to self-determination and are encouraged to participate in decisions about their health.

Principle Two

Each member exercises professional judgment in the best interest of the patient, at a level consistent with his or her scope of practice to ensure that patient needs are met.

Principle Three

Each member preserves the confidentiality of patient information acquired in the course of his or her professional practice and does not divulge this information except where authorized by the patient, required by law, or where there is a compelling need to share information in order to protect the patient or another person from harm.

Principle Four

Each member respects the autonomy, individuality and dignity of each patient and provides care with respect for human rights and without discrimination. No patient shall be deprived of access to pharmaceutical services because of the personal convictions or religious beliefs of a member. Where such circumstances occur, the member refers the patient to a pharmacist who can meet the patient's needs.

Principle Five

Each member acts with honesty and integrity.

Principle Six

Each member commits to continually improve his or her professional competence.

Principle Seven

Each member collaborates with other health care professionals to achieve the best possible outcomes for the patient, understanding the individual roles and contributions of other health care providers and consulting with or referring to them as appropriate.

Principle Eight

Each member practices under conditions which neither compromise professional standards nor impose such conditions on others.

Glossary

A

adverse drug event
an illness, injury, reaction, or the experience of serious symptoms resulting from the use of a medication

B

best practice
methods and processes that have been proven to produce optimal results

C

constructive dismissal
termination in which an employer provokes the employee to resign when he or she doesn't really want to leave the job

controlled act
in Ontario, under the *Regulated Health Professions Act*, a specific act or procedure that may be performed only by a specific health professional

controlled substance
Any substance, including but not restricted to the category of drugs, that is the subject of government regulation

co-payment
a percentage of the total drug cost that the patient must pay

D

deductible
a set fee that the patient must pay per prescription

delegate
legally assign to a subordinate health professional (in Ontario, under the *Registered Health Professions Act*)

delisting
in the context of pharmacy, the process of deregulating a substance by removing it from a list of controlled substances, thereby changing its legal classification

designated drug product
a drug listed in the Ontario Drug Benefit Program formulary for which the government offers reimbursement

designated manager
a pharmacist who has been appointed by the pharmacy owner or operator as having the ultimate legal responsibility for the pharmacy's compliance with laws, standards, and guidelines

discrimination
unequal treatment that occurs because of race, ancestry, place of origin, colour, ethnic origin, citizenship, creed, sex, sexual orientation, age, marital status, family status or disability

double doctoring
A practice by which the patient obtains duplicate or multiple prescriptions for the same drug from different doctors, usually for illicit resal

Drug Identification Number (DIN)
a number assigned by Health Canada to every product defined as a drug under Canada's *Food and Drugs Act*

E

ethical distress
discomfort related to activities in a professional's environment that are inconsistent with his or her moral convictions

ethics
principles of right and wrong conduct

F

formulary
a list of prescription drugs covered by a particular drug benefit plan

H

harassment
comments or conduct that may reasonably be predicted to be unwelcome

I

independent double-check
a best practice in which any product dispensed must be independently verified by a peer

internal responsibility system
a system created by the Ontario *Occupational Health and Safety Act* that imposes role-specific workplace safety duties on all workplace parties

J

jurisdiction
the parliamentary body that created a law, and the political unit to which it applies

L

lawsuit
a non-criminal proceeding brought by a plaintiff against a defendant to redress an alleged wrong

legislation
laws introduced into a parliament and passed by a formal vote

listed drug product
a drug listed in the Ontario Drug Benefit Program formulary

listed substance
a non-drug item, such as vitamins or nutritional supplements, listed in the Ontario Drug Benefit Program formulary

M

malfeasance
wrongful conduct by a professional who has a duty of care to the public

mediation
a process in which a neutral third party attempts to help parties in a dispute reach an agreement

medication discrepancy
a medication error that is discovered before the medicine reaches the patient

medication error
an error that occurs during the process of prescribing, transcribing, dispensing, administering, or monitoring a drug

morals
principles, values, convictions, or beliefs, held by individuals or shared by groups, that influence perceptions of the rightness or wrongness of actions

N

negligence
an act committed without intention to cause harm, but which a reasonable person would anticipate might cause harm

O

offences
acts or omissions committed that run contrary to a statute

open access plan
a drug benefit plan that covers any drug approved by Health Canada and prescribed by a physician

over-the-counter (OTC) drugs
medicines that are sold directly to consumers without a prescription from a health-care professional

P

pharmacy
the custody, compounding, and dispensing of drugs; the provision of non-prescription drugs, health-care aids, and devices; and the provision of information related to drug use

pharmacy benefit manager (PBM)
a company contracted by insurers and government programs to manage pharmacy networks, drug-use trends, patient outcomes, and disease protocols with the aim of saving money

policies
guidelines, codes, rules, and statements of expectations created by governments or non-governmental bodies

private drug insurance plan/private drug benefit plan
drug coverage plan that does not rely on government funds

private insurance
insurance provided by a third-party company

professional ethics
the analytical application of morals to problems that enables compliance with professional duties

R

reference-based coverage
drug insurance that limits the amount reimbursed to the cost of a particular drug with proven effectiveness

regulations
laws created under a statute to support its administration

remediation
practice assistance, study, and skill development imposed by the Ontario College of Pharmacists Quality Assurance Program on professionals who do not meet standards of competence

reportable drug
a drug the details of purchase or sale of which must be recorded to permit reporting to a regulatory agency

revoke
cancel officially

root cause analysis (RCA)
a process to identify and remedy problems with a view to avoiding recurrence

S

schedule
in the context of legislation or regulations, an appendix containing a list, chart, or other collection of data

scope of practice
the decisions, actions, and procedures that are permitted for a licensed professional

severance pay
a lump sum negotiated between an employer and an employee on termination of the employment contract

T

targeted substance
in Canada, benzodiazepines and other drugs included in Schedule 1 of the *Benzodiazepines and Other Targeted Substances Regulations* made under the *Controlled Drugs and Substances Act*

termination pay
a lump sum required by law that represents pay in lieu of termination notice, typically one week's pay per year spent working for the employer

W

Workplace Hazardous Materials Information System (WHMIS)
a Canada-wide system designed to inform employers and workers about hazardous materials used in the workplace—for example, via labels, material safety data sheets, and educational programs

Index

Credits

Images

Chapter 1: Corbis/image100; Chapter 2: Florian Franke/Corbis; Chapter 3: Canadian Press/J.C. Moczulski; Chapter 4: SCPhotos/Alamy; Chapter 5: Jim West/Alamy; Chapter 6: Mira/Alamy; Chapter 7: Bubbles Photolibrary/Alamy; Chapter 8: Ruth Bonneville/Bloomberg/Getty; Appendixes: Joe Raedle/Getty.